VISUAL DESIGN FUNDAMENTALS: A DIGITAL APPROACH

THIRD EDITION

ALAN HASHIMOTO
MIKE CLAYTON

Charles River Media
A part of Course Technology, Cengage Learning

COURSE TECHNOLOGY
CENGAGE Learning

Australia, Brazil, Japan, Korea, Mexico, Singapore, Spain, United Kingdom, United States

COURSE TECHNOLOGY
CENGAGE Learning™

**Visual Design Fundamentals:
A Digital Approach, Third Edition**
Alan Hashimoto and Mike Clayton

**Publisher and General Manager,
Course Technology PTR:** Stacy L. Hiquet

Associate Director of Marketing: Sarah Panella

Content Project Manager: Jessica McNavich

Marketing Manager: Jordan Casey

Executive Editor: Kevin Harreld

Project and Copy Editor: Marta Justak

CRM Editorial Services Coordinator: Jen Blaney

Interior Layout: Shawn Morningstar

Cover Designer: Mike Tanamachi

CD_ROM Producer: Brandon Penticuff

Indexer: Valerie Haynes Perry

Proofreader: Sue Boshers

Printed in China by China Translation &
Printing Services Limited.
3 4 5 6 7 14 13 12

For product information and technology assistance,
contact us at

**Cengage Learning Customer and Sales Support,
1-800-354-9706**

For permission to use material from this text or
product, submit all requests online at
cengage.com/permissions

Further permissions questions can be emailed to
permissionrequest@cengage.com

Microsoft Windows® is a registered trademark of Microsoft
Corporation in the United States and other countries.
Apple® Mac OS® is a trademark of Apple Inc., registered
in the U.S. and other countries.   Adobe® Illustrator®,
Adobe Photoshop®, Adobe Illustrator CS4®, and Adobe
Photoshop CS4® are all registered trademarks of Adobe
Systems Incorporated.

All other trademarks are the property of their respective
owners.

Library of Congress Control Number: 2008935093

ISBN-13: 978-1-58450-581-5

ISBN-10: 1-58450-581-8

Course Technology
25 Thomson Place
Boston, MA 02210
USA

Cengage Learning is a leading provider of customized learning solutions with office locations around the globe, including Singapore, the United Kingdom, Australia, Mexico,
Brazil, and Japan. Locate your local office at:
international.cengage.com/region

Cengage Learning products are represented in Canada by
Nelson Education, Ltd.

For your lifelong learning solutions, visit **courseptr.com**
Visit our corporate website at **cengage.com**

To my heroes, Mom and Dad, who both
passed away since my last edition.
They were role models in every way and helped me
see the important things in life.

—*Alan Hashimoto*

This is for Min and all of my little "A"s.

—*Mike Clayton*

ACKNOWLEDGMENTS

First, I would like to thank Mike Clayton for his great contributions to this book and his family who put up with all the madness.

I want to thank the many talented artists, designers, and students who permitted me to use their great work. I would also like to acknowledge the graphics students and faculty at The University of the Incarnate Word and Utah State University for their participation and artwork.

Special thanks to Jon Anderson and Glen Edwards, my first design instructors, and the many administrators, colleagues, students, artist agents, art directors, and clients who put up with me through the years and gave me the wisdom to write this book.

I would like to personally thank my wife Amy Hopkins for keeping me sane and healthy throughout this whole process.

Many thanks to Marta Justak for her great work and for keeping Mike and me in line and on track and to Jennifer Blaney for leading the way.

—Alan Hashimoto

Special thanks to Alan Hashimoto for being my mentor for the past 11 years and taking me under his wing. I truly would not be where I am today without him and his expert guidance.

I would also like to thank the dozens of students who have taken my foundations design course over the last four years and have knowingly and unknowingly contributed to this book.

Thanks to my fellow professors and administrators at the University of the Incarnate Word for their continued support for our program.

Mindy, I love you... and that's all there is to it.

Last of all, thanks to Marta and Jennifer for making this edition go a little smoother than the first two.

—Mike Clayton

ABOUT THE AUTHORS

Alan Hashimoto (Logan, UT) is an associate professor in the field of graphic design and computer art at Utah State University. Alan has created over 400 nationally published visual design solutions for more than a hundred national and international corporations, advertising firms, and design studios. His design experience includes corporate identities, packaging, editorial layout, illustration, interactive design, and animation. He is also the author of the first and second editions of *Visual Design Fundaments: A Digital Approach*.

Mike Clayton (San Antonio, TX) is the director and an associate professor of Computer Graphic Arts at the University of the Incarnate Word. He teaches Web and interactive design courses, as well as foundations design. He has a BFA and MFA in Graphic Design from Utah State University.

Credits

Alan Hashimoto / Mike Clayton
Inside: Technical Theory and Tutorials by Mike Clayton
Contributing Author: Danielle Fagan

CONTENTS

INTRODUCTION

Digital technology has become integrated into every aspect of visual communications. New digital techniques and tools for designers and artists are being invented every day. Many more options and solutions for design and art projects can be explored in greater detail and in less time. The ease of use and inexpensive cost of hardware and software has given the public the ability to create computer-generated graphics and artwork. However, the availability of technology and the advances in imaging and production techniques will not cover up what is essentially a bad design. The history of design teaches us that the same elements and principles of design have always existed, regardless of medium or technique. As the market place and exhibition rooms become saturated with digitally produced images, knowledge of the fundamentals of design becomes even more important. To create sophisticated visuals, which entertain and communicate effectively, an artist or designer cannot ignore what defines design. The intent of this book is to provide a basic understanding of design and how to integrate this knowledge into digitally produced two-dimensional images.

PURPOSEFUL ORGANIZATION

Design can be defined as *purposeful organization*. As it relates to this book, the term *design* will be narrowed to include only the visual aspect of design and more specifically to those visuals that can be represented two-dimensionally.

So what is meant by "purposeful organization of visuals represented two-dimensionally?" Purposeful organization is the opposite of chance. Everything is thought out, planned, and placed or arranged with reason. *Visuals* are things we can see. They consist of one or more of the following elements: line, shape, space, volume, value, color, and texture. These elements are organized using the "principles" of design. Design principles are concepts and ideas that use the elements of design to create visuals. A design that both communicates and is aesthetically pleasing is dependent on a clear understanding and effective application of these principles.

"Two-dimensional" refers to height and width. The images contained in this book are reproduced on paper or observed on a monitor. They are all examples of two-dimensional visuals. One-dimensional design refers only to length. A true one-dimensional design could not be seen because it has no width. A line is often referred to as one-dimensional; however, a line has width and is in reality two-dimensional. This book looks past this fact and defines lines as one-dimensional. Three-dimensional visuals have length and width but also depth. Examples of three-dimensional designs are packaging, industrial design, sculpture, interiors, and architecture.

HOW TO USE THIS BOOK

There are two primary concepts of design: content and form. The designs and format of this book will follow these ideas. Content is the subject matter, concept, or solution to a design problem. Form is the actual visual that is created. Not all art is created using both of these ideas. Some visuals are purely conceptual with no need to be presented in form. Some visuals are created only for visual pleasure without subject matter or a problem to be solved. The focus of this book is on visuals that communicate, which extend beyond art that is created solely for aesthetic purposes. Each chapter examines and explains important content, outlines and gives instruction on process. Digital prints demonstrating specific content will be the final form resulting from the understanding of fundamental design theory and use of digital tools and techniques.

Classic art combined with contemporary design and illustration will be combined to explore the classic nature of the concepts in this book. To aid in the practical usage of the fundamentals of design, there will be a series of projects designed to inform and expand the knowledge and experience of the reader. These projects will also encourage the exploration of alternative creative options. Accompanying these projects will be tutorials detailing classic digital techniques and procedures. These tutorials will give the reader the basic tools to complete each project.

BACKGROUND AND TECHNOLOGY REQUIREMENTS

Specific subject matter and personal expression will not be a necessary part of these projects, making it easier to focus on the specific element or principle being discussed. Because of the universal nature of these exercises, they will be applicable across a variety of design areas. Readers who are well trained in software will discover the classic art of design behind all the technology. Others who have art training but little experience in the area of digital tools will begin to see the relationship between art and technology by completing digitally produced design projects.

DESIGN ELEMENTS

INTRODUCTION

This chapter introduces the most basic ideas concerning the elements that make up a visual design. The next chapter will present simple concepts explaining how these elements are organized and what types of relationships are established. The goal of these first chapters is to give a general overview of design and how we can use this knowledge to recognize good design, regardless of the technique or medium. The following chapters will focus on the computer and related software as one of many ways to create visual designs.

ELEMENTS OF DESIGN

Line, shape, negative space, volume, value, color, and texture are the elements of design. These elements, used together or separately to create all visuals, are called the *principles of design*. To a visual designer, the elements of design are the same as notes to a musician or words to a writer. They are the tools used to create their masterpieces. Similarly, design principles can be compared to the rules that apply to composing a musical score or the grammatical structure and rules required for writing a novel. A designer can use the elements and principles of design in many ways, which are discussed in Chapter 2, "Principles of Design." For now, let's look at defining each of these elements.

Line

Lines are the most basic element of design. They are a child's first visual means of expression and the foundation for most works of art (Figures 1.1 and 1.2).

FIGURE 1.1   Child's drawing.
(*Monsters* © 2008. Reprinted with permission from Oliver Hashimoto.)

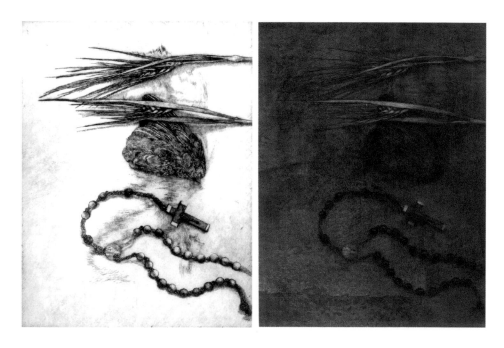

FIGURE 1.2   Foundation etching and color print.
(*Sparrow's Wing and a Prayer* © 2008. Reprinted with permission from Adrian Van Suchtelen.)

Many designers use lines to think through concepts and create preliminary sketches that communicate their ideas quickly (Figures 1.3, 1.4).

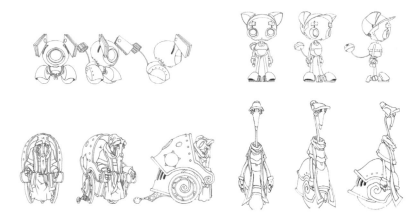

FIGURE 1.3   Preliminary character studies for a 3D animation.
(*Illumination* © 2008. Reprinted with permission from Jess Ung.)

FIGURE 1.4   A preliminary drawing and 3D character models based on this drawing.
(*Munchin* from "After Oz" © 2008. Reprinted with permission from Scott Moore.)

The emotional expression and communicative quality of lines are often underestimated. Lines can be thin and delicate or thick and strong. They are curved and organic or sharp and mechanical (see Figure 1.5).

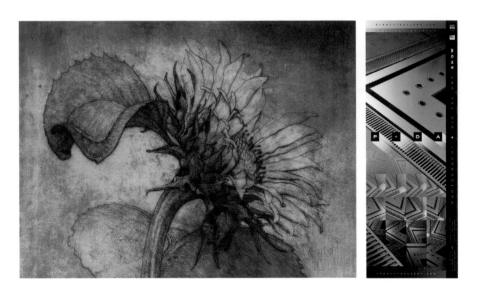

FIGURE 1.5   Left: The drawing uses thin and delicate organic lines. (*Summer Sunflower* © 2008. Reprinted with permission from Adrian Van Suchtelen.)   Right: The design uses thick mechanical lines. (*Photography and Digital Art Show Poster* © 2008. Reprinted with permission from Patrick Wilkey, www.visiocommunications.com.)

A line can define the outside contours of a shape, multiple lines can create value, and repeated lines can produce patterns and textures (Figures 1.5, 1.6, 1.7).

FIGURE 1.6   This design uses lines to describe the outside contours of a shape. The petals located in the upper part of the flower, as well as inside the flower, are shapes created by contour lines. In contrast, the lines at the lower part of the petals located by the stem are not exactly contour lines but lines that are placed close together to create the illusion of form. (*Tulipomania: Priscilla's* © 2008. Reprinted with permission from Adrian Van Suchtelen.)

In Figures 1.7 and 1.8, notice how the subtle differences in cross-hatching or use of the direction of the lines creates different visual textures and values.

FIGURE 1.7   This print uses lines to describe a variety of patterns.
(*Kadode* © 2006. Reprinted with permission from Koichi Yamamoto.)

FIGURE 1.8   A print that uses multiple lines to create value.
(*Kai no shiro* © 2006. Reprinted with permission from Koichi Yamamoto.)

Line and Design

Line can be defined as having only length or one dimension. There are two types of lines: visual lines and implied lines. The more commonly used *visual line* is defined as a line that can be seen. Figures 1.1 through 1.8 are examples of visual lines. In mathematical terms, a line is the distance between two points.

A true 1D line cannot be seen because it has length but no visible width. This type of line is called an *implied line*. An implied line forms an invisible connection between other elements to form a line.

Figure 1.9 gives a few examples of visual and implied lines. The line at the top is a visual line. The line in the middle is an implied line. Notice how the footprints do not touch but seem to connect to form a line. The line at the bottom is an implied line using type. Notice how each letter is separate but seems to connect to form a line.

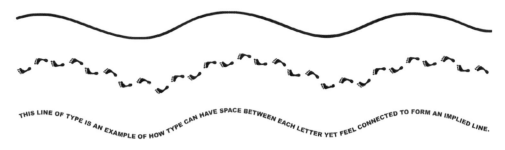

FIGURE 1.9   Visual and implied lines.

Line Direction

One of the most important characteristics of a line is direction. *Line direction* is the feeling of movement created by the structure and placement of elements in a composition. This feeling of motion, or lack of motion, is based on our experiences with gravity. For example, vertical lines suggest stability because when we stand up perfectly straight and well balanced, we feel stable. A soldier standing at attention is a good example. Large buildings surging straight up into the sky also seem well planted and powerful. Figure 1.10 with the vertical line direction diagrammed on the right is a good example of vertical line direction. The asparagus shows strength and stability.

Figure 1.11 is another example of vertical line direction. Although there are other line directions, the vertical lines dominate. Notice how the vertical shapes of the warrior and horse express the feelings of power and stability. The diagonal line direction pointing upward creates action and also adds to the feeling of power. The horizontal line direction is very subtle and not dominant.

Horizontal lines may also feel stable, but they can provide a sense of calmness that vertical lines do not have. Think about how landscapes and seascapes stretching out horizontally seem relaxed and soothing. When we are at rest, our bodies are usually horizontal, providing the sense of calm required for sleep. Figure 1.12 shows a horizontal line direction that gives the painting a tranquil feeling.

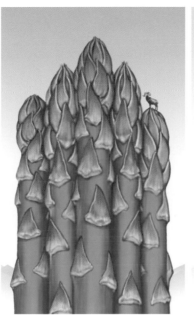
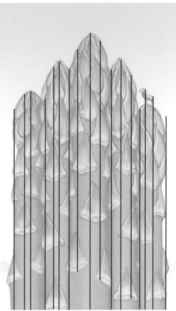

FIGURE 1.10   Vertical line direction. The diagram at the right helps illustrate line direction.
(*Asparagus with Goat* © 2006. Reprinted with permission from Alan Hashimoto.)

FIGURE 1.11   The vertical line direction dominates other line directions. The diagram at the right helps illustrate this point. (*Young Warrior*© 2008. Reprinted with permission from Glen Edwards.)

FIGURE 1.12   The horizontal line direction is identified more clearly by the right composition.
(*Chest Deep* © 2008. Reprinted with permission from Glen Edwards.)

Diagonal lines communicate motion and tension. When you are running or participating in any physical sport, your body is usually angled forward. Likewise, an object that is tilting and about to fall gives you a tense feeling as you anticipate the action. See an example of this in Figure 1.13.

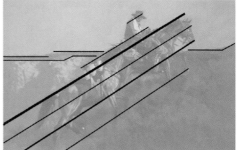

FIGURE 1.13   A composition using diagonal line direction to communicate action.
The diagonal line direction is identified more clearly by the composition on the right.
(*Over the Ridge* © 2008. Reprinted with permission from Glen Edwards.)

Figure 1.14 is a perfect example of how line direction affects the mood and feeling of a design. The design on the left is a painting that has been cropped to show a horizontal line direction. The design on the right is the same painting but left in its original state. Notice how different each composition feels even though the colors and objects are basically the same.

FIGURE 1.14   The composition on the left has a distinct horizontal line direction. The composition on the right is the original painting with an obvious implied vertical line direction.
(*Squash* © 2006. Reprinted with permission from Christopher Terry.)

Shape

Shape has both length and width and is 2D without mass or depth.

When we see an object at a great distance, the first thing we notice is its shape. We do not see specific lines, values, or colors because details at a distance blend together to form a basic shape. From far away, we can only recognize the basic shape of a person. As the person approaches, we will be able to discern gender or basic attire because more details will come into focus. Shape is the element that communicates the identity of objects most immediately and directly. We usually do not need to see every line, value, color, or texture to recognize an object. We identify objects by their shapes.

The main objective of any successful graphic designer is to communicate visual information in a unique and efficient way. The competition for visual attention in an environment bombarded by images, coupled with the public's short attention span, makes the understanding and creative use of shapes a necessity because of its ability to communicate visual messages quickly and directly.

Shape and Design

Shapes can be designed in several different ways. They can be realistic, distorted, stylized, abstract, and nonobjective.

Realism

Realism is the way we observe images in nature with all the proportions and dimensions of the natural world. Figure 1.15 is an example of realism. All the objects are represented in a way we would expect to see them without distortion or exaggeration. The object placement is natural and not unusual. The textures and lighting obey the laws of nature and do not seem to be manipulated.

FIGURE 1.15   A painting using realism.
(*Bowl of Oranges* © 2003. Reprinted with permission from Christopher Terry.)

Realism is used to communicate a visual image accurately to the largest audience possible. Everyone can relate to the images we see in real life. A well-drafted painting or drawing of a mountain can be easily understood as a mountain by almost anybody. Most designs for mass communication use realism to ensure the visual message is understood with little or no doubt. It may not be the most unique or efficient way of using shape, but the images are interpreted with little effort.

Distortion

When realistic shapes are manipulated or changed but are still recognizable as natural objects, it is called *distortion*. Distortion can be used to emphasize or deemphasize a natural shape to aid in expressing a particular feeling or idea. The legs of an athlete are drawn extremely long to emphasize his ability to run. The head of a person may be painted larger in proportion to the body to portray that the person is really smart or extremely thick headed. Figure 1.16 shows designs that are all examples of distortion. The illustration on the right and the drawing in the center use distortion to emphasize the eating habits of Idaho. The illustration on the left is a watercolor that distorts the lower part of these figures to emphasize their lack of mobility.

FIGURE 1.16   Designs that use distortion.   (Right: *Scenic Idaho* © 2006. Reprinted with permission from Marcella Gillenwater. Center: *Scenic Idaho Drawing* © 2006. Reprinted with permission from Marcella Gillenwater. Left: *Old* © 2006 Reprinted with permission from Marcella Gillenwater.)

Abstraction

Another way designers and artists use shape and distortion is through abstraction. *Abstraction* is the process of reducing natural shapes down to their simplest form.

Trademarks and other commercial symbols use abstraction to communicate the maximum amount of visual information delivered through a minimal amount of shapes. Pictographs or information symbols are just one example of how abstraction is used. Road signs, buttons on a DVD player, and Web site navigation symbols must be simple and read quickly. Trademarks are another example of how abstracted symbols deliver information simply and directly. At a glance, all the aspirations, products, services, and integrity of a company are represented in a single image. Figure 1.17 shows five trademarks (and related type) that communicate using abstracted shapes. Notice how these five simple graphic examples express the essence of what might be very complex objects or ideas.

FIGURE 1.17   Simple graphics express the essence of objects or ideas.
(Top left: *Powerplug Logo* © 2008. Top right: *Angel Moon Spa Logo* © 2008.
Bottom left: *Global Organics Logo* © 2008. Bottom right: *Keane Optics Logo* © 2008. Center: *RMI Logo* © 2008.
All logos are reprinted with permission from Patrick Wilkey, www.visiocommunications.com.)

Stylization

There are varying degrees of abstraction depending on the amount of visual information needed to communicate the content of a design. If more realism is needed, and the abstraction is slight, it is called *stylization*. Many artists and illustrators use stylization to create and establish a unique look to their work. Their simplified images may also be interpreted with less effort, which makes the specific visual message more obvious (see Figure 1.18).

FIGURE 1.18   Movie poster concept using stylization to emphasize the dynamics of the city and mysterious futuristic atmosphere.   (*Future Quest* © 2008. Reprinted with permission from Alan Hashimoto.)

Nonobjective

When shapes in a design have no recognizable visual representation to anything in nature, they are defined as *nonobjective*. Figure 1.19 shows two designs that use nonobjective shapes. The design on the left is a digitally enhanced photographic design. The design on the right is a computer-generated virtual 3D model. Even though there are no recognizable objects, nonobjective designs, such as these, are still visually interesting. The types of shapes, their placement, and color relationships can be designed to create interest.

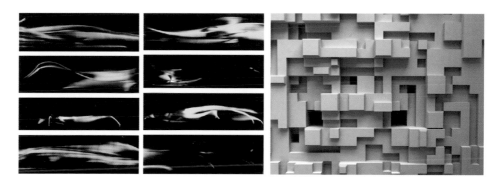

FIGURE 1.19 Designs that use nonobjective shapes.
(Left: *The Rapture* © 2008. Reprinted with permission from Christopher Gauthier, gauthierphotography.com.
Right: *Shades of Blue* © 2008. Reprinted with the permission of Anson Call.)

Because there is no subject matter distracting the viewer, elements and principles of design are isolated and observed clearly. We have to rely on the element or principle itself to begin to understand and appreciate these types of compositions.

A successful nonobjective design can still carry emotional content. In fact, the design may be easier to recognize because we are not trying to find meaning in "real" objects or concerning ourselves with how the subjects are being represented or presented. We can simply see the color blue and feel cool, or look at a large shape next to a small shape and sense the contrast.

Rectilinear Shapes

There are two very different types of shapes, rectilinear and curvilinear. *Rectilinear* shapes are sharp and angular. They often reflect the characteristics of man-made mechanical objects that are rigid and geometric in nature. Figure 1.20 shows a composition using rectilinear shapes.

Around the turn of the century, during the Industrial Revolution, rectilinear shapes were commonly seen in design and in fine art. They reflected the new mechanized world and related social issues that dominated society at that time.

FIGURE 1.20 The angular and mechanical quality of the shapes gives the feeling of organization and structure, which is typical of designs using rectilinear shapes.
(*Beamrider* © 2003. Reprinted with permission from Alan Hashimoto.)

Futurism, Constructivism, Cubism, and Art Deco were a few of the art and design movements that were influenced by the new world of mass production and machines. These movements are still very popular and often imitated by contemporary designers involved in every facet of design from graphic design to architecture.

The following is a brief description of a few of the historic design styles and art movements that use rectilinear shapes and are still relevant to contemporary design.

Cubism (1908–1920): Cubism was developed in Paris and can be described as the breaking up of space and realism into abstract or nonobjective shapes or forms. Cubists created this effect by overlapping or connecting rectilinear shapes. Multiple points of view seen at one time are also characteristic of Cubism.

Futurism (1909–1919): Futurism began in Italy and was based on the glorification of the machine and denunciation of classical art and culture of the past. Aggressive praise of new technology led to violent manifestos. Motion, dynamics, and speed are characteristics of Futurism. Many of the Futurist attitudes and beliefs are the beginnings of the more contemporary punk movement. Figure 1.21 shows a contemporary book design about Futurism.

FIGURE 1.21   This cover, etched on a copper plate, uses typography design influenced by the Futurists.   (*Futurista* © 2003. Reprinted with permission from Holly Craven.)

Constructivism (1910–1921): Constructivism in relationship to art is a movement that incorporated minimal, geometric, and orderly nonobjective shapes with an idealistic attitude that tried to find a new approach to art and architecture that could deal with the social and economic problems of the day. The early principles of constructivism began in Russia and were heavily influenced by both the Cubist and Futurist art movements. Constructivism is still used today in industrial, interior, and graphic design. Figure 1.22 shows a few examples of Constructivist influenced designs. The design on the left is a Constructivist influenced trademark. The example on the right is a contemporary title design dealing with Constructivism using typography design from the period. The larger design at the top is the main title. The three designs below are minor titles.

FIGURE 1.22   Constructivist influenced designs.   (*Van Doesburg* © 2003. Reprinted with permission from Mike Clayton. *Constructivist Titles* © 2003. Reprinted with permission from Nancy Wride.)

Art Deco (1920s and 1930s): Geometric simple shapes and streamlined design of machines characterize Art Deco. It began in Europe as an ornament and surface decoration style based on the concepts of Art Nouveau. Art Deco gained popularity in the United States in interior design and architecture. The Chrysler Building and Empire State Buildings in New York City are examples. Theaters, restaurants, hotels, ocean liners, furniture, sculpture, clothing, jewelry, and graphic design became heavily influenced by Art Deco. Figure 1.23 shows a few examples of Art Deco. The two fonts on the left reflect the simple geometric shapes characteristic of Art Deco. The package illustration and two trademarks are contemporary examples of the commercial influence of Art Deco.

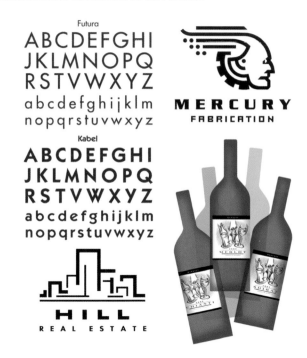

FIGURE 1.23   The commercial influence of Art Deco.

(Hypothetical Logo for Mercury Fabrication © 2006, *Hill Real Estate Logo* © 2006, and *Wine Label proposed for Marquee Wines* © 2006 are reprinted by permission from Patrick Wilkey, www.visiocommunications.com.)

Curvilinear Shapes

In contrast, shapes that are organic, curved, and round are called *curvilinear*. They are based on life forms that exist in nature (see Figure 1.24). Art Nouveau and some Psychedelic art of the 1960s are just two examples of art and design movements that use curvilinear shapes.

FIGURE 1.24 Curvilinear compositions influenced by Art Nouveau.
(Left: *Vinegar Label* © 2006. Reprinted with permission from Alan Hashimoto. Right: *Visio Communications Holiday Promotions* © 2006. Reprinted with permission from Patrick Wilkey, www.visiocommunications.com.)

The following is a brief description of design styles and art movements that use curvilinear shapes and are still relevant to contemporary design.

Art Nouveau (1880s and 1890s): Art Nouveau is a decorative art style characterized by detailed patterns of curving lines and shapes. The Art Nouveau artists wanted to unify all arts and center them on man and his life. This movement had many names in other countries based on the major artists' names, magazine titles, or firm names. In France, it was known as *Style Guimard*; in Germany, *Jugendstil*; and in Italy, *Stile Liberty*. Figure 1.25 shows examples influenced by Art Nouveau. The trademark on the left and illustration on the right are contemporary examples of the organic, free-flowing shapes that are characteristic of Art Nouveau.

Psychedelic Art (1969–1978): Psychedelia is a style of design influenced by the hippie culture of the 1960s. It borrowed from past art movements such as Art Nouveau, Op Art, and Pop Art. Bright colors, organic shapes, and decorative typefaces are typical of Psychedelic art. Graffiti artists and Gen X designers often use images and designs based on Psychedelic art. (Figure 1.26).

FIGURE 1.25   Designs influenced by Art Nouveau.   (*Holiday Promotions* © 2006.
Reprinted with permission from Patrick Wilkey, www.visiocommunications.com.)

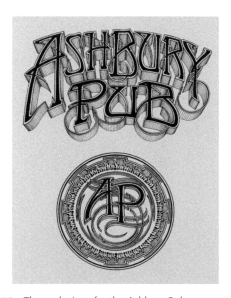

FIGURE 1.26   These designs for the Ashbury Pub are contemporary
examples of a logo influenced by Psychedelic art and design.
(*Ashbury Pub* © 2003. Reprinted with permission from Alan Hashimoto.)

Many more historic art and design movements contributed to the contemporary design of rectilinear and curvilinear shapes. Some of these are Arts and Crafts, Baroque, Bauhaus, De Stijl, Pre-Raphaelites, and Rococo.

Negative Space

Negative space is the empty area surrounding a positive shape. When designing with recognizable subject matter, identifying positive shape and negative space is easy. The relationship between this shape and space is called *figure/ground*. The figure is the positive shape, and the background is the negative space. In Figure 1.27, the larger image to the left is the original illustration as it was published. The smaller darkened image at the top right indicates the figure or positive shape. The smaller darkened image at the bottom right indicates the ground or negative space.

FIGURE 1.27   Figure/ground.
(*Green Thumb Olympics* © 2008. Reprinted with permission from Alan Hashimoto.)

When a design is composed of nonobjective shapes, the term *figure/ground* does not necessarily apply. Any nonobjective shape may be viewed as either a positive shape or a negative space. This becomes important because it emphasizes the fact that as we design positive shapes, we are also designing negative space.

In some designs, the negative space is confused with the positive shape and vice versa. This technique adds interest to designs and reminds us that negative space is a design element not to be ignored. In Figure 1.28, the example on the left is a painting that combines color and shapes that confuse. Which is the figure? Which is the ground? The example on the upper right is a design where the positive shape and negative space are interchangeable and confused to add interest to a design. The logo on the bottom right purposely uses figure/ground confusion to form the letters e and c.

FIGURE 1.28   Figure/ground confusion.
(Detail: *Hell's Kitchen d* © 2008. Reprinted with permission from Woody Shephard.
Zoo Figure Ground Tee-Shirt Illustration © 2003. Reprinted with permission from Bob Winward.
Ecology Center © 2008. Reprinted with permission from Alan Hashimoto.)

To understand negative space fully, the surface boundaries around a design must be defined. This area is called the *picture frame*. The picture frame will aid in creating and defining those areas that are positive shapes or negative space. Figure 1.29 shows examples of how the picture frame affects these elements. Notice how the absence of a picture frame in the top-left design makes the positive shape feel like part of the entire page. The picture frames in the other examples illustrate the change in negative space and how different formats can affect the entire design. The upper-right design feels much more active because there is less negative space. The lower-left design is more tranquil because of the horizontal line direction and added negative space. The lower-right design is more stoic in nature because of the added vertical negative space and line direction.

FIGURE 1.29   The picture frame affects the entire design.
(*Beethoven* © 2003. Reprinted with permission from Alan Hashimoto.)

Volume

Volume defines 3D visuals that have length, width, and depth. Images of this element can be represented in 2D in this book; however, realistically, volume must be observed from an assortment of angles and observed in an actual environment. This could be done virtually using a time-based medium such as a CD-ROM, DVD, or video, but because it would be viewed on a monitor, it would still technically be a 2D image. This book deals with volume indirectly and attempts to include 3D examples when discussing the elements and principles. Interior design, architecture, industrial design, and sculpture share the same basic principles of design as 2D shapes.

Value

Value describes light and dark. It is dependent on light, without which value does not exist. Light permits us to see the contrast of values that make up shape and form. Extreme contrast of values in a design gives a sense of clarity and depth, as shown in the painting on the right in Figure 1.30. Similar values may give a sense of subtlety, as shown in the design on the left in Figure 1.30.

FIGURE 1.30   Left: Similar values. Right: Extreme contrast of values.
(Left: *Quaking Aspen* © 2008. Reprinted with permission from Adrian Van Suchtelen.
Right: *Winter Forest* © 2008. Reprinted with permission from Adrian Van Suchtelen.)

Value and Design

When values are very light, the term *high key* is used. Lighter values suggest a brighter, happier mood, as seen in the painting on the left in Figure 1.31. Conversely, dark values are called *low key*. They usually feel somber and serious, as seen in the design on the right in Figure 1.31.

Value is also used to describe volume in 2D by imitating the way light reveals a form or object. The lightest values are in the direct line of light whereas the darker values are in shadow, as seen in Figure 1.32. This print uses a light source coming from the right to reveal the beehive. The light is so direct and intense that the shaded part of the beehive is lost in the long shadow stretching to the left.

There will be more information concerning value and design in Chapter 10, "Design Project 4: Value." It includes a project that will analyze value as a design element.

FIGURE 1.31   Left: High-key design. Right: Low-key design. (Left: *Jacob's Chair*© 2006. Reprinted with permission from Koichi Yamamoto. Right: *Sheep Skull* © 2008. Reprinted with permission from Adrian Van Suchtelen.)

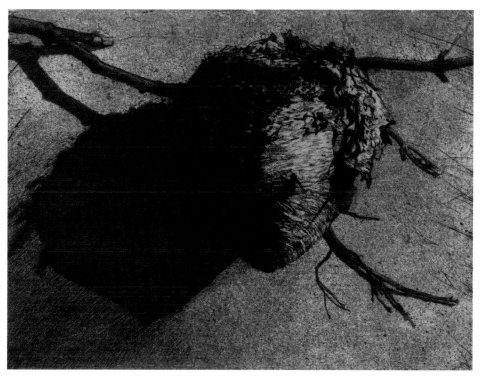

FIGURE 1.32   Compositions using light to reveal form.
(*Beehive* © 2008. Reprinted with permission from Adrian Van Suchtelen.)

Color

Color is essentially an element of light. If you have ever looked at natural light shining through a prism, you can see how light can be broken down into various colors. A surface that is painted red reflects only the red rays and absorbs the rest of the colored rays. Green paint absorbs all the rays except the green rays, which are reflected. This kind of color produced from reflected light is called *subtractive*. Color that is made from emitted light, such as a computer monitor, is combined to make that color and is referred to as *additive*. When discussing color mixing, these two systems are very different from each other. If you combine the primary subtractive colors of yellow, red, and blue, you will get a muddy gray. If you combine the primary additive colors of red, green, and blue, you will get a white light.

Many other theories associated with color will be discussed in Chapter 11. Color as a design element will also be included in design projects from Chapters 10, "Design Project 4: Value," 11, "Design Project 5: Color and Color Theory," and 12, "Design Project 6: Typeface Design."

Texture

Texture is the surface quality of an object. There are two types of texture: tactile and implied. *Implied* texture is texture that we can see but cannot feel or touch. Technically, it is not texture at all—it is the illusion of texture. *Tactile* texture is texture we can actually touch and feel. Looking at Figure 1.33, the painting on the left uses implied textures on almost every surface. The actual ceramic jar portrayed by a photograph on the right is an example of tactile texture; however, the photograph itself is an example of implied texture.

SUMMARY

Now that the elements have been identified, you should be able to point out many examples of these elements in the art and design you observe every day. Look at the type and images in a printed poster, art book, or design magazine. What kind of line direction is being used for the image? What kind of line direction is being used for the layout? What kinds of shapes are being used? Are the shapes examples of realism, nonobjective, distortion, abstraction, or stylization? Are the shapes organic, mechanical, or a mixture of both?

Look at examples of trademarks. Are they using abstraction or stylization to communicate the identity of their business? Is the negative shape or space being used as an example of figure/ground to increase the communicative content of their identity?

FIGURE 1.33   Left: Implied texture. Right: Tactile texture.
(Left: *Offering* © 2006. Reprinted with permission from Christopher Terry.
Right: *Bottle* © 2008. Reprinted with permission from J. Daniel Murphy.)

Take a closer look at your own photographs or photographs in a book or magazine. What kind of value is being used? Is it high key or low key? Are the values contrasting or similar?

Try to find examples of tactile texture and implied texture. Observe the difference.

As a visual designer, you should try to increase your observation skills by looking more carefully at images. In many ways, it is like physical exercise. If you practice, it becomes more natural. The more you observe, the broader your visual vocabulary will become. The more images you have in your vocabulary, the more options you will have to create your own original art and design.

2

PRINCIPLES OF DESIGN

INTRODUCTION

This chapter is a general overview of the "principles of design." There have been volumes of books dealing with this subject. The purpose of this book is to summarize and generalize all of this material. There should be enough content to give the reader a little insight into the process of looking at designs and determining why they are interesting or boring. Through observation and making many of your own conclusions, the images in this book should help you begin to understand what makes a design and why you may or may not like or understand it.

PRINCIPLES OF DESIGN

The *elements* of design refer to "what" are used and the *principles* of design refer to "how" they are used. The use of each principle is specific to the individual problem to be solved. Once the problem is researched and well defined, the elements can be selected, and the principles can be applied. Design is about making these visual choices. This chapter will concentrate on the many ways that design elements can be used and what to be aware of when creating and analyzing successful design projects.

GESTALT

Understanding how the eye and mind work together to perceive and organize visuals is an absolute necessity for any designer. The principles of design outlined in this chapter use results from psychological studies based on human perception of visual elements. The most widely accepted study on this subject is included in the Gestalt theory of visual perception. Generally speaking, it states that humans inherently look for order or a relationship between various elements. They observe and analyze individual parts of an image as separate components and have the tendency to group these parts into a larger, greater image that may be very different from the components (see Figure 2.1).

The design on the upper left in Figure 2.1 is an example of how similar shapes group themselves to form a diamond. This diamond shape is clearly evident to a viewer and can be seen with little effort on the viewer's part. The lower-left design is an example of how similar colors, symbols, and letters have grouped themselves to form the American flag. The design on the right is an example of shapes, which are not physically connected, but form a relationship between each other and become a greater shape, different from its parts.

FIGURE 2.1   Gestalt theory examples.   (Upper left: *Gestalt Example* © 2006. Reprinted with permission from Alan Hashimoto. Lower left: *Assembly* @ 2006. Reprinted with permission from Phillip Kesler. Right: *Transcendental Birthday Party* © 2006. Reprinted with permission from Brisida Magro.)

These three examples represent just a few of the many fundamental ideas associated with Gestalt theory. The following sections will explore the relationship between the elements and principles of design using Gestalt theory as evidence of how we naturally organize images.

Unity or Harmony

Unity expresses the idea that things belong together. *Harmony* is another word that might be used in place of unity. The idea that we tend to group similar elements visually and try to find the relationships that exist between them is an example of how the design principle of unity is incorporated into the Gestalt theory of visual perception. A design that is void of unity is usually chaotic and uncomfortable to view. The simple design on the left in Figure 2.2 is an example of unity. Notice how the similarity of shapes and their placement creates unity throughout the entire composition, even though the sizes or the shapes vary. In contrast, the simple design on the right is void of unity. Notice how the lack of unity between shapes causes the composition to feel chaotic.

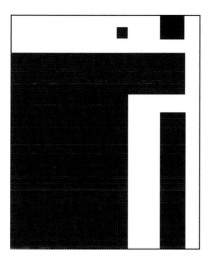

FIGURE 2.2   Left: Unity. Right: Lack of unity.

Unity can be accomplished in many different ways, including placement, repetition, and continuation. Each of these principles connected to unity can be applied to any element of design, including line, shape, and value. These ideas will be defined and discussed in the following sections. Unity and color will be discussed in Chapter 11, "Design Project 5: Color and Color Theory."

Unity and Placement Using Line

The placement of elements next to each other is one way to create unity. In creating text for a layout, notice how lines of type are organized to group information that is related. The design on the left in Figure 2.3 is a page from an article that uses the placement of lines of type and surround space to create a relationship between various forms of information. The design on the right emphasizes the shapes and values that are formed by these lines of type.

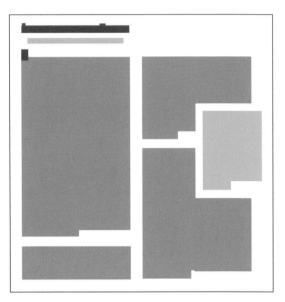

FIGURE 2.3   Lines of type that are organized to group information.

The placement of lines or type in relationship to each other can affect the entire look of the shape, value, and legibility of a paragraph. The space between each line of type is referred to as *leading*. The closer the lines of type, or less leading there is, the denser and darker the shape of the paragraph appears. Figure 2.4 illustrates a paragraph with less leading and a paragraph with more leading. Notice the relationship between the lines of type. Can you see the differences in value? Which is easier to read?

Placing lines of type *flush* (vertically lined up to one side) or *justified* (vertically lined up on both sides) is a way of giving unity to a block of text. Notice in Figure 2.5 how flush and justified arrangements of type give the paragraph unity. Figure 2.5 also shows an example of the same information arranged randomly, which makes the paragraph less readable and more chaotic.

Digital technology has become integrated into every aspect of visual communications. New digital techniques and tools for designers and artists are being invented every day. Many more options and solutions for design and art projects can be explored in greater detail and in less time. The ease of use and inexpensive cost of hardware and software has given the public the ability to create computer generated graphics and artwork. However, the availability of technology and the advances in imaging and production techniques will not cover up what is essentially a bad design. The history of design teaches us that the same elements and principles of design have always existed regardless of medium or technique. As the market place and exhibition rooms become saturated with digitally produced images, knowledge of the fundamentals of design becomes even more important. To create sophisticated visuals, which entertain and communicate effectively, an artist or designer cannot ignore what defines design. The intent of this book is to provide a basic understanding of design and how to integrate this knowledge into digitally produced two-dimensional images.

Digital technology has become integrated into every aspect of visual communications. New digital techniques and tools for designers and artists are being invented every day. Many more options and solutions for design and art projects can be explored in greater detail and in less time. The ease of use and inexpensive cost of hardware and software has given the public the ability to create computer generated graphics and artwork. However, the availability of technology and the advances in imaging and production techniques will not cover up what is essentially a bad design. The history of design teaches us that the same elements and principles of design have always existed regardless of medium or technique. As the market place and exhibition rooms become saturated with digitally produced images, knowledge of the fundamentals of design becomes even more important. To create sophisticated visuals, which entertain and communicate effectively, an artist or designer cannot ignore what defines design. The intent of this book is to provide a basic understanding of design and how to integrate this knowledge into digitally produced two-dimensional images.

FIGURE 2.4   A paragraph with more leading (left) and a paragraph with less leading (right).

Placing lines of type flush (vertically lined up to one side) or justified (vertically lined up on both sides) is a way of giving unity to a block of text. Notice in figure 2.7 how flush and justified arrangements of type give the paragraph unity. Figure 2.7 also shows an example of the same information arranged more randomly making the paragraph less readable and chaotic. Figure 2.7 Example of type arrangement that is flush to the right and type arrangement that is justified, and a type arrangement that is random, less readable, and chaotic.

Placing lines of type flush (vertically lined up to one side) or justified (vertically lined up on both sides) is a way of giving unity to a block of text. Notice in figure 2.7 how flush and justified arrangements of type give the paragraph unity. Figure 2.7 also shows an example of the same information arranged more randomly making the paragraph less readable and chaotic. Figure 2.7 Example of type arrangement that is flush to the right and type arrangement that is justified, and a type arrangement that is random, less readable, and chaotic.

Placing lines of type flush (vertically lined up to one side) or justified (vertically lined up on both sides) is a way of giving unity to block of text.

Notice in figure 2.7 how flush and justified arrangements of type give the paragraph unity. Figure 2.7 also shows an example of the same information arranged more randomly making the paragraph less readable and chaotic.

Figure 2.7 Example of type arrangement that is flush to the right and type arrangement that is justified, and a type arrangement that is random, less readable, and chaotic.

FIGURE 2.5   Type arrangement that is flush to the left, type arrangement that is justified, and a type arrangement that is random.

Unity and Placement Using Shape

Notice the relationship between the shapes in the Figure 2.6. All of the shapes in the left design are placed far apart and all are too close to the *picture frame* (outside boundaries of a design). When shapes are placed closer to the picture frame and further away from each other, they will form a strong relationship to the picture frame and a weak relationship to each other. When this happens, the edges of the composition will receive the attention, and the middle feels open and empty.

FIGURE 2.6 Unity and placement.

Figure 2.7 shows an example of a title set closer together (tight) and an example of the same title set farther apart (loose). Notice how the example of type set close together creates a fast-paced feeling. Tightly set type is used for ads and billboards that promote products for people "on the go" or that need to be read very quickly. The bottom line of type is an example of the same type set loosely, creating a title that must be read at a slower pace. Elegance and spaciousness are the feelings this type may give to a product name or title.

THE MULTIMEDIA MARCHING BAND

THE MULTIMEDIA MARCHING BAND

FIGURE 2.7 Type set close together and the same type set loose.

This idea may be useful when designing type for titles or headlines. A fast-paced feeling can be achieved by setting type closer together. In contrast, a slower, calmer feeling is created when type is set farther apart. In visual design, distance is equal to time. This means that the larger the distance between elements of a design, the more time it will take for the viewer to recognize the relationship. This creates a feeling that more time is passing by. Titles with type spaced far apart can still feel unified by using letters from the same font and placing the letters on the same line, commonly called a *baseline*.

Designs that use shapes placed randomly can seem active and fun. If the visual message is short and simple, these designs can be effective; however, most designs demand a more complex and detailed visual message that needs to be communicated very quickly. Creating easy-to-recognize relationships between visuals becomes absolutely necessary. Similar line directions, related shapes, and lining up edges of shapes and lines of type can help in unifying a design. Figures 2.8 and 2.9 illustrate how the same shapes may be organized to created chaos or stability.

Looking at Figure 2.8, the shapes in the left design are placed at random and seem chaotic. In the right design, the same shapes are placed together to take advantage of similar line direction and related aspects of the shapes themselves. Notice how the triangle feels less tense when placed with the heavier, more stable side facedown. This occurs because of our relationship to gravity.

In Figure 2.9, the left design illustrates how neglecting to establish unity between type and lines of type can make reading a message difficult. The design on the right uses the same type but delivers the visual message quickly and more effectively.

 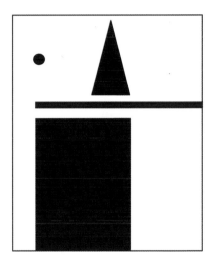

FIGURE 2.8   Shapes placed at random (left) and shapes placed with similar line direction and related aspects of the shapes themselves.

VISUAL DESIGN
FUNDAMENTALS:
A Digital Approach

VISUAL DESIGN
FUNDAMENTALS:
A Digital Approach

FIGURE 2.9   Unity between type and lines of type.

Repetition Using Line

Repetition is also a characteristic of unity that can be applied to any element of design. The idea is that a part of a design repeats somewhere else in a composition to create unity. Figure 2.10 is an example of how repetition of a line can unify a composition. The simple design on the left is made up of three shapes and one contour line describing the outside of a circle. The shapes seem to feel unified, but the circle seems out of place. The design on the right illustrates how repeating a line similar to the circle can make the entire composition more harmonious. The newly added line is larger to give the design variety and interest that will be discussed later in this chapter.

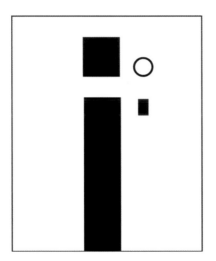 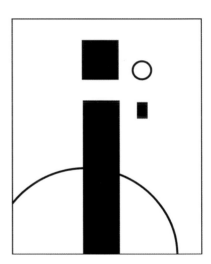

FIGURE 2.10   Example of how repetition of a line can unify a composition.

Other examples of repetition and line creating unity are shown in Figure 2.11. These illustrations use a consistent repeated line width in conjunction with shape to create unity.

As stated earlier in Chapter 1, direction is a characteristic of lines. Repetition of a common line direction can help relate all parts of a design. Figure 2.12 is an example of how repeating the vertical line directions of primary shapes unifies a design. The design on the left contains shapes that seem unrelated. Through the use of a vertical line direction, the shapes in the right design appear to be more unified.

Figure 2.13 is an example of a diagonal line direction unifying all the elements into a harmonic dynamic design. This illustration for an electronics catalog cover shows a diagonal line direction creating unity between all of the circuit board shapes and the racing automobile.

FIGURE 2.11   Repeated line width creating unity. (Upper left: *Safe* © 2008. Reprinted with permission from Jordan Leary. Lower left: *Medscries4 Coach Logo* © 2008. Reprinted with permission from Patrick Wilkey, www.visiocommunications.com. Right: *Franklin Covey Lifestyles Illustration* © 2008. Reprinted with permission from Patrick Wilkey, www.visiocommunications.com.)

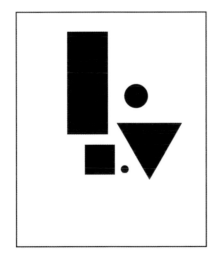
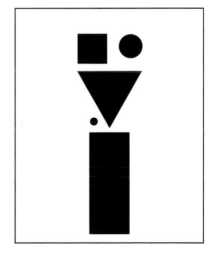

FIGURE 2.12   Repeated line direction and unity.

FIGURE 2.13   Diagonal line direction creating unity.
(*Electronic Race* © 2008. Reprinted with permission from Alan Hashimoto.)

Repetition Using Shape

As discussed earlier, there are two different types of shapes: rectilinear and curvilinear. Designs that consist of the same or similar types of shapes are usually harmonious. Figure 2.14 shows a design with similar rectilinear shapes and a design with similar curvilinear shapes. Both feel very unified. A third design makes use of both shapes in one composition, illustrating the idea that both types of shapes can be present in a unified design. The idea that these shapes are different from each other but can exist in the same design is a good example of balancing unity with variety.

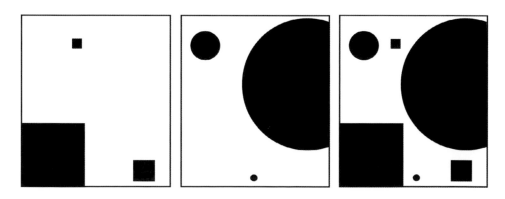

FIGURE 2.14
Left: Similar rectilinear shapes. Middle: Curvilinear shapes.
Right: Both types of shapes are combined and unified.

Many designs that emphasize unity usually use either curvilinear or rectilinear shapes. The two designs in Figure 2.15 use both types of shapes but allow one or the other to dominate. The focus on the design on the left is mainly on rectilinear shapes. The design on the right uses primarily curvilinear shapes.

FIGURE 2.15 Two designs that are curvilinear and rectilinear
(Left: *Programming for the Future* © 2008. Reprinted with permission from Alan Hashimoto.
Right: *Tulipomania: Sorbet Vanitas* © 2008. Reprinted with permission from Adrian Van Suchtelen.)

RHYTHM

Another design principle closely related to repetition is rhythm. *Rhythm* creates unity by repeating exact or slightly different elements in a predictable manner. It differs from repetition in the degree of duplication of elements and a feeling of pacing. Rhythm depends on a more exact duplication of elements, as seen in Figure 2.16. In Figure 2.16, the design on the left is an example of a design that uses repetition of shapes, not rhythm. The design on the right is an example of rhythm. Rhythm uses repetition to produce feelings of predictability and pacing. The viewer can anticipate that the following shape in this design will dip lower to duplicate the position of the fourth shape and be equal distance from the fifth shape.

There are two other types of rhythm: *alternating rhythm* and *progressive rhythm*. In alternating rhythm, two contrasting elements are created. These two elements are repeated over and over, one right after the other. Progressive rhythm relies on a progressive change in a series of elements that are repeated. These elements change from one element to the next in increasing or diminishing size or weight. Figure 2.17 will help define these types of rhythm and illustrate a few concepts associated with them. The first design on the left is an example of alternating rhythm. The second design from the left is an example of progressive rhythm. Notice how your eye follows the design downward until it almost leaves the picture frame. This is not what a designer wants if the point is to keep the viewer's interest. The third design from the left solves this problem by creating a shape at the bottom that stops the progressive rhythm. This bottom shape feels unified because it is aligned with another shape located near the top. Notice how your eye is stopped from going out of the picture frame and back up to the top. The design farthest to the right is an example of progressive rhythm that progresses in two different directions. It is also an example of alternating rhythm because of the alternating thick and thin shapes.

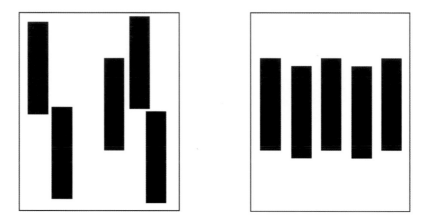

FIGURE 2.16   Repetition and rhythm.

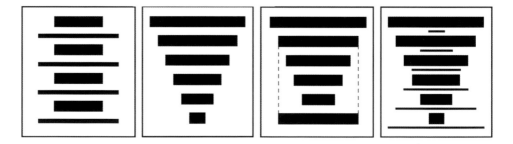

FIGURE 2.17   Rhythm examples.

In Figure 2.18, examples of progressive rhythm are exemplified in the snowflake design on the upper left and teepees in the painting on the upper right. Alternating rhythm is used in the design on the lower left and the photograph on the lower right. An alternating pattern of pine leaves rotates in a circular pattern around the bright star. In the photograph on the lower right, an alternating pattern of a hay field creates an interesting visual effect.

FIGURE 2.18 Progressive rhythm and alternating rhythm examples.
(Upper left: *Holiday Greeting Card Illustration* © 2008. Reprinted with permission from Patrick Wilkey,
www.visiocommunications.com. Upper right: *Welcome Visitors* © 2008. Reprinted with permission from Glen Edwards.
Lower left: *Holiday Greeting Card Illustration* © 2008. Reprinted with permission from Patrick Wilkey,
www.visiocommunications.com. Lower right: *Hayrolls, Aerial, Minnesota* © Reprinted with permission from
Patrick Cone Photography.)

Unity Using Value

Unity can be achieved through the use of repeated values in a design. Through the use of value, unrelated shapes may be designed into a unified composition. Figure 2.19 illustrates an example of how this can be done. The example on the left shows several unrelated shapes. Similar values create unity between these shapes in the middle design. If placement and line direction were also considered, these shapes would have an even greater sense of harmony, as exemplified in the design on the right.

Figure 2.20 shows examples of how similar values can be used to create unity. The print on the left uses lighter values that help create the feeling of harmony between the various elements in the center and dark values around the edge to create interest through contrast. The print on the right uses similar dark values to create unity. The darker values make the design seem heavier.

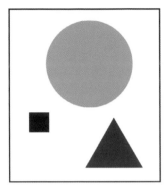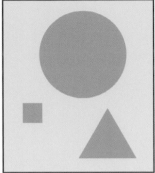

FIGURE 2.19   Unrelated shapes, shapes with similar values, and shapes with harmony through placement.

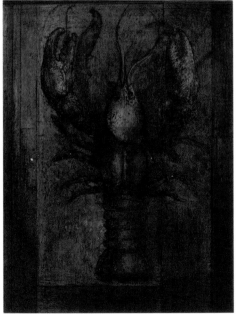

FIGURE 2.20   Similar values creating unity.
(Left: *Sunflower* © 2008. Reprinted with permission from Adrian Van Suchtelen.
Right: *Bear River Crayfish* © 2008. Reprinted with permission from Adrian Van Suchtelen.)

Unity and Continuity

Another less obvious way to create unity is continuity. *Continuity* uses the idea that something is carried over or connected to another element. A grid or guides to organize information and images in magazines, books, and Web sites is a common example of how continuity is achieved. Grids are used to make reading and viewing large amounts of material easier by creating a rhythm and consistent structure so the eye and mind do not have to work to adjust to unexpected changes and unorganized information. Figure 2.21 uses vertical and horizontal guides to indicate where visuals and text can be placed. Notice how the repetitious grid is broken by a few images to give the layout interest through variety. If the placement of images is carefully thought out, the continuity of the grid can be broken, but the basic rhythm will still exist. Compare this to a simple piece of music. You can hear a consistent rhythm even though the melody might not always follow every beat. Some notes will be held for more than one count yet the rhythm is not affected. Figure 2.22 is another example of how the rhythmic underlying structure of a layout organizes information and how this information can have variety through the size and placement of written and visual information.

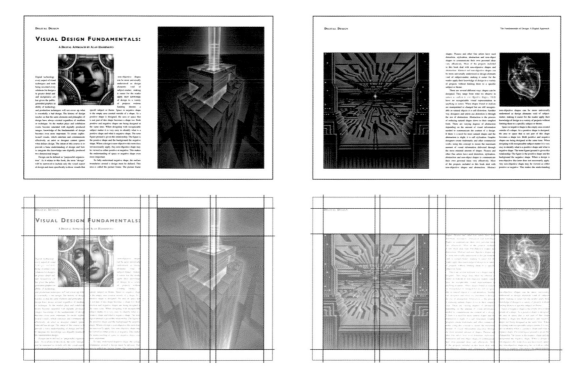

FIGURE 2.21   A basic grid structure used for a simple double-page spread layout.

FIGURE 2.22   Four simple double-page layouts that use a grid structure for unity and varying sizes of images and type for variety.   (*See Everything: Portraits of a City Reflecting Upon Itself, a photographic essay* © 2008. Reprinted with permission from Patrick Wilkey, www.visiocommunications.com.)

Continuity can apply to any series of art or design projects. The element or elements that are being carried over can be related to line, line direction, shapes, values, colors, forms, or texture. Figure 2.23 is an example of how the principle of continuity can be observed in the relationship between illustrated images. Continuity is created in similar fashions by the theme, style, color, values, and basic composition.

Continuity is also used in establishing corporate identities. Trademarks, product labels, equipment, packaging, business literature, and other promotional and associated material must be consistent to ensure that the identity of a company is reinforced and remembered. Figure 2.24 is an example of how continuity can be used to create a consistent identity for a group of promotional materials.

FIGURE 2.23   Continuity using four related storybook illustrations.
(*What's Wrong Chuck?* © 2008. Reprinted with permission from Scott Wakefield.)

FIGURE 2.24   These promotional materials support a product's identity by using the principle of continuity. (Left: *Common Knowledge Stationery, Visio Communications Self-promotional Mailer* © 2008. Right: *Visio Communications* © 2008. Reprinted with permission from Patrick Wilkey, www.visiocommunications.com.)

Variety

When everything is overly structured and unified, the result can be so predictable and repetitive that it becomes boring. *Variety* introduces interest through contrast. *Contrast* refers to the differences between elements. Unity attempts to accomplish the opposite by establishing similarity between elements.

Although they are very different from each other, unity and variety have two things in common: 1) they can both be applied to any or all elements of design, and 2) most successful designs are composed of a balance between these two principles. Too much variety causes chaos. Too much unity is boring. Find the perfect balance. and you may have created a masterpiece (see Figure 2.25).

 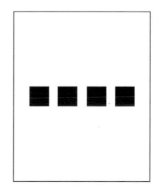

FIGURE 2.25   Left: Too much variety. Right: Too much unity.

Variety and Line

To create variety, line can be used as a contrasting design element. Contrasting thick and thin lines, as well as different line directions, creates interest and adds more variety to overly unified designs. Figure 2.26 is an example of two designs using contrasting lines to create variety.

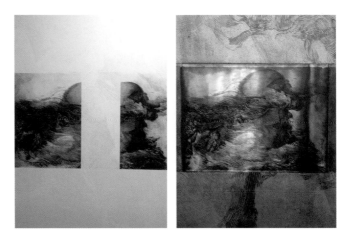

FIGURE 2.26   Two compositions incorporating contrasting widths of lines to create interest.
(*Untitled* © 2006. Reprinted with permission from Koichi Yamamoto.)

Figure 2.27 is a composition using contrasting line directions to create variety. Notice how the main line direction is vertical, and the less important elliptical line direction is still very noticeable, but only after we get the overall feeling that this composition feels vertical.

FIGURE 2.27   Left: A book cover that shows the hierarchy of contrasting line directions.
Right: Inverted image illustrates this point. (*Orbit* © 2008. Reprinted with permission from Alan Hashimoto.)

Variety and Visual Weight

Shapes may contrast in a variety of ways to create interest. They can vary in size or visual weight. *Visual weight* is the feeling that a design element is heavy or light, depending on the attention that element is given. This term usually applies to the size of a shape. Large shapes seem heavier than small shapes.

Visual weight is most commonly related to visual size, but it can also be applied to the value of a shape. If the value of a shape has little contrast with the background, the visual weight will seem light; the same shape may seem heavier if the values are more contrasted. Figure 2.28 uses simple shapes to make this point obvious. The design on the left shows a large shape that is closer in value to the background, which gives the feeling of less visual weight. The same shape in the design on the right feels heavier because of the contrast in value. The three smaller shapes are used to emphasize and give reference to the large shape's visual weight in both designs.

 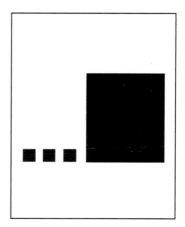

FIGURE 2.28 Simple designs illustrate how visual weight is influenced by value.

Variety and Contrasting Types of Shapes

Another way that shape can be used to create variety is to contrast different types of shapes, such as thick and thin shapes, tall and short shapes, rectilinear and curvilinear shapes. The two compositions in Figure 2.29 use a variety of different types of shapes to create interest through contrast.

The design on the left of Figure 2.29 creates interest by contrasting the organic shapes of leaves with very simple geometric lines and shapes. In the design at the right, the round shape of the magnifying glass and eye is in distinct contrast to the other surrounding sharp shapes.

FIGURE 2.29   Variety and contrasting shapes.

(Left: *Mountain Ash Leaves* © 2008. Reprinted with permission from Adrian Van Suchtelen. Right: *Visio Communications Bid Pack Illustration* © 2008. Reprinted with permission from Patrick Wilkey, www.visiocommunications.com.)

If all elements have variety and are different from one another, the result is chaos and disorder. Variety must be used with unity to create a successful design. There must be similarity, harmony, and variety to add interest. It is up to the designer to balance these two principles. A design can emphasize unity or variety, but both principles should be present. Figure 2.30 uses simple shapes to illustrate this concept. The design on the left emphasizes unity over variety. All of the shapes are very similar, but there is variation in the size of each shape. The design on the right emphasizes variety over unity. You can see a variety of shapes and sizes unified by placement and repetition of each shape placed throughout the entire design.

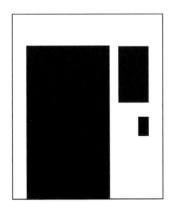

FIGURE 2.30   A design that emphasizes unity over variety, and a design that emphasizes variety over unity.

FOCAL POINT AND VISUAL HIERARCHY

A *focal point* is an element that is given emphasis so it will attract attention. It is a way to catch the viewer's attention and make the viewer look deeper into a design. Contrast is one way to create a focal point by making an element different from its surroundings; however, unity must be part of a focal point to ensure it will still fit into the overall composition. Beginning with the simple design on the left in Figure 2.31 and continuing to the design on the right, a focal point is created using line direction, different types of shapes, contrasting values, and contrasting color.

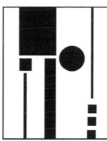

FIGURE 2.31   Focal point created using line direction, different types of shapes, contrasting values, and contrasting color.

Another way of creating a focal point is by the positioning of an element. If a shape, value, or color is isolated and positioned away from the majority of the other elements, it will receive more attention and become a focal point. Figure 2.32 is an example of a Web site that creates a focal point using placement, as well as other elements, to create a focal point. The page on the left uses positioning to separate unrelated information and group related information. Size and value are used to organize this information in terms of importance. The page on the right positions the "pop-up" window in the center and surrounds the light value with darker values, giving this page an obvious focal point.

FIGURE 2.32   Two pages from a Web site that show obvious focal points using placement, value, and size variation. (*Alison Ragguette* © 2008. Reprinted with permission from Jiong Li.)

Many designs have several focal points. These must be organized carefully. They cannot all command attention at the same time. When a design consists of many different areas of emphasis, the concept of hierarchy must be introduced. The idea of *visual hierarchy* is to organize each area of emphasis so that it does not conflict or take away attention from another area of emphasis. Focal points must be viewed one at a time in stages. One focal point will get the most attention. The viewer's eye will then move to another subtler focal point and from there to another. The careful staging of focal points and areas of emphasis will lead the viewer from one part of a design to the next until the entire design has been viewed in detail. Areas of lesser emphasis are called *accents*. They keep the viewer's attention in the subtlest areas of a design.

Figure 2.33 illustrates two examples of visual hierarchy. The illustration on the left is composed of three main groups of shapes: 1) The Indian and horse, 2) cabinet and water pitcher, and 3) stand with wheel. The Indian and horse represent the largest group of shapes, and the contrast in color from the background makes it the most obvious place to begin looking at the composition. The cabinet and pitcher would be observed next and then the smaller stand and wheel. Value also plays a part in guiding us from one area to the other. We see the white on the horse first. Then our eye is drawn to the white pitcher, basin, and towel. From there our attention goes to a tiny white shape on the handle that is connected to the wheel, which helps our eye continue to the lower left and then up to the whiteness in the sky and over again to the white color of the horse.

The illustration on the right is made up of farm animal shapes in a variety of sizes. Starting with the smallest animation in the upper-left corner, our eye travels to the right, and we end up in the right side of the composition with the largest animal. Because of the contrast in value, our eye goes left to the pig. The cool green and blue colors contrasted by the warm browns and oranges help lead our eye back to the smallest animal in the upper-left corner. We can continue to look at the entire illustration again.

FIGURE 2.33   Two illustrations that emphasize visual hierarchy. (Left: *Left Behind* © 2008. Reprinted with permission from Glen Edwards. Right: *I Could Chuck You Duck!* © 2008. Reprinted with permission from Scott Wakefield.)

Not all designs have focal points. Generally speaking, the absence of a focal point usually results in the entire composition being seen as a pattern. A pattern is a repetition of a similar or exact element of design. Patterns do not communicate individual elements as quickly as a design using visual hierarchy because there are no beginnings or ending points of interest. Figure 2.34 shows four examples of designs that have no focal point. The design on the left is a painting that uses a variety of shapes and lines, but no focal point is evident. The design in the upper right is a repetitive pattern that uses similar shapes. The middle-right and lower-right designs are self-generating designs created through programming software. They are also patterns with no specific focal point.

FIGURE 2.34   Compositions with no specific focal point. (Left: *Ox Killer Hollow* © 2008 Reprinted with permission Woody Shephard. Upper right: *Knotwork* © 2008, Middle right: *Turner Layout* © 2008, Lower right: *Phoenix Layout* © 2008. Reprinted with permission from Jordan Leary.)

BALANCE

The visual principle that a design is weighted equally is called *balance*. Visual balance gives a natural feeling that is achieved by distributing weight equally on both sides of a composition. Things that are tipped, leaning, or heavy to one side or the other make us feel uneasy and exemplify *imbalance*. Figure 2.35 is a diagram of a balanced design and a diagram of an imbalanced design.

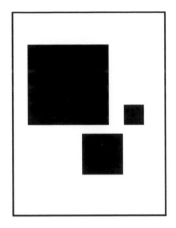 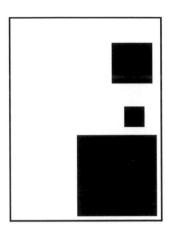

FIGURE 2.35   These two diagrams illustrate balance in the left design and imbalance on the right.

When one side of a design is exactly the same as the other side, it is called *symmetrical balance*. It is also referred to as *classical balance* because of the historical significance of symmetry in Greek and Roman architecture. *Formal* is another term given to symmetrical balance. It is based on the fact that symmetrical designs give the feeling of stability and permanence. Figure 2.36 is an example of symmetrical balance.

FIGURE 2.36   A design that is symmetrically balanced.

Balanced designs, which use elements that are very different from each other, are referred to as *asymmetrically balanced*. The weight of the design is distributed unevenly, but balance is still maintained. Figure 2.37 is an example of asymmetrical balance. These individual double-page spreads are all asymmetrically balanced. Continuity and harmony are maintained through the use of a similar grid structure, colors, and theme.

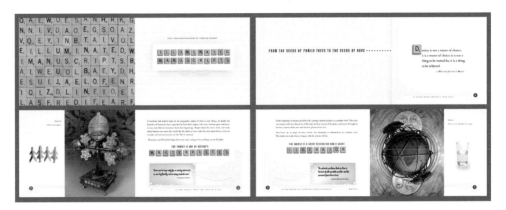

FIGURE 2.37   A design that is asymmetrically balanced. (*Illuminated Manuscripts*: Four double-page spreads © 2008. Reprinted with permission from Patrick Wilkey, www.visiocommunications.com.)

Both symmetrical and asymmetrical designs use a *fulcrum,* or center balancing point, to achieve balance. The fulcrum for symmetry is in the center of a composition. In asymmetry, the fulcrum is shifted to one side or the other to maintain the balance between dissimilar elements. Figure 2.38 shows the location of the fulcrum for a symmetrical design on the left and the location of the fulcrum of an asymmetrical design on the right.

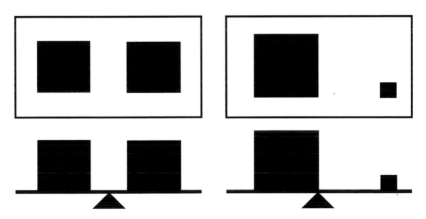

FIGURE 2.38   The location of the fulcrum for a symmetrical design (left) and asymmetrical design (right).

Radial balance is another kind of balance. It can be described as balance that radiates out from a central focal point. It can be either symmetrical or asymmetrical depending on the location of its focal point. This type of balance is commonly used when a dynamic focal point is required. All of the attention from anywhere in the design will lead back to a single source, as seen in Figure 2.39. Advertising and packaging use radial balance to attract and hold a viewer's attention in a single spot so that a visual message has time to be delivered. The next time you go grocery shopping, notice how many packages use radial balance to grab and hold your attention.

FIGURE 2.39   Left: Asymmetrical radial balance. Right: Symmetrical balance.   (Left: *Asimov Book Cover* © 2008. Reprinted with permission from Alan Hashimoto. Upper right: *Aries* © 2008. Reprinted with permission from Alan Hashimoto. Lower right: *Time Package* © 2008. Reprinted with permission from Alan Hashimoto.)

SUMMARY

The concepts and ideas associated with Gestalt theories and the principles of design can apply to many different forms of design other than two-dimensional. Take a closer look at a piece of furniture or an example of industrial design, and see if you can identify the harmony and variety in its design. Do any of these examples make use of continuity, repetition, rhythm, or contrast? Are they asymmetrically balanced or symmetrically balanced?

The design principles can be found in the organization and design of almost anything. Have you ever organized a party? You assumed that for a successful social function everyone should have something in common. You also knew that if everyone had the same experiences, interests, and hobbies it would get boring. This is an example of balancing harmony with variety. Can you think of any experiences that are good examples of continuity, repetition, rhythm, contrast, and balance?

The elements and principles of design are the foundation for every project in this book. These concepts are universal, but the specifics of how they will be used are dependent on the design problem to be solved. The next step and chapter deal with the procedures associated with defining design problems and creating visual solutions using the elements and principles of design.

3

INTRODUCTION TO CONTENT AND FORM: PROBLEM SOLVING AND THE DIGITAL PROCESS

INTRODUCTION

Now that the elements and principles of design have been defined, the next step is to make this information relevant to each individual by solving specific design problems and creating original designs digitally. This chapter will introduce you to the steps involved in conceptualization and give basic information concerning digital tools and their use.

To begin, there are two primary concepts dealing with visual design: content and form. *Content* is the subject matter, concept, or solution to a design problem. *Form* is the actual physical visual created as a final finished object or image.

Another concept that is related to both content and form is *process*. *Process* is the procedure and steps necessary for the creation of a visual. It can be divided into two very different ideas: conceptual and production. *Conceptual process* is the "thinking" part of design content. It involves the organization of a series of steps that will lead to the idea and solution to a visual problem. After the conceptual process is completed, the process of *production* may begin. The *production process* deals with "doing." It is the organization and implementation of the steps involved with the physical creation of the visual form.

All the following chapters have been designed to take advantage of these universal and classic design concepts. Each chapter deals with specific design elements and principles. A design project will be presented for you to solve, followed by a tutorial that will help you complete this project digitally.

The following section explains the general ideas and procedures associated with each of these concepts as they relate to the seven projects in this book. Each project will be discussed in more detail in the following chapters.

INTRODUCTION TO DESIGN PROJECTS

The previous two chapters were concerned with the general content that makes up most visual designs. With the exception of color, which will be detailed later in Chapter 11, "Design Project 5: Color and Color Theory," these chapters covered the basic elements and principles of design that should be evident when designing any visual. Each of the following chapters introduces an element or principle that requires you to create an original design following basic rules. Beginning with a simple designed shape using elementary digital techniques and tools, each project builds from the preceding chapter, adding a new design element, principle, digital technique, or tool. The final project uses all the elements and principles to create a very involved design using most of the tools and techniques introduced in each tutorial. The following is a brief description of the seven projects included in this book. You should get a basic idea of how these projects build onto one another to create increasingly more difficult and sophisticated designs. The final form of each of these designs will be a tabloid-size digital print.

Design Project 1: The first project is divided into four related but different designs. Each design examines four basic methods of abstraction using a combination of design principles and elements. Each method will have its own chapter and design project (see Chapters 4-8). After the introduction to content and process in these chapters, you will be introduced to some of the basic tools and techniques Adobe Illustrator uses to create simple designs.

Design Project 2: Chapter 8 "Using Methods of Abstraction to Create a Logo" reinforces what has been taught in the first project through the process of designing and creating a logo. Exploration of picture frames and the selection of type help in solving this design problem.

Design Project 3: Chapter 9 "Figure Abstraction and Nonobjective Shape" is also about shape as a design element subject to the principles of harmony and variety. Stylized figures are abstracted and distorted to demonstrate the principles of continuity, symmetrical balance, and open form versus closed form. More involved digital tools and techniques are also introduced.

Design Project 4: Value as a design element is the focus of the project in Chapter 10 "Value." A basic value study of photographic composition is the basis for this project. Examining the basic design of photographs and understanding how to create value digitally are the main topics.

Design Project 5: Chapter 11 "Color and Color Theory" combines all the design principles associated with shape and value, but it is expanded to include the element of color. Color theory and color schemes are used to create designs from multiple sources. Digital color and how to mix and apply color are covered in this project.

Design Project 6: Chapter 12 "Typeface Design" deals with the relationship among value, shape, letterforms, and type used as text. Text type, as a design element, and its association with pattern and implied texture are emphasized. More information concerning digital type and how to create and manipulate type are discussed in the tutorials.

Design Project 7: In Chapter 13 "Digital Montage/Collage" a collage using photography and illustrated images encompasses the elements that make up this next project. Color, value, shape, and line are used to create a composition that will demonstrate all the principles associated with design. Digital paint programs, tools, and techniques make up most of the tutorials. Another part of this project focuses on implied textures and patterns. Experimentation with the various filters incorporated with paint programs are explored. More involved tools and techniques related to raster imaging are the topic of tutorials.

CONCEPTUAL PROCESS

As mentioned earlier, the conceptual process is the "thinking" part of designing. The following procedures should aid you in this first part of the design process.

Step 1: Research and Define the Problem

The first step in the conceptual process is to ask questions and gather as much information and research as possible about the design project. After examining all this material, parameters and guidelines are created to make the design problem easier to define. After the problem to be solved is clear, the process of focusing on a solution can begin.

Step 2: Preliminary Solutions, Organized List of Options, and Thumbnail Sketches

A single problem may have an infinite number of solutions. These solutions may be narrowed through a process of objective reasoning, close observation, and educated guessing. You might want to organize options by writing them down in lists, which makes your ideas more concrete and easier to examine and compare. Think about the specific reasons why one design choice may be better than another. If there are no specific reasons for that choice, it might not be the best pick. The definition of design is planned organization. If a design is "planned," then decisions concerning design choices should be clear.

After exploring all your preliminary alternatives, give them a visual representation by creating small, quick sketches called *thumbnails*. Thumbnails should be concerned with only the most basic information. They should be small and not detailed to allow for the maximum number of ideas in the least amount of time. By quickly getting these visuals onto paper with a pencil or pen, thumbnails allow for more intuitive thinking and make it easier to quickly change direction to explore alternative views and approaches to visual problem solving. Figure 3.1 illustrates how the object of thumbnail sketches is to produce as many ideas as possible and not worry too much about details.

FIGURE 3.1 Quickly drawn thumbnail sketches on the left are very crude, but convey the essence of a variety of ideas. The solution to this design project has been narrowed to the two designs on the upper right. Located on the lower right is the final finished solution for a corporate logo.

(*RELM* © 2008. Reprinted with permission from Raymond Earl and Alan Hashimoto.)

Well-executed thumbnails of people should convey simple characteristics and gestures that express the personality and nature of the subject. The sketches should not be too concerned about all the specifics that can be added later. Figure 3.2 shows examples of some selected thumbnail sketches used to visualize characters for an animation. These very simple preliminary drawings were created quickly, but they communicate clearly the basic characteristics of each figure or model. Notice the emotional quality of line and how drawing style can vary and reflect the personality of each character even at this preliminary stage.

FIGURE 3.2   A variety of quickly-drawn thumbnail character sketches.
(Top two rows of thumbnail sketches © 2003. Reprinted with permission from Nathan Tufts.
Bottom row of thumbnail sketches © 2003. Reprinted with permission from Jon Pitcher.)

You do not need drawing experience to create thumbnails. Simple lines and shapes can represent objects and object placement. Details can be added later using other tools or software. Figure 3.3 is a good example of how simple lines drawn abstractly represent placement of subject matter in an illustration.

FIGURE 3.3 A thumbnail sketch and the finished illustration it inspired.
(*Barrel Pond Romance* © 2003. Reprinted with permission from Alan Hashimoto.)

Step 3: Roughs—Refined Preliminary Visual Design Solutions and Alternatives

After a decision concerning several design solutions has been reached, these solutions should be expanded and refined as roughs. *Roughs* are preliminary options of a design that communicate in more detail than thumbnails. Roughs are placed side by side so they can be compared, contrasted, and analyzed so that decisions concerning specific design options can be made. In Figure 3.4, the two designs located on the top row and the bottom-left design are examples of three rough alternatives for an advertising campaign dealing with education and the future. The lower-right design is the final design that was selected.

Roughs help the designer focus on alternatives without having to commit to a final decisive solution. Roughs should clearly communicate problem-solving concepts, position and proportions of shapes and objects, value and color, and general composition.

Experimentation with new methods for creating the final project can be tested and developed at this stage if necessary.

Step 4: Composites or Comps

Comps are the final preliminary step before the finished design is created. A final concept or concepts should be chosen, and all the elements involved should be put into position. Tools and techniques should have been thoroughly tested and chosen by this point. The comp should be as similar to the final solution as time and resources permit.

FIGURE 3.4   Three rough alternatives and the final design.
(*The Future of Education* © 2003. Reprinted with permission from Alan Hashimoto.)

Many times, the comp follows the exact techniques of the final design and may even appear to have all the details and refinements of a finished design. The main purpose of a comp is for presentation and discussion of last-minute changes before expensive and time-consuming production begins. Figure 3.5 is an example of a pencil comp.

If a final solution uses a dark background, using light-colored pencils on black board seems to duplicate the effects of the finish more accurately and efficiently without spending too much time. The time saved on the production aspect of a comp can be applied to the conceptual phase so more original and alternative ideas can be explored. The color comp at the top of Figure 3.6 was created in two hours. The comp in the lower-left side of Figure 3.6 was drawn in less than an hour.

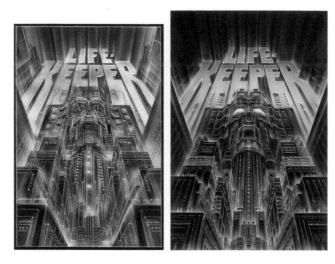

FIGURE 3.5   A comp and the finished art created from this comp.
(*Life Keeper* © 2006. Reprinted with permission from Alan Hashimoto.)

FIGURE 3.6   Top is a comp and the finished art made from this comp. Bottom left is a comp and the finished art created from this comp. (*Marc Aramian, Soundscape* © 2003. Reprinted with permission from Alan Hashimoto. *Hierarchy Search* © 2003. Reprinted with permission from Alan Hashimoto.)

Step 5: The Final Design or Finish

After completing the preliminary steps, final decisions are made. The final or finish is the result, which is the last step in the conceptual process. The production process can now take place. Mass production processes such as printing will use the finish as a guide to compare the actual product or print with the finished design. In animation, textures, models, environments, and sound can now be edited together into the final video or film.

The final phase of the conceptual process as it relates to the projects in this book will lead to a 2D design created digitally as a print. The "Production Process" section in this chapter examines the basic concepts of digital hardware and software necessary for the production part of the process.

The various steps involved in the conceptual process may seem time consuming, but they are very necessary to ensure that the design problem is thoroughly understood and researched beforehand, and the best solution is selected. In most cases, these steps will save time by avoiding misunderstandings, mistakes, and changes to finished designs. Figure 3.7 illustrates the various steps involved in the conceptual process. The content or visual problem being solved deals with a design for a skateboard. The upper-left design is the rough sketch chosen for the final design. The center-top and lower-left designs are preliminary roughs where line and value solutions are worked out. The lower-center design is the final line and value study. Color decisions and other design elements are combined to create the final art on the far right.

FIGURE 3.7   Rough sketches, line and value studies, and final design.
(*Grassroots Skateboards* © 2008. Reprinted with permission from Dave Smellie.)

The conceptual process is used for all types of design. Figures 3.8 and 3.9 are two examples of digital dimensional animated designs that use rough sketches, comps, or composite preliminary art, mockettes or clay sculptures, and basic un-textured digital models to analyze the final form and eventually create the finished design.

FIGURE 3.8 The sketch on the left shows the back of the figure. The sketch in the middle is the front. The clay mockette is used to study the entire figure in three dimensions. Below is a sequence of frames showing the digital figure engaged in an animated walk cycle.

(*Tin Man* © 2008. Reprinted with permission from Scott Moore.)

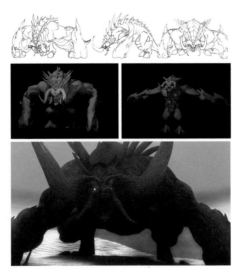

FIGURE 3.9 The rough sketches on top show various views of the figure. The two rendered models in the center illustrate the figure in a crouched and upright position to test the structure, movement, and how it will be lit. Below is a frame from the animation showing the setting, texture, and lighting.

(*Razor Back* © 2008. Reprinted with permission from Jess Ung and Beau Hacking.)

PRODUCTION PROCESS

The projects in this book are to be created using a computer and related software. The following is an introduction to the most basic digital concepts dealing with the production process. Each chapter will introduce new and increasingly advanced digital production concepts, tools, and techniques.

Computer Applications Used in Design

Looking back through the history of graphic design, each era had its own unique set of tools. Some had letterpresses, some had drafting tools, and some were designed by collage. Over the past 30 years, computers have become a key component in the world of art and design.

For the past few decades, designers have used computers to create digital imagery. Setting type became easier, color-correcting photographs became simpler, and the user was given a 3D space in which to work.

As you know, the operating system of a computer is the environment that manages all the programs or applications and file systems. Two major operating systems are the Microsoft Windows OS (PC) and the Apple Macintosh OS (Mac).

Along with the OS, software applications can be installed that allow you to do a variety of tasks. You can use software to surf the Internet, check your email, write papers, listen to music, make a movie, do your taxes, or play video games. Other applications can help you work toward a career as a digital artist and designer.

The OSs are coded differently, which allows some operations to be more efficient than others. Different OSs often require a specific version of software. For instance, an application specifically written for Windows cannot be installed on a Macintosh and vice versa. Most major software developers create applications that are available for the PC and the Mac.

Software Applications for Graphics

Software applications used to create images can be divided into two main categories: paint programs (bitmap) and object-oriented (vector) programs. Each type of software is unique and has its own distinct purpose in creating and modifying visuals. Paint programs, such as Adobe Photoshop, create a variety of bitmap (pixel-based) images, whereas object-oriented programs, such as Adobe Illustrator, create vector (mathematically based) images.

For the purposes of this book, the industry standard in software is represented. For bitmap images, the industry standard is Adobe Photoshop, and for vector graphics, the industry standard is Adobe Illustrator.

Paint Programs: Bitmap Graphics

If you look closely at a painting, you will see that every bit of the canvas is covered with bright hues and tempered shadows. Imagine that canvas in your head and divide the picture into little squares of single colors. Those little squares make up the image.

Each of those little squares of color is called a *pixel* (short for picture element). A bitmap is an image made up of dozens of millions of those little pixels. For example, the ever-lovable "smiley" in Figure 3.10 is made up of 256 pixels (16 rows of 16 pixels) that are easy to see. In Figure 3.11, the pixels are harder to see because there are so many. The more pixels an image contains, the higher the image quality. This is called *resolution*, or a ratio of pixels per inch.

FIGURE 3.10   This smiley is made up of 256 pieces of information or bits.

FIGURE 3.11   A detail from the bitmap image reveals that the image is made up of many pixels.

Images that are created to be viewed on the Internet are examples of low-resolution images. Because they are designed specifically to be seen on a computer screen, a high number of pixels is not required. You can see the individual pixels in images like this.

In magazines, newspapers, books, or anything printed, an image's resolution is a different story. The quality of the image needs to be higher in printed works. Some magazines and high-end publications use images that have 2,400 pixels per inch (ppi). That's a little less than 5.8 million pixels per square inch (ppi) or 5,760,000 pixels, to be exact.

Each pixel (or piece of information) takes up space. Images that have a high ppi tend to have very large file sizes and require a lot of disk space. One of the benefits of a small pixel count in Web images is that they can be downloaded (or transferred) quickly.

Images can be created directly in paint programs using the drawing tools available in the software. Images can also be scanned from photographs, drawings, paintings, objects, fabric, and so on. Images can also be captured via digital cameras, video cameras, and Web cams. The computer rewrites the image as pixels, which allows you to take the image into a program such as Photoshop for image manipulation, color correction, compositing, and a variety of other uses.

After an image is created, the file can be saved in many formats for later use. Each format has its own unique qualities. A TIFF (Tagged Image File Format) is a cross-platform graphic that can be read on both PCs and Macs. These images are meant for printing because they have a large tolerance for color depth. As you scan your images for the projects you will do in this book, save the files as TIFF for the best results. (They have file extension .tif.)

Object-Oriented Programs: Vector Graphics

Vector-based images are defined by mathematical equations. A full-color rendered vector image appears on the left side of Figure 3.12 and on the right, you can see the lines that were used to create it.

Images are drawn using the point-and-line system. To draw a straight line, all you need are two points and the line in between. You'll use those points and lines to draw simple or complex images. In Figure 3.13, there are two circles. The circle on the left is made up of 64 points and 64 lines. The circle on the right uses 4 points and 4 curved lines. These curved lines, called Bézier Curves, can be used to simplify the path and the object.

Vector drawings normally have small file sizes because they contain only mathematical data about the placement of the points and the angles of the curves. These files are size independent and can be scaled to size with no degradation of the image. Illustrator saves these files with the extension .ai (for Adobe Illustrator).

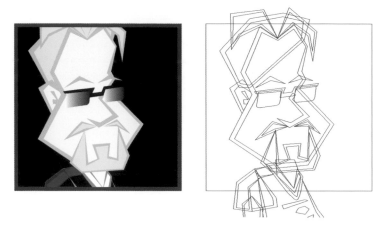

FIGURE 3.12   The image on the left is the vector illustration. On the right are the points and lines that it took to make the drawing. (*Avatar* © 2000. Reprinted with permission from Michael Clayton.)

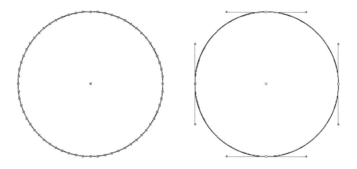

FIGURE 3.13   The principle of point, curve, and line is demonstrated with these two circles.

HOW TO USE DESIGN APPLICATIONS AND THIS BOOK

This text contains many assignments, projects, and tutorials to help you learn the basics of these two software applications used for design by both students and professionals.

We will begin with the object-oriented program, Adobe Illustrator CS4, using the tools to create and modify basic shapes. Step-by-step tutorials are included to show you how to use the different tools, panels, and settings available in this program.

Toward the end of this text, your attention will turn to bitmap files and paint programs. For this section, Adobe Photoshop CS4 will be used. Again, tutorials will show you the basic tools and concepts that can be used.

Along the way, you will be introduced to new tools, commands, and panels. Each of these can be accessed using panels, menus, and the menu bar along the top of the screen. These will be written in such a way that they can be easily identified. For example, when you need to open a new document, you'll see "choose File > New." The ">" indicates that a menu or submenu is available under that option. To open a new document, you would select File from the top menu and then New (Figure 3.14).

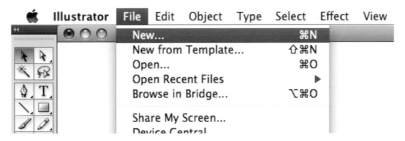

FIGURE 3.14   Choose File from the main menu and then select New to open a new document.

Some menus also have submenus. For example, the instruction, "to move this object to the back, select Object > Arrange > Send to Back," requires you to select the Object menu, then mouse down to Arrange, and then over to the Send to Back option (Figure 3.15).

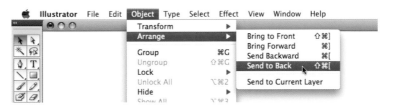

FIGURE 3.15   Choose Object from the main menu, then Arrange, and then
Send to Back from the submenu.

Simple keyboard combinations (called *shortcuts*) can access most tools. These shortcuts follow the name of the tool of the menu option in parentheses. For example:

To open a new file, choose File > New (PC: Ctrl + N; Mac: Command + N).

The keyboard shortcuts are different for the PC and Mac, but normally they only differ by one key (see Figure 3.16). On the PC, the primary key for a shortcut is the Control key. On the Mac, it's the Command (or Apple) key. In this case, to open a new document on a PC, you hold down the Ctrl key and press "N." On the Mac, you press the Command key and the "N" key.

FIGURE 3.16 Location of the Ctrl key on the PC (left) and the Command key on a Mac (right).

Some tools in the toolbar can be accessed, switched, or activated with a simple key press. For example, in the instruction, "Select the Direct Selection Tool (A)," pressing the "A" key on the keyboard would switch the current tool to the desired tool (Figure 3.17).

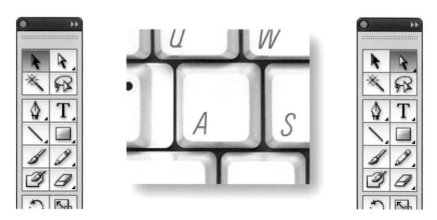

FIGURE 3.17 Pressing the "A" key can activate the Direct Selection Tool without physically selecting the tool on the toolbar.

By using these software applications on your computer coupled with this book, you will have a tool that can become very powerful and pivotal in your career as a designer. Not only will you learn the software, but you will also gain an understanding of the thought process involved in creating great designs.

SUMMARY

You are now ready to begin using your knowledge of problem solving and digital production processes as they relate to the elements and principles of design. To review, you should be able to answer the following questions.

- Name and identify the elements of design. (Answers: line, shape, space or negative shape, form, value, color, texture)
- Name and identify the main principles of design. (Answers: harmony or unity and variety). (Additional answers could be listed under these two main principles. Harmony: repetition, rhythm, continuity. Variety: contrast.
- What is content? What is form? (See definitions) What primary concept is related to both? (*Process* is related to both).
- What two concepts are part of process? (Answers: conceptual "thinking" and production "doing.")
- List the steps involved with "conceptual process". (Answers: 1) Research and define the problem. 2) Organize a list of options, thumbnail sketches. 3) Refine preliminary solutions and alternatives, roughs. 4) Composites or comps. 5) Final design or finish.)
- List and describe the two main categories of graphics software. (Answers: Object oriented [drawing program], Bitmap [paint program].)

The following are exercises that will help you understand the design process. Think of a fairly complex object and without actually looking at it, visualize it in your mind. Very quickly complete a few thumbnail drawings. This object could be a machine such as a kitchen appliance, flower, animal, or just about anything that has several parts to it. After you have several simple sketches, look at the real-life object if possible. A photograph could work, too. Take a close look and see how many details or proportions you may have missed. Do another series of drawings after studying the real object. Notice how much more you have added. This is a good example of why research is so important. We think we know what something looks like, but upon closer inspection and research, we can see there are so many things we may miss. Study this object again and draw it from different angles and views. Notice how the object can be visually altered, depending on how we view it. This is an example of why we must try as many options as possible to experiment and find the best way to portray any object. Later on in this book, you will see how drawing something by hand before you scan it helps define many of the subtle details of an object. This drawing can be used as a map that guides you toward a finished solution.

4

DESIGN PROJECT 1 (PART 1): ABSTRACTION THROUGH SIMPLIFICATION

INTRODUCTION TO ABSTRACTION

In this project, you will use the process of abstraction to explore some of the ways in which the previously introduced elements and principles of design are used in visual communication.

Beginning with a given object, you will use drawing to evaluate and understand the visual aspects of the object. Then you will make a specific series of design alterations to explore some of the methods commonly used in the type of abstraction found in symbol design. This project addresses basic drawing and observation skills, and then uses the concepts of simplification, repetition, line and shape, and a combination thereof. You will use these concepts through cropping, scaling, repetition, using line to imply shape, and combining shapes into a unified whole.

An important part of this project is to explore and compare many possibilities within each of the methods used. Then each study is evaluated, and based on this evaluation, the best solutions are refined and finished.

FOUR BASIC METHODS OF ABSTRACTION

The purpose of this project is to allow you to examine and compare several of the methods commonly used in visual communications to abstract an object. Abstraction is the process of reducing an image or object to a simpler form. Because abstraction reduces the amount of visual information that a viewer must take in and decode, this method frequently allows for faster and more memorable visual communication and is commonly found in the design of visual symbols, trademarks, posters, and illustrations.

This project is broken down into four basic methods of abstraction. Each of these is applied to the same object so that you can see how a different design process affects the final design and the visual communication. Chapter 4 deals with abstraction through simplification, Chapter 5 examines abstraction through repetition, Chapter 6 addresses abstraction using line and shape, and Chapter 7 explores abstraction using a combination of object and type.

METHOD ONE: SIMPLIFICATION

This part of the project deals with one of the most commonly used methods of abstracting an object—that of eliminating some visual information to focus attention on the essential qualities of the object or to emphasize some particular aspect of the object. Using this method first allows the designer to study the subject matter in careful detail and, through experimentation, explore the basic shapes and the shape relationships found within that object.

CONTENT: THE BASIC PROBLEM DEFINED

Each of the methods of abstraction is based on an initial series of black-and-white marker drawings of a simple man-made mechanical object (Figure 4.1).

FIGURE 4.1   Drawings can be made from a simple man-made
mechanical object, such as a hole punch.

Because these drawings will be used as the basis for all the subsequent methods of abstraction, be sure to pay attention to the accuracy of proportions and to shape relationships within the object (Figure 4.2). Although these should be simplified drawings of the object, they should not be silhouettes. The drawings should explore how the eye distinguishes various parts of the object and how light falling on the object helps a viewer understand the shapes within the object. Texture, color, and volume are not used in this project, so these qualities of the object should be either eliminated or translated to shape.

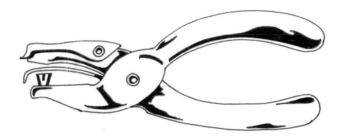

FIGURE 4.2   A simple drawing of an object.

Based on the drawings, do a series of studies within a specified frame that explores how to simplify the object (Figure 4.3). These simplification studies will explore positive and negative shape relationships to better understand unity, variety, and the relationship between positive and negative shapes. These studies will also allow you to explore what kinds of visual cues are necessary for the recognition of an object.

FIGURE 4.3   Studies from a simple drawing of a cordless phone.
(Abstraction Studies—Phone © 2005. Reprinted with permission from Robin Parker.)

Background: Shape

The most important design element used in this portion of the project is shape. What kinds of shapes are found within the object and how can both positive and negative shapes be used to create unity, variety, and recognition within the composition?

In some cases, an object is easily read as a white or dark shape that is surrounded by a contrasting background. This background is sometimes referred to as a *negative shape*. As shown on the left in Figure 4.4, many visual designs contain both positive and negative shapes that are equal in importance and in structure. In the design on the right, neither the light shape nor the dark shape can be considered to be background. The shapes appear interchangeable. Designers use this concept to achieve multiple images within a simple enclosing form. This use of shape creates visual interest and allows the designer to communicate more visual information without making a design complex (Figure 4.5).

FIGURE 4.4   Positive shape and negative shape. The design on the left has shapes that are equal in importance. The one on the right does not.

FIGURE 4.5   The relationships that exist among objects, letters, and figure ground. (*Dino Park Logo, Boise Zoo Tee-Shirt Logo* © 2003. Reprinted with permission from Bob Winward.)

To create unity within a composition, the basic shapes should relate. Good design is based on relationships. Relating simple geometric shapes to each other is easier than unifying complex organic shapes and simple geometric shapes. Successful use of this concept allows the designer to achieve a good "fit" between the elements used in a composition.

Variety within this type of composition can be achieved by exploring the use of position and scale of the shapes and by varying shapes of the same type.

Recognition of an object frequently depends on understanding just which shapes are the necessary visual cues to that object. Some parts of an object are more important in identifying that object than others (Figure 4.6).

FIGURE 4.6   A design where the parts of the object are important to its identification.
(*Abstractions—Hole Punch* © 2004. Reprinted with permission from Matt Tovar.)

Conceptual Process

Now that you have the problem defined and all of the background for this stage of the project, you can begin the conceptual process outlined in Chapter 3. The following are the steps that you must take to complete this process.

1. Choose a simple man-made object for the project. This should be something familiar and not too complex or detailed. This project relies on understanding and using simple shapes. Some examples of the types of objects that might be used for this assignment are a cellular or cordless phone, spring-type clothespin, hole punch, channel lock pliers, or an adjustable compass (Figure 4.7). Do not select objects that rely on texture or color because these elements will not be part of this project.

2. Draw your object four to five times with the goal of improving the drawing each time (Figure 4.8). Do not do silhouette drawings. You need to try a number of different ways that you might represent the highlights and shadows that you see using only solid value shapes rather than "shading." As you do each initial drawing, be careful to observe and improve the overall proportions and shapes within the drawing.

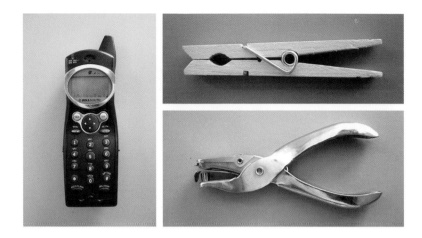

FIGURE 4.7   Objects that can be used for this project include a cordless phone, spring-type clothespin, or a hole punch.

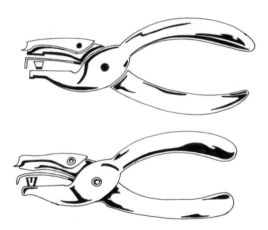

FIGURE 4.8   Two simple drawings of a hole punch.

3. To study certain areas of the drawings, you will need a pair of L-shaped cropping frames and a template of 4" × 4" squares. Make a pair of L-shaped cropping frames from black or dark gray mat board or a thick cover stock. These should be at least 8" long (Figure 4.9).
4. Make a template of squares that are 4" × 4" and 0.5" apart (Figure 4.9). Don't draw on this sheet. Place another piece of transparent or translucent paper—such as tracing paper—on top of this template and do your design work on the top sheet. When you fill this top sheet, you can replace it and keep working without having to redraw your initial squares.

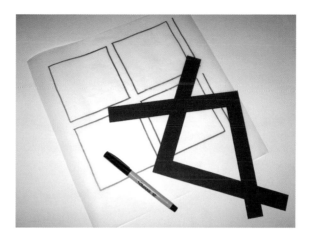

FIGURE 4.9   Cropping frames and a template of 4" x 4" squares.

5. Adjust the cropping frames to show a square area in one of your drawings. Move the frame around until you have isolated what you think would be an interesting composition and then draw that composition inside one of your squares (Figure 4.10).

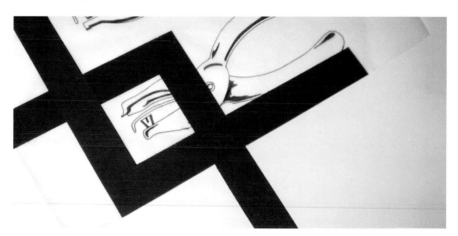

FIGURE 4.10   Use the cropping frame to focus on an interesting area of the simple drawings.

6. Move the frame around to find other possible compositions, and draw the ones that you find interesting on the tracing paper within the 4" × 4" squares with a black marker. Work in solid, filled-in shapes rather than outlined shapes. You can fill the shape with black and leave the background white, but you should also use white shapes within a black background (Figure 4.11).

FIGURE 4.11   Study taken from a detail of a simple drawing using the cropping frames.

7. Don't forget to adjust the cropping frames so that you are looking at both close-up and more complete versions of the object (Figure 4.12). Experimenting with scale is an important part of this project. Also, experiment with changing the angle of the object within the cropping frames.

FIGURE 4.12   Remember to adjust your cropping frames to change the scale and rotation of the area for the study.

8. You should do at least 25 of these initial compositions.
9. After you have completed your initial exploratory studies, evaluate them to select those with the strongest overall compositions and the most visual interest, and then refine these. Some of the things you should consider in selecting the best compositions are balance, unity through the use of similar shapes, variety to create interest, and recognition of the object. In Figure 4.13, the two compositions shown within the red rectangle were selected for further refinement. In each case, the shape of the positive object and the negative or background areas was compatible and interesting. The object is not "floating" within the frame but relates to the space around it. Both create an interesting shape within the surrounding negative space, and, in both cases, the object is identifiable. The shapes within the object itself are compatible because they are equally simple and use variations of the same types of shapes. The example in the blue square was not selected for further refinement because identification of the object would have been more difficult, and the surrounding space was less interesting.

FIGURE 4.13 Evaluating the first studies.
(*Abstraction Studies—Phone* © 2005. Reprinted with permission from Robin Parker.)

10. The refinement drawings should be done within the same square format. Based on the drawings that you select from your initial studies, do at least 10 refinement studies (Figure 4.14). Some of these may be variations from the same initial design study so that you can explore different ways of solving the problems that you see.

FIGURE 4.14   Ten refined drawings.
(*Abstraction Revisions—Phone* © 2005. Reprinted with permission from Robin Parker.)

11. From these 10 refined studies, select three to be scanned and converted to final Illustrator files (Figure 4.15).

The "Production Process" part of this chapter explains scanning and the steps required to create the finished design. Computer hardware and software can help with multiple options and alternatives after the initial design is realized. Digital methods will also ensure the accuracy and well-crafted production of your designs.

FIGURE 4.15   Three final studies completed in Illustrator.
(Top row: *Abstractions—Phone* © 2005. Reprinted with permission from Robin Parker.
Bottom row: *Abstractions—Clothespin* © 2005. Reprinted with permission from Jeremy Kenisky.)

Production Process

After the conceptual process of creating the final three studies is complete, scan the three final marker drawings into the computer. Using the object-oriented program, Adobe Illustrator, trace the drawings and complete the production process. The final form will be a digital file either for print or to be viewed on a computer monitor. The following sections deal with all the digital tools and techniques you will need to complete this project. The basics of scanning and more involved drawing tools will be outlined step-by-step in tutorials designed to create the final forms.

Scanning Basics

After you have finished creating the final studies for this section of the project, you are ready to go to the next step, which is to scan your final drawings for each design into the computer and bring them into Illustrator for tracing.

TUTORIAL   **SCANNING**

Have you ever used a copy machine? It is a lot like using a scanner. A scanner is a device that is connected to your computer and is used to make a digital copy of your photograph or drawing, which can then be edited using software on your computer (Figure 4.16).

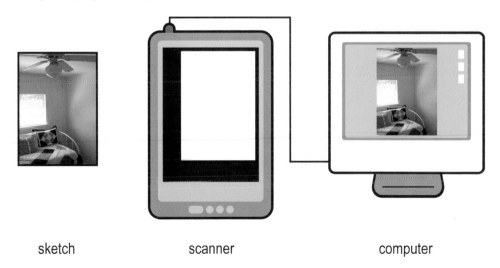

sketch   scanner   computer

FIGURE 4.16   To scan, you need three things: an image, a scanner, and a computer.

Although there are many kinds of scanners, the most popular is the desktop scanner. A few years ago, scanners were expensive, but today you can buy a scanner for less than $50. Scanners are so inexpensive that they are often bundled free with computer purchases. Any desktop scanner will do for this exercise, as will any scanning software.

1. With the computer and scanner powered on, open the top lid of the scanner and place your sketches face down on the scanning bed. Most scanners scan from top to bottom, so place your page in the top-right corner of the glass.
2. Close the lid on the scanner.
3. Launch the software you will use to scan your image.

Most scanners come with software that you can install on your computer. However, the best software comes with drivers for Photoshop, so that you can directly import or scan your image into Photoshop.

You may want to refer to the manual that came with your scanner or the Help section of the software that was packaged with it if you have any installation questions.

For Photoshop CS4 users with the necessary drivers installed, launch Photoshop CS4, choose File > Import from the menu bar, and select the appropriate application/scanner.

(The default setting for each scanner and software might be different. Following are general things to look for.)

4. Preview the image. This might require pressing a button named "Preview," or some scanners may automatically begin by previewing the image.

A *preview* is a quick scan of your image. Most software allows you to preset different qualities and settings before doing a final scan. A scanner "reads" every line of an image as the scanning head passes down along the scanning bed. It imports that information line-by-line into the computer (Figure 4.17). Some scanners scan in multiple passes so patience may be necessary.

5. Crop the area that you want to scan.

The software should allow you to crop the area of an image, so that you don't waste time scanning empty areas of the document. The selection box can be moved by mousing over the edges of the box until arrows appear that allow you to adjust the selection in or out and up or down (Figure 4.18).

6. Set the resolution of your image to 72 ppi (pixels per inch).

The resolution of the image is important. The higher the ppi, the better the quality of the image (Figure 4.19). When the resolution is set to 300 ppi, the scanner scans 300 pixels (the basic unit of measurement in computer graphics) of information per inch. For high-quality archiving scans or scanning for printed publications, a higher quality is necessary. When a scanner scans at 300 ppi, it is often much slower.

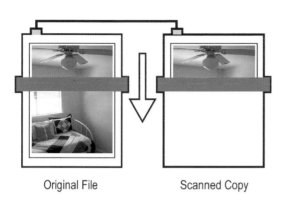

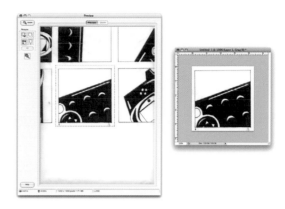

FIGURE 4.17   A scanner reads the image line-by-line and sends that information to the computer.

FIGURE 4.18   Use the scanning software's built-in cropping tools to select the area that you want to scan.

FIGURE 4.19   This image has been scanned at a size of 1" × 1" at three different resolutions: 300 ppi (left), 150 ppi (middle), and 72 ppi (right). The images have been scaled to 200%. The 300 ppi image has more dots, which gives it a finer print quality.

Because you need only to use these images on the screen, it is a waste to scan more information than you need. Your monitor's basic resolution is 72 ppi, so by scanning at that resolution you will easily be able to get the information that you need.

If you want to find a common ground, scan at 150 ppi. Although the scan will be better than a 72-ppi image, it will not have the excess information a 300-ppi scan would have.

7. Click Scan or Save. Now sit back and let the scanner do the work.

If you are scanning into Photoshop, you will have to save the image. Do so by selecting File > Save. In the Save dialog box, select a location to save your image to, name the file, and save it as a TIFF file. A TIFF file is a multipurpose file that can handle multiple color depths with equal ease.

If you scanned the image using some other software, save the file onto the desktop or in a specific location.

8. Repeat this process until all of your drawings have been scanned.

Scanning is simple. Follow the simple steps and you can scan in anything: photographs, paper, fabric, lace, soft textures, and so on. Further on in the text are other exercises that will require scanning. Refer to this section, as you need to.

TUTORIAL   ## CREATING A NEW DOCUMENT

To begin working in Illustrator CS4, you must create a new document. This file is where you will trace over the designs that you have scanned for this part of the project.

You can create a new document for each of the three final studies, or you can create multiple Artboards (new to CS4) and trace all three in one document.

The document can be set to any size and orientation. For this project, you will use the following basic settings:

- Name: Phase A
- Number of Artboards: 3
- Spacing: 1.5 inches
- Width: 4 inches
- Height: 4 inches
- Units: Inches
- Orientation: Portrait

1. Launch Adobe Illustrator CS4 and create a new document by selecting File > New (PC: Ctrl + N; Mac: Command + N). Make sure that the Artboard Setup is set according to Figure 4.20.

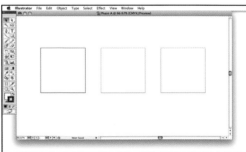

FIGURE 4.20   Create a new document with these specifications.

2. If your Rulers are not visible, select View > Show Rulers (PC: Ctrl + R; Mac: Command + R). A horizontal and vertical ruler showing inches will appear.
3. Save the document by choosing File > Save (PC: Ctrl + S; Mac: Command + S). The document might already have a name.

You should save your document frequently. You never know when your power might go out, the machine may freeze up, or another of a dozen things happen. You might want to make a projects folder that you can use to store the files from this text.

<table>
<tr><td>**TUTORIAL**</td><td>**PLACING AN IMAGE INTO ILLUSTRATOR CS4 FOR TRACING**</td></tr>
</table>

Follow these steps to insert an image into the Illustrator document.

1. Choose File > Place to open the Place dialog box. Find the file that you want to place, select it, and click Place. For this example, the image ch04_phone_study.tif is used. It is located in the Chapter 4 folder on the CD-ROM.

ON THE CD

If you choose to uncheck the Link box, the image file will be embedded in the document, increasing the file size. If it remains checked, you must keep the image that you have placed in the same location at all times. Illustrator will look for it each time the file is opened. If you have moved the file, the program will prompt you to find it. The file is now placed within the page (Figure 4.21).

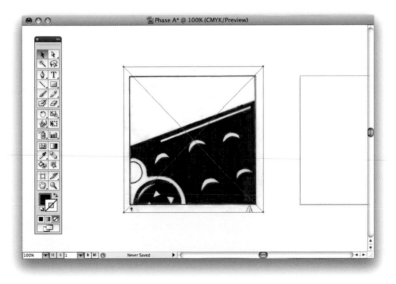

FIGURE 4.21 The image of the drawing is now placed in the page.

2. Open your Layers panel by selecting Window > Layers. (Your Layers panel may already be visible.) In your Layers panel, there should only be one layer named "Layer 1."

3. To change the name of this layer, double-click the name of the layer to open the Layer Options dialog box or choose Options for "Layer 1"... from the Options menu of the Layer panel (Figure 4.22).

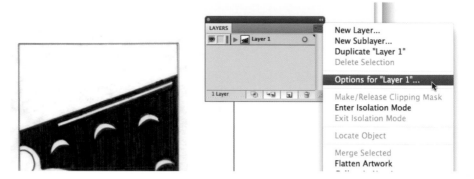

FIGURE 4.22   Opening the Layer Options dialog box.

4. In the Layer Options dialog box, name the layer "Tracing Image" (Figure 4.23).

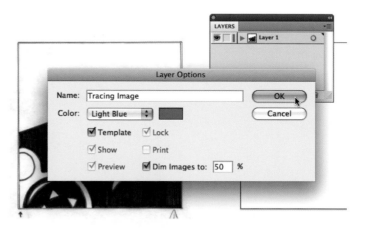

FIGURE 4.23   The Layer Options dialog box.

5. While in the Layer Options dialog box, check the Template box. This setting locks the layer so that it cannot be edited, makes it so the contents of the layer cannot be printed, and dims the image so that it can be easily traced. Click OK.

You will notice that the image is less bright and easier to look at.

6. Create a new layer by clicking on the New Layer icon in the Layers panel (Figure 4.24).

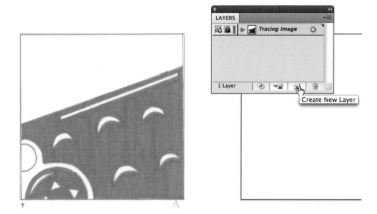

FIGURE 4.24   Location of the Create New Layer button.

7. Name the layer "Tracings." Follow Step 4, previously mentioned, to name the new layer.
8. Make sure that the Tracing Image layer is locked by checking for the lock in the Lock box (Figure 4.25).

A locked layer will keep you from inadvertently moving or working on the layer with the image.

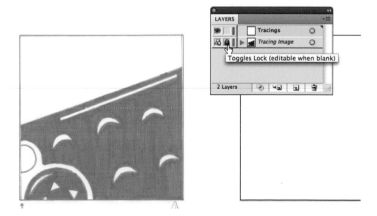

FIGURE 4.25   Click the Toggle Lock area of the layer in the Layers Panel.

9. Open the Layer Options for the Tracing Image layer by double-clicking on the Tracing Image layer or by selecting the layer and choosing the appropriate option from the Layer Option menu. Notice that the Print box is unchecked. (This happened when you checked the Template box in Step 5.) Click OK.

The layer will not print with this box unchecked. As you trace your thumbnails, you may periodically want to print them out to see how they look. If you do so, the information on that layer will not print, making it easier to see your tracings (Figure 4.26). You can set any layer not to print.

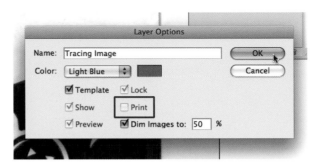

FIGURE 4.26   With the Print box unchecked in the Tracing Image layer, only the Tracings layer will print.

You are now ready to trace over your drawing.

TUTORIAL   **BASIC DRAWING TOOLS**

The Tools panel (Windows > Tools) is the home of all the tools used in this program. This is sometimes referred to as the *Toolbox.*

More than 70 tools are housed in the Tools panel. If they were all displayed at the same time, the screen would be too crowded, so you can "hide" certain tools until you need them. If you take a closer look at the Tools panel in Illustrator, you will see that some of the tools have a small triangle in the bottom right-hand corner; this is a visual clue to let the user know that other tools are nested under that tool. To reveal those tools, click and hold down your mouse button until the tools pop up. Then, with your mouse button still pressed, drag over to the desired tool and release the mouse. The tool will now be selected. For example, under the Rectangle tool in Illustrator CS4 are five other tools: the Rounded Rectangle tool, the Ellipse tool, the Polygon tool, the Star tool, and the Flare tool (Figure 4.27).

You need to become familiar with a few basic drawing tools in order to create this first design. For this example, you will use the two basic Shape Tools: Rectangle tool and Ellipse tool.

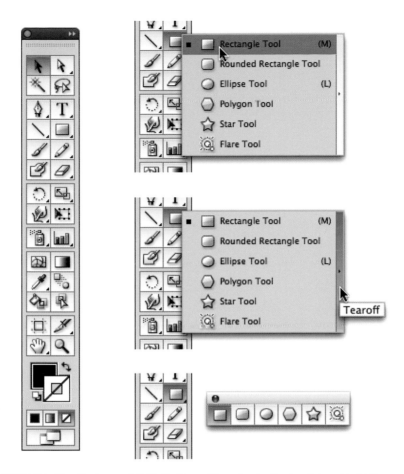

FIGURE 4.27   The Tools panel (left). To "tear off" a subset of tools, click and hold the mouse
down on the main tool (top right). Drag the cursor over to the tear tab on the
right (middle right) and then release the mouse to "tear off" the subset (lower right).

The Rectangle tool creates rectangular shapes (rectangles and squares), whereas
the Ellipse tool creates elliptical shapes (ovals and circles). Almost all of the tools
within Illustrator are that literal in their name and description.

The Rectangle and Ellipse Tools

The Rectangle tool (M) can be used to draw rectangles and squares. To use the
Rectangle tool, click on the tool in the Tools panel or press the M key on your
keyboard. You draw a rectangle by clicking on the Artboard, holding down the
mouse button, and dragging out the perimeter of the shape (Figure 4.28).

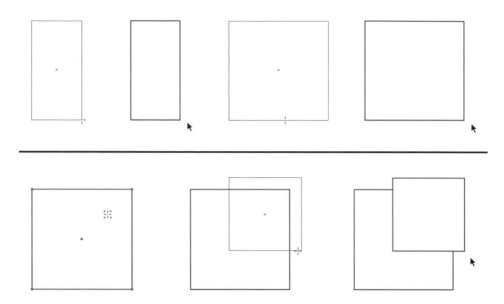

FIGURE 4.28   Using the Rectangle tool with the modifier keys of Shift and Alt/Option allows you to draw squares and draw from the inside out.

Adding modifier keys to the Rectangle tool can help you draw in different ways. In Figure 4.28, the top left pair of images shows a rectangle being drawn, as described previously. When you hold down the Shift key while drawing a rectangle, the shape is forced (or constrained) to a square, as demonstrated in the top-right pair of images. In the lower half of the image, the Alt (PC) or Option (Mac) key is added to draw from the center out. Using both modifier keys allows you to draw a square from the center out.

The Ellipse tool (L) works in much the same way as the Rectangle tool. The tool is located in the subset underneath the Rectangle tool (Figure 4.29), or it can be activated by pressing the L key. The tool initially draws oval shapes, but with the Shift modifier key, the shape is constrained to a circle. By using the Alt (PC) or Option (Mac) keys, you can also draw from the center out. This helps when you have to draw shapes with a precise center.

By nature, each shape that is drawn has a fill and stroke. A *fill* is a color or pattern within an object. The *stroke* is the visible line of a path or an object. These values are set through the Fill box and the Stroke box near the bottom of the Tools panel (Figure 4.30). Click on the Fill or Stroke box to bring it to the front. A fill or stroke can be taken away by clicking on the None icon (the white square with the red diagonal line) at the left of the row of icons below the boxes on the Tools panel.

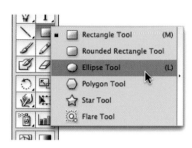

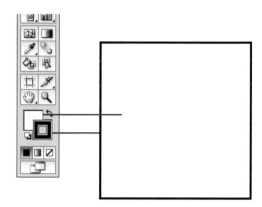

FIGURE 4.29   The location of the Ellipse tool in the Rectangle tool subset.

FIGURE 4.30   The locations of the Fill and Stroke boxes in the Tools panel and their effects on shapes.

USING BASIC SHAPES TO CREATE THE FIRST DESIGN

With the image placed in the document and the tracings layer created and selected, you are ready to create the design using basic shapes.

1. Select the Rectangle tool (M) by choosing it from the Tools panel.
2. Click once anywhere on the Artboard (the area within the document) to open the Rectangle dialog box.
3. Enter 6 into the Width field and 3.5 into the Height field. Click OK.

A rectangle that is 6" × 3.5" is placed on the Artboard. The Rectangle dialog box allows you to directly input numbers for a precise measurement for a rectangle. You could create a rectangle the traditional way and eyeball it to be the approximate size, but this method is easier and more accurate.

4. Remove the fill from the new shape by clicking on the None button while the Fill box is at the front in the Tools panel.
5. From the Tools panel, click on the Selection tool (V), the black arrow, or the first icon in the first row. Place the cursor just outside the upper-right corner of the selected shape.

The cursor changes from an arrow into a curve with an arrow on both sides. (This is the symbol for rotating an object.) Refer to Figure 4.31 for the next few steps.

6. With the rotation symbol visible, click and hold the mouse button while slightly moving the symbol counterclockwise until the angle of the top line of the rectangle matches the angle of the drawing. Release the mouse button when you have it right. If you make a mistake, simply place the cursor outside the corner until the symbol appears, press the mouse button, and continue.

7. Using the Selection tool, click on the top line of the shape, hold the mouse button down, and move the shape into position, as shown in Figure 4.31.
8. Choose the Ellipse tool from under the Rectangle tool (in the hidden subset) or press the L key to activate the tool.

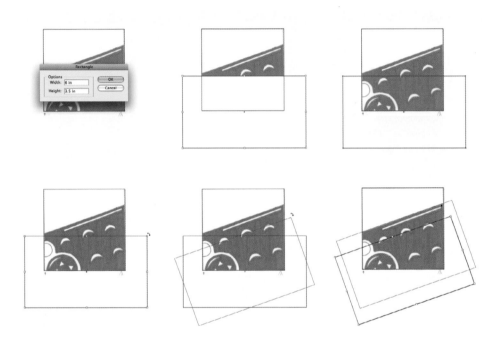

FIGURE 4.31   The process of creating the first rectangle, changing its fill to None, rotating it, and positioning it for its correct placement in the design.

THE PATHFINDER PANEL

The next step is to create the sliver moon shape for the buttons by using the tools in the Pathfinder panel to "punch out" the shape. The Pathfinder is used to create complex shapes by simply merging, cropping, adding, and subtracting the areas of different shapes.

1. Open the Pathfinder panel by selecting Window > Pathfinder.

The Pathfinder can do just about anything when it comes to combining the area of two or more shapes. The following is a list of buttons included in the Pathfinder and how they affect shapes. There are two types of tools included in the Pathfinder: the Shape Modes and the Pathfinders (Figure 4.32).

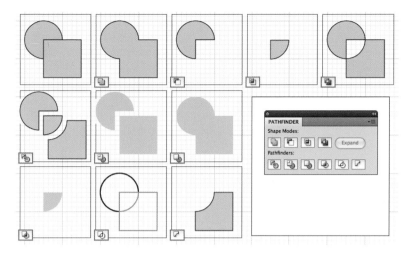

FIGURE 4.32   The Pathfinder (top row) Original Shapes, Unite, Minus Front, Intersect, Exclude; (middle row) Divide, Trim, Merge; (bottom row) Crop, Outline, and Minus Back.

The Shape Modes

When using the Shape Mode option, the objects themselves do not combine; instead, they are shared in creating the new shape. To combine them into one continuous path, select the shape and click on the Expand button in the Pathfinder panel. This will merge the paths into one. You can use the following methods to create new shapes:

> **Unite:** This function combines the areas of the shapes into one shape.
> **Minus Front:** This function subtracts the shape in the front from the shape behind it.
> **Intersect:** This function leaves behind only the areas of the shape that share the same space.
> **Exclude:** This function is the opposite of the Intersect operation. It deletes the area that shapes share.

The Pathfinder Tools

When using these operations, the integrity of the shapes is altered, resulting in one or more paths (both complete and incomplete). By default, these resulting shapes are grouped together and can be moved individually by either ungrouping the objects or using the Direct Selection (A) tool. You can use the following methods to create new shapes:

> **Divide:** This operation separates all overlapped areas into their own shapes. If two shapes are overlapped, the result is three shapes.

Trim: In this function, the shape on top subtracts its area from the image behind while leaving the shape intact. This results in two shapes, the image in front (untouched) and the image behind (with the overlapping area cropped out). Both shapes are complete paths.

Merge: Like the Unite mode, this function joins the two shapes into one shape with one complete path.

Crop: Like the Intersect mode, this function leaves behind only the overlapped areas of the shapes and results in one complete path.

Outline: When you use this operation on two overlapping shapes, the result is three paths. The overlapped areas are rendered as a complete path, with the two outlying paths left open but intact.

Minus Back: Instead of subtracting the shape in front from the one behind, this function does just the opposite. It subtracts the area of the overlapping shape in the back from the one in the front, resulting in a complete path.

To create the sliver shape for the button using two overlapping circles, follow these steps.

1. Click on the Artboard to open the Ellipse dialog box and enter 0.6 into both fields. Click OK (see Figure 4.33, left).

Much like the Rectangle dialog box, the Ellipse dialog box lets you enter precise information for an exact measurement.

2. With the Selection tool (V), move the newly created circle to the position shown in Figure 4.33 (right).

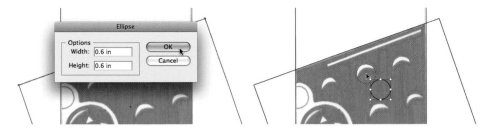

FIGURE 4.33 The Ellipse dialog box (left). Move the circle into the position shown (right).

3. Change the fill of the shape to white by clicking on the Color button, which is the first square in the row underneath the Fill and Stroke boxes in the Tools panel (Figure 4.34).
4. With the circle selected, choose Edit > Copy (PC: Ctrl + C; Mac: Command + C) to copy the shape to the clipboard (Figure 4.35).

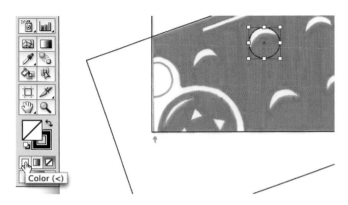

FIGURE 4.34   The location of the Color button under the Fill box.

The clipboard is a temporary storage place for information that you want to duplicate. In most programs, only one object can be stored in the clipboard at a time. The circle will remain in the clipboard until a new object is copied.

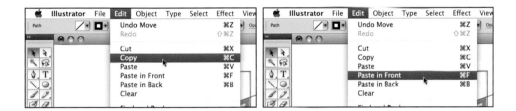

FIGURE 4.35   Locations of the Copy command and Paste in Front command in the pull-down menus.

5. Choose Edit > Paste in Front (PC: Ctrl + F; Mac: Command + F) to paste a copy of the circle directly in front of the one that you copied (Figure 4.35).
6. Using the Selection tool, move the newly pasted circle into the position shown in Figure 4.36.

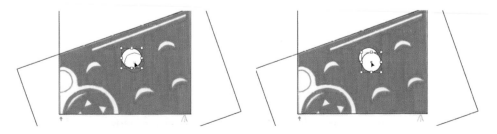

FIGURE 4.36   Move the new circle into position over the original circle.

7. Select both circles by clicking on one of them, holding down the Shift key, and clicking the other circle. With both circles selected, click on the Minus Front (first row, second icon) in the Pathfinder panel (Figure 4.37).

A compound shape is made up of several simple shapes that take on the characteristics of the topmost shape. The individual shapes within a compound shape can be edited separately. A simple shape has only one path and its own attributes.

Illustrator CS4 and Compound Shapes

In Illustrator CS4, shapes created as a result of the Pathfinder Tools are automatically converted into simple paths. If you want the resulting shape to be a Compound Path (meaning you can go back and edit the separate shapes within the resulting shape), you must press the Alt key (PC) or the Option key (Mac) for the shape to be a compound one.

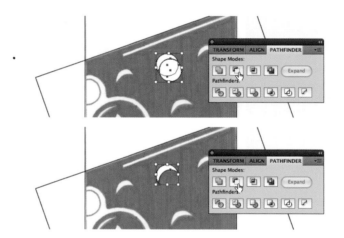

FIGURE 4.37   Use the Minus Front from the Pathfinder to create the sliver shape from the two circles.

8. Copy and paste the new sliver shape four times using the Selection tool to move them over to the appropriate places in the design.

When you have repeating shapes like this in a design, it's better to create one and copy and paste it over and over, rather than making new ones each time. If the design calls for them to be different shapes and sizes, simply repeat the Pathfinder process to make the shapes that you need.

9. Use the Ellipse tool to create the two circles shown on the left of Figure 4.38. Select both circles using the Shift key method and choose Edit > Copy (PC: Ctrl + C; Mac: Command + C) to copy them to the clipboard. You will need to paste them later on.

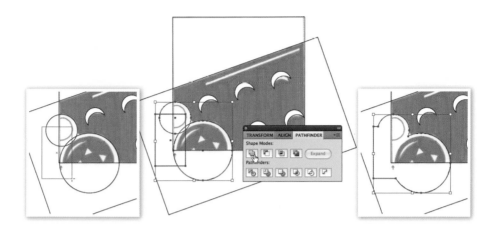

FIGURE 4.38   The process of creating a complex shape using simple shapes and the Pathfinder.

10. After the circles are copied, use the Rectangle tool to create the rectangle shape on the left of Figure 4.38. Select all three shapes and combine their areas using the Unite button (first row, first icon). Click on the Expand button to make the compound shape a single shape.

Resizing Shapes

When you use the Selection tool to choose an object, little white boxes appear in the corners and in the middle of the sides. These handles are used to make minor transformations to the object. In the first step of this exercise, you rotated a rectangle by mousing over outside of the corners and clicking and dragging the mouse. If you mouse over the corners themselves, you will actually change the scale of the shape. Follow these steps to make copies of the two circles you copied a few minutes ago:

1. Choose Edit > Paste in Front to paste the copies of the copied circles in front of the originals (Figure 4.39).

   Rather than trying to line them up perfectly on your own, use the Paste in Front command to place copies right on top of the originals.

2. Click on the stroke of the larger of the two circles to select it. While holding down the Shift and Alt (PC) or Option (Mac) keys, put your cursor on the bottom-right handle and click and drag inward, resizing the circle until it matches the one shown in Figure 4.40. Do the same to the other circle.

FIGURE 4.39   The location of the Paste in Front command from the pull-down menus.

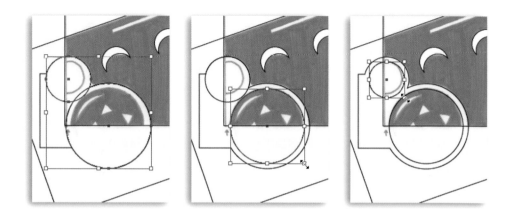

FIGURE 4.40   Resize the circles as shown here.

The Polygon Tool

Another of the tools hidden in the Rectangle subset is the Polygon tool. This tool is used to create multisided shapes from triangles to decagons and higher. The easiest way to use this tool is to single-click on the Artboard and enter in your numbers:

1. Choose the Polygon tool from the Rectangle tool subset.
2. Click once on the Artboard to open the Polygon dialog box.
3. Create a triangle by entering 0.15 into the Radius field and 3 into the Sides field (Figure 4.41).
4. Set the Fill and Stroke to the default settings by selecting the triangle with the Selection tool and clicking on the Default Fill and Stroke (D) icon to the lower left of the Fill and Stroke boxes in the Tools panel (Figure 4.42).
5. Move the new triangle into the area of the circles on the left.
6. Use the Zoom tool to enlarge an area of the Artboard, as shown in Figure 4.43.

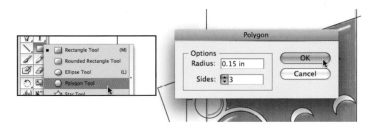

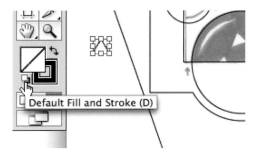

FIGURE 4.41   The location of the Polygon tool (left). The Polygon dialog box (right).

FIGURE 4.42   The location of the Default Fill and Stroke icon.

Zooming Out

Pressing the Alt or Option key while the Zoom tool is being used allows you to zoom back out.

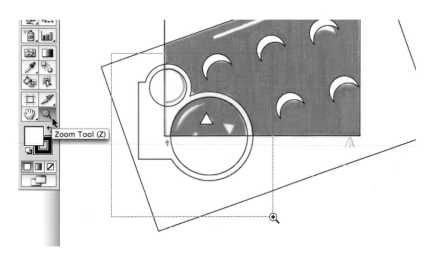

FIGURE 4.43   The location of the Zoom tool (left). Use the Zoom tool by either clicking on the artwork or clicking and dragging a marquee around the area you want to enlarge (right).

7. Position the triangle, as shown in Figure 4.44, and rotate it to match the angle of the drawing.

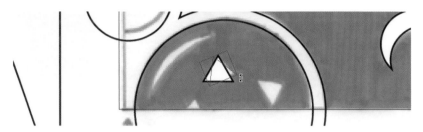

FIGURE 4.44   Position the triangle in the button area.

8. Copy and paste the triangle two more times and position them accordingly (Figure 4.45).

FIGURE 4.45   Position the other triangles, as shown in the drawing.

Polygon Tool Tip: Using the Arrow Keys

You can also use the Polygon tool like any of the other shape tools and just click and drag it to make shapes. As you draw the shape, press the Up Arrow key to add a side to the shape (for example, square to pentagon to hexagon, and so on) or the Down Arrow key to lower the number of sides.

The Pathfinder Revisited

The stacking order of shapes when using the Pathfinder is crucial. To create the little sliver of a highlight on the button, use this method of subtracting the area of two overlapping circles:

1. Draw two circles, as shown in Figure 4.46. Draw the smaller of the two circles first so that the larger of the two circles is on top.
2. Select both circles; choose Minus Front to create the large sliver shape for the design.

FIGURE 4.46   Subtract the area of the topmost image from the one beneath it to get the sliver shape.

The Hand Tool

For the last few steps, you have been zoomed in to the lower half of the design. The next step is to create the line near the middle of the design. You can use the scroll bars at the left to scroll up to the middle of the Artboard, but there is an easier way.

The Hand tool (H) lets you "move" the artwork around and change the area within the window:

1. Activate the Hand tool (H) and click on the Artboard to "grab" it.
2. With the mouse button pressed, drag the mouse around to move the board (Figure 4.47).

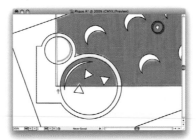 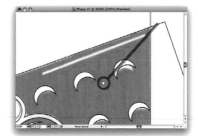

FIGURE 4.47   Use the Hand tool to move around the Artboard.

3. Move the artwork so that you see the white diagonal line of the drawings near the top of the first rectangle.
4. Release the mouse to stop the moving or to reposition the hand and move the Artboard again.

Hand Tool Tip: The Spacebar

This is a very good trick to use to navigate around the Artboard and focus your attention on a different part of the design. The spacebar can be pressed to temporarily toggle the Hand tool. Hold down the spacebar to activate the Hand tool, and then release the spacebar to go back to the last tool you used.

The Line Segment Tool

This tool is used to draw a straight line. The Line Segment tool is one of the easiest tools to use. You simply click, drag, and let go to create a line.

1. Choose the Line Segment tool (\) from the Tools panel (fourth row, first icon).
2. Draw a line segment by placing the cursor at the lower left of the line, holding down the mouse button, and then dragging up and to the right near the end of the line (Figure 4.48).

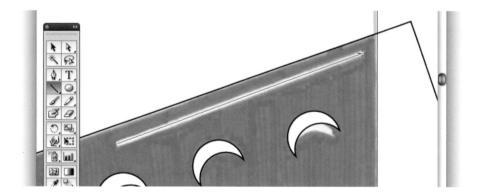

FIGURE 4.48 Draw a line segment by placing the cursor at the lower-left corner and drawing up and to the right.

3. Release the mouse button to set the line. Leave the line as it is, since you will change the properties of it later.

FINISHING THE DESIGN

Some of the shapes do not have a fill. Some have both a fill and a stroke. Now you need to make all of the right color selections to finish up this design.

Setting the Fills and Strokes

Set the fills and strokes of the shapes by following these steps:

1. Choose Select > All (PC: Ctrl + A; Mac: Command + A) to select every object that is not locked (Figure 4.49).

FIGURE 4.49   The Select > All pull-down menu.

2. Click on the Default Fill and Stroke (D) icon in the Tools panel to reset all fills to white and all strokes to a 1-point black line (Figure 4.50).

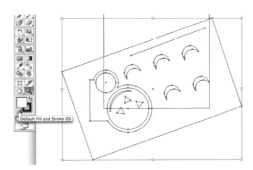

FIGURE 4.50   Set all the shapes back to their default fill (white) and stroke (black).

3. Select the large rectangle and click on the Swap Fill and Stroke (Shift + X) icon to the upper right of the Fill and Stroke boxes (Figure 4.51).

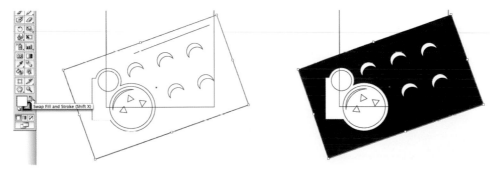

FIGURE 4.51   Swap the fill and stroke colors using the Swap Fill and Stroke icon (left).

4. Do the same to the two round buttons on the left, as shown in Figure 4.52.

FIGURE 4.52   Swap the fill and stroke on the circle shapes shown.

5. With the Selection tool, carefully select the line segment in the middle part of the design. Swap the fill and stroke so that the line is white.
6. Open the Stroke panel (Figure 4.53) by choosing Window > Stroke (PC: Ctrl + F10; Mac: Command + F10).

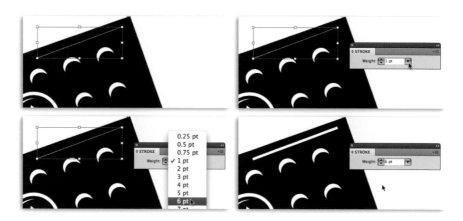

FIGURE 4.53   Select the line segment and make it have a white 6-point stroke.

7. With the line segment selected, choose 6 points from the menu or enter it into the field.

The colors are set, and everything looks good. You can remove the strokes from the sliver shapes and the other white shapes if you want to.

Clipping Masks

All the major shapes are drawn, but as you can clearly see, almost all of them appear outside of the 4" × 4" square the drawing was created in. We need to clean up the design by hiding all of those unwanted shapes.

A Clipping Mask will allows you to use shapes as a mask to reveal only the area of the image that overlaps. To create a clipping, follow these steps:

1. Using the Rectangle tool, click once on the Artboard and make a square that is 4" × 4". Click OK.
2. Place this square over the top of the shapes so that it fits in the area of the drawing (Figure 4.54).

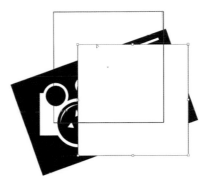

FIGURE 4.54   Move the square shape for the Clipping Mask over the original square shape of the drawing to position the mask.

3. With the rectangle selected, choose Edit > Copy (PC: Ctrl + C; Mac: Command + C) to copy the rectangle to the clipboard for later use.
4. Select everything on the Artboard by choosing Select > All (PC: Ctrl + A; Mac: Command + A).
5. Choose Object > Clipping Mask > Make (PC: Ctrl + 7; Mac: Command + 7) to set the mask (Figure 4.55).

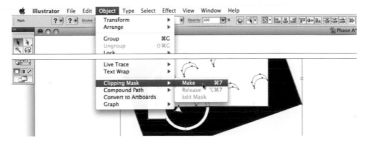

FIGURE 4.55   Choose Object > Clipping Mask > Make from the pull-down menu to set the mask.

The white box disappears and only allows the areas that overlap the shape to come through. The integrity of the paths is still there, and the Clipping Mask can be released (Object > Clipping Masks > Release); however, it looks so much better when it's cleaned up (Figure 4.56).

FIGURE 4.56 The result of applying the shape as a Clipping Mask. The information is still there, but it is just hidden by the shape.

All that is left to do is put in the background shapes, and the design is finished. Remember that square sitting on the clipboard? It is the right size, shape, and color to act as your background for the design:

6. Choose Edit > Paste in Back (PC: Ctrl + B; Mac: Command + B).
7. Select the Rectangle tool and make a rectangle that is 5" × 5", black, and with no stroke. Center the rectangle on the design.
8. With the new rectangle selected, choose Object > Arrange > Send to Back (PC: Ctrl + Shift + [; Mac: Command + Shift + [ ) to send the shape to the back of the design.
9. Paste another copy of the 4" × 4" rectangle (in your clipboard) in front of the design using Edit > Paste in Front (PC: Ctrl + F; Mac: Command + F). Set the Fill of that rectangle to None (Figure 4.57).

FIGURE 4.57 Paste a copy of the 4" × 4" square in front of the design and swap the fill and stroke so that the Stroke is white and the Fill is None. This will be the border.

10. Set the Stroke to white and make it a 3-point wide line (Figure 4.58).

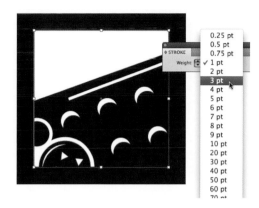

FIGURE 4.58   Set the Stroke to 3 points to complete the border.

The design is finished and ready to print (Figure 4.59). Because the design is only 4" × 4", it will fit on a letter-sized sheet of paper.

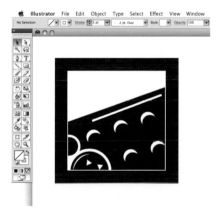

FIGURE 4.59   The finished design in Illustrator CS4.

Remember that the Tracing Image layer is locked and set not to print. At this time, you might want to delete the Tracing Image layer so that the file does not take up that much more space. To delete the Tracing Image layer, follow these instructions:

11. In the Layers panel, click on the Tracing Image layer.
12. In the bottom-right corner of the Layer panel is a Trash Can icon. Click that icon to delete the layer.
13. A message pops up asking if you are sure that you want to delete the layer and its contents. Click YES.

TUTORIAL   ## USING THE PEN TOOL TO CREATE ORGANIC SHAPES

The first design was simple because it was composed of simple shapes and line segments. Some of the objects and studies will not be so geometric. Some of the drawings might be extremely organic, and combining squares and circles will not help much in solving those problems.

In the case of studies that are more organic, such as the study from the hole punch shown in Figure 4.60, you will need a different drawing tool to achieve this solution. This tool is called the Pen tool (Figure 4.61).

FIGURE 4.60   A study taken from the first drawings of the hole punch.

FIGURE 4.61   The location of the Pen tool in the Tools panel.

Using the Pen Tool

The process of using the Pen tool is a simple matter of clicking. To draw, click once to insert a point and then move the mouse and click again. You have now recreated the simplest form of drawing: the line. By subsequently moving the mouse and clicking, you can add more points and lines to your shape. If you bring the cursor back over the first point, a small circle will appear next to the pen cursor, allowing you to close the line.

Bézier Curves

To draw a straight line in Illustrator using the Pen tool (P), start by clicking the mouse to place a point. After releasing the mouse, move the cursor to the desired location for the end of the line and click again. This time, do not release the mouse button. Simply drag the mouse slowly in any direction. Watch the line between the points as it bends in a slight curve. This is called a *Bézier curve*.

French mathematician Pierre Bézier developed the curve in the 1960s for use with CAD (Computer-Aided Drafting) programs. At least three points are used to define the curve (Figure 4.62). The two endpoints of the curve are called the *anchor points*, whereas the other point (or points) defines the actual curvature. That point is called a *handle* (which is also referred to as a *tangent point* or *node*). By moving the handles, you can modify the shape of the curve.

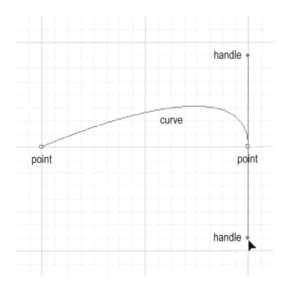

FIGURE 4.62   The basic parts of a Bézier curve are point, curve, and handle. The distance and angle of the handle in relationship to the point create the curve.

The Basics of Bézier Curves

Creating and manipulating Bézier curves is a simple process. Carefully use the following exercises for practice. Go over them again and again until you feel that you have a grasp of the basic concepts.

With the Pen tool (P) selected, click once somewhere on the document.

Move the mouse about 2 inches to the right of that line and press the mouse button, but do not release it yet. With the mouse button pressed, slowly drag the mouse up about 1 inch. The line that is usually straight is now curved. By dragging the handle below the point, the curve is the top. Likewise, if you move the mouse up, the curve bends down. The further away from the point you go, the more intense the curve will be (Figure 4.63).

Pulling Points

Dragging the cursor is often called pulling. *By pulling the cursor after placing a point, you are creating a curve.* Pulling *is a term that is used frequently in this text.*

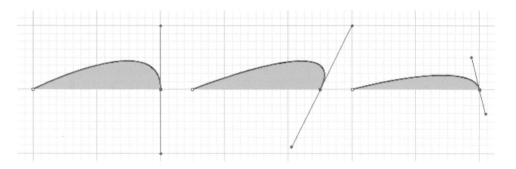

FIGURE 4.63   As you create the curve, move the mouse back and forth to see what kind of a curve you are drawing.

Take some time and experiment with these tools. Attempt to draw a path with multiple points and varying curves by clicking and dragging the mouse. As you make a handle, move the mouse around freely and watch the blue preview line show you how the curve would be if you were to let go of the mouse button. By alternating curve direction and angles, see if you can recreate any of the paths shown in Figure 4.64. Remember that Illustrator still auto-fills the path even though it is not complete. To turn off the auto fill, simply change the Fill swatch to None.

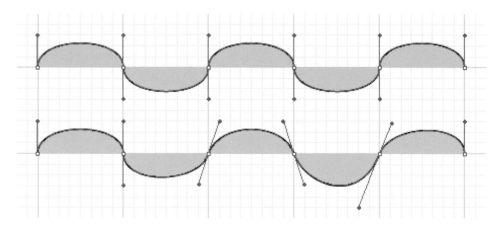

FIGURE 4.64   Complex paths that show variations in handle length and angle. All the points and handles are shown for your reference.

Alternating between clicking points and clicking and dragging points can give you a combination of straight and curved lines. Simply click and click to create straight-line segments, and alternately click and drag to create curved lines (Figure 4.65).

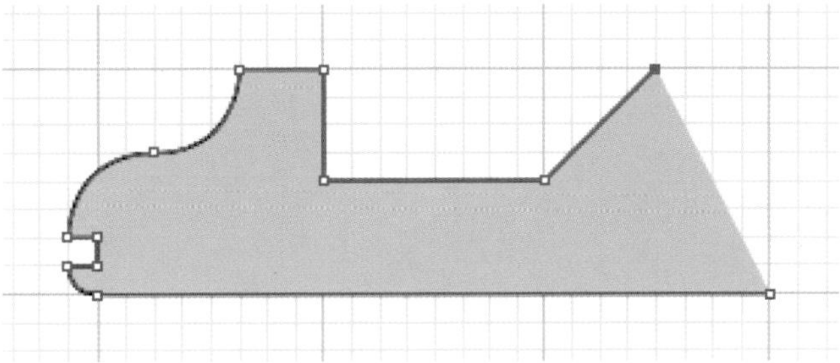

FIGURE 4.65   You can draw objects that contain both straight and curved lines. To close a path, simply click on the first point of your path to complete it.

Modifying Curves by Pulling Handles

As you use the Pen tool (P) to draw, along the way you might make mistakes and need to go back and modify the curves. Because the handles control the curve, you can move the handle using the Direct Selection tool (A)—sometimes referred to as the *Open Arrow* and change the curve. By moving the handle's angle, the direction of the curve can be changed. By increasing and decreasing the distance from the handle and the point, you can change the height of the curve. Use these steps to practice pulling handles:

1. Using the Pen tool (P), create a curve similar to the one pictured in Figure 4.66. Place a point, without dragging, and then place another point 2 inches away, but drag the mouse so that the curve appears.

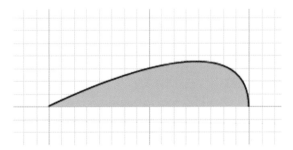

FIGURE 4.66   A simple Bézier curve.

2. Using the Direct Selection tool (A), select the top handle (Figure 4.67) and click and drag it to the left. Watch the blue preview of the curve move to the left and become more even (Figure 4.68). With the handle still selected, move the handle to the right and watch the curve bend toward and then over the point.

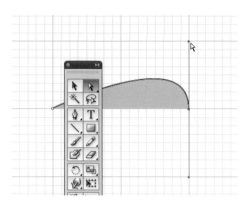

FIGURE 4.67   Use the Direct Selection tool to select the top handle.

FIGURE 4.68   Move the handle to the left and watch the preview line show the new curve. Move the handle to the right over the point and watch the preview line bend, creating a nice curve.

3. Delete the path, using the Selection tool (V), by selecting the path and pressing the Delete key.
4. Using the Ellipse tool (L), draw a circle that is 1" × 1" (Figure 4.69).

As you can see, a circle is made up of four points and four curves. Using the Selection tool (V), you can scale the shape vertically, horizontally, and diagonally. By using the Direct Selection tool (A), you can modify its shape. Using the Direct Selection tool (A), drag a marquee around the top-most point of the circle. Notice that the handles for that point appear, as do the top handles for the points at its middle edges. The other handles will not be affected by the next step.

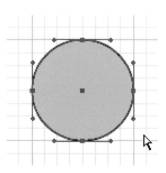

FIGURE 4.69   A circle contains four points and four curves.

5. Click on the top-right handle and drag it to the right about .5 inch (Figure 4.70).

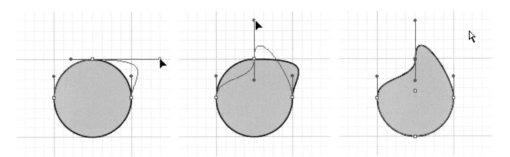

FIGURE 4.70   As you move the handles, the preview line shows you how the curve will change with the new placement of the handle.

The blue preview line shows the new curve. The curve looks strange because you are moving only one handle, straight across. If you move the handle up or down, the curve becomes more dynamic.

6. Select the same handle that you just moved and drag it up. While dragging the handle, hold down the Shift key. The handle is now constrained to 45° angles. Move the handle into the same position as the handle shown in the middle of Figure 4.71.

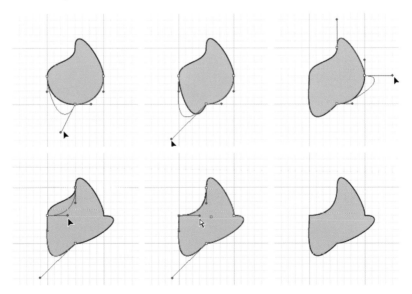

FIGURE 4.71   Holding down the appropriate key, click the desired handle to move only that handle. Notice that the handles do not move together anymore. Remember to select the point first and then the handle.

7. Notice that the handles move together or in tandem. This is done by default but can be remedied by holding down the Alt key on a PC or the Option key on a Mac as you drag the handle. (Refer to Figure 4.71 for the next few steps.)
8. Using the Direct Selection tool (A), select the bottom point of the shape. (We can't call it a circle anymore.)
9. Press and hold the proper key on the keyboard (PC: Alt; Mac: Option). A plus sign (+) will appear near the right of the cursor. This sign is a visual clue that you are about to modify the handle. Select the handle on the left, and while holding down the mouse button and the proper key, drag the handle down .5 inch. These handles do not move together and will not from this point on. After you have moved one handle independently from the other, they will not work in tandem anymore.

Hold down the correct key on the keyboard before clicking the handle! If you hold down the key after you have selected the handle, the path will be duplicated. If this happens, undo the last command (PC: Ctrl + Z; Mac: Command + Z) and try again. By nature, the Alt and Option keys are used to drag duplicates of selected shapes from the original.

10. Select the point on the right and, while holding down the proper key, select the bottom handle and pull it up and to the right, as shown in the third panel of Figure 4.71.
11. Select the point on the left side of the shape and move its top handle down and inside the shape toward the right. Also hold down the Shift key to constrain the handle to 45° increments, which results in the shape in the sixth panel of Figure 4.71.

By pulling these handles, you can create and modify curves and begin to venture into more complicated drawing techniques.

The Direct Selection tool can also be used to move points, lines, and objects that reside within groups. Whereas the Selection tool allows you to move groups and entire objects, the Direct Selection tool lets you select things (points, lines, handles, and so on) within objects and groups.

Tracing the Hole Punch Study

With the basics of the Pen tool defined, creating the shapes for the hole punch study will be easier. It will take some patience on your part and a combination of straight and curved lines to complete some of the intricate shapes.

For the first part of this exercise, refer to Figure 4.72. The image is separated into steps beginning at the top left.

1. Start by creating a new document in Illustrator CS4 (File > New) and placing the image ch04_hole_punch_study.tif (File > Place) into the document.

2. Double-click on Layer 1 in the Layers panel to open the Layer Options. Check the Dim Image To and Lock boxes and uncheck the Print box. Set the Dim Images To number to 30. Name the layer "Tracing Image." Click OK.

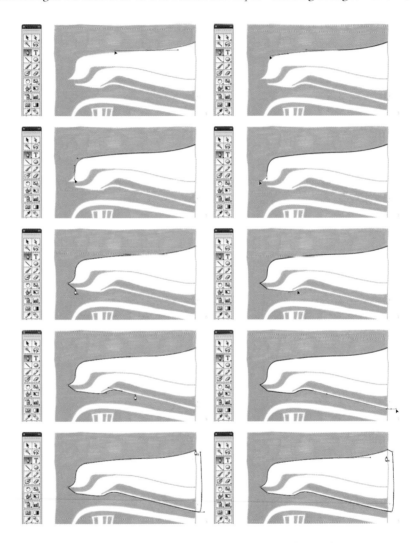

FIGURE 4.72   Steps in creating the top shape of the hole punch study.

Dimming Images

By dimming the images to 30%, the stroke is easier to see. You can set it lower if you want to, but 30% is enough. Remember that with the Print box unchecked, when you print the file, that layer will not print.

3. Click on the New Layer button and name that layer "Tracing Layer."
4. Use the Zoom Tool to zoom in on the top part of the image if necessary so that you can trace the top shape in the study.
5. Select the Pen Tool (P) from the Tools panel. Set the Fill to None and keep the Stroke black.
6. Start making the path by clicking on the upper-right corner of the shape, as shown earlier in the top-left panel of Figure 4.72.
7. Click again about a third of the way across the image to set another point. As you click, drag a handle out of the point by holding the mouse button down as you set the point.

Keep Practicing

This technique might take some getting used to, so use the Edit > Undo command (PC: Ctrl + Z; Mac: Command + Z) to undo the last step you did. Do not rush it. Try to get a feel for the tool and the angle of the curve by moving the mouse up and down as you "pull" the curve out. Experimentation is key in this process. If you are really struggling with this, ask one of your classmates for help.

8. Continue around the perimeter of the shape, clicking and setting points you need to create the shapes. To set a corner point, simply click the mouse button. To set a smooth point, pull the handles out of the point as you set the point and move them up and down to change the curve.
9. As you come back around to completing the shape, click on the first point that you set to "close" the shape.

Use the Pen tool (P) to draw the other shapes that you see in the design. Use Figure 4.73 as a guide as to the order that the shapes should be drawn. Doing it in this order helps you stack the shapes correctly so that when filled, they will be in the correct order and not hidden behind other shapes.

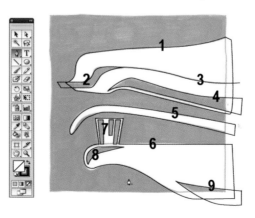

FIGURE 4.73   The suggested order that you should use when drawing the shapes.

Finishing the Design

With the shapes drawn, you are ready to fill them with the appropriate color and set the Clipping Mask. Refer to Figure 4.74 for this part of the tutorial.

1. Select all the shapes (Select > All) and set their fill and stroke to the default by clicking on the Default Fill and Stroke (D) button in the Tools panel.
2. Choose the shapes shown in the second panel of Figure 4.74 that need to be set to black and swap their fill and stroke colors using the Swap Fill and Stroke Color (Shift X) button.

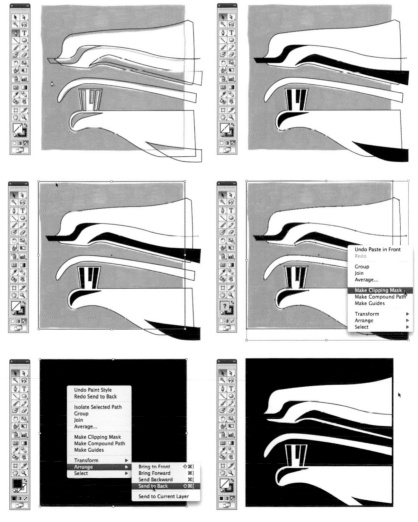

FIGURE 4.74   Finish the design by coloring the shapes, setting a Clipping Mask, adding a black background, and adding the border.

3. Make a rectangle that is 4" × 4" and move it so that it is over the design. This is similar to what you did to finish the phone design.
4. Copy the rectangle (Edit > Copy) to the clipboard for later use.
5. Select all the shapes (Select > All) and right-click the middle of the design. (Mac users with a single button mouse can access the right-click menu while holding down the Ctrl key when clicking.) In this menu, choose Make Clipping Mask to set the Clipping Mask.
6. Paste a copy of the rectangle behind the design (Edit > Paste in Back) and swap its fill and stroke so that it is black.
7. Paste another copy of the rectangle in front of the design (Edit > Paste in Front) and set the stroke to 6 points.

This design is now complete. Delete the Tracing Image layer if you want.

You may find that your studies and final designs contain both geometric and organic shapes. Use a combination of the tools described in this chapter to complete the digital production process of this phase of the project. In later projects, these tools will be reused and reinforced, and you will be introduced to new uses for them.

SUMMARY

This first project is probably the most difficult in terms of both the content and production process. It presents new ideas and involves procedures that could be very difficult if you have no previous experience in design theory or digital production. This is why the first project is divided into four parts. All the basic concepts and procedures needed to create the rest of the projects are introduced here. The projects in the following chapters will build from this one, and there will be less production material to consider as the book progresses.

As you have experienced from the first part of this project, design is based on structure. There are many rules to learn before you can create intuitive designs without the underlying organization of the basic elements and principles of design. Think about the times you have succeeded in improvising in an activity that required a basic foundation before you really felt like you knew what you were doing. A comparison may be drawn to a sport that requires finesse that can only be acquired from the continual practice of its basic principles. Too often, our only experience with visual creativity has come from purely intuitive processes. However, if you want to use visual expression as design, understanding the fundamentals of how we see and what we are all looking for becomes a necessity. You must understand the beats per measure and the key you are composing or playing in if you are going to improvise through music. You have to know the rules and the physical requirements if you are going to compete or perform in a sport. In the same way, the fundamentals of design, and how to create it, must be understood before you can improvise and perform successfully.

5

DESIGN PROJECT 1 (PART 2): ABSTRACTION THROUGH REPETITION

METHOD TWO: REPETITION

Another frequently used method of abstracting an object is to repeat all or parts of the object. This allows the designer to create a more complex design in which the composition may be unified by the repetition of shape. In this method, the designer may repeat the entire object a number of times or may elect to repeat only parts of the object. This type of abstraction is in part based on the previously introduced method of simplification because objects used in repetition studies are most often very simple in their individual forms.

In Figure 5.1, the example uses the same simplified shape of a person (as seen on the right) and repeats it over and over to create a group of people, which ultimately defines the shape of a brain. We do not see the entire shape of the people shape, but we know what they represent.

In Figure 5.2, the repetitions of the leaf shapes are not as important as the negative space that creates the outline of the dove. This use of positive and negative shape helps your mind try to close the gaps and bring closure to the image.

FIGURE 5.1   Example of a logo unified by the repetition of a shape. (*Creative Club of San Antonio* © 2006. Reprinted with permission from The Bradford Lawton Design Group, www.bradfordlawton.com.)

FIGURE 5.2   The use of positive and negative shape creates closure. (*Ecumenical Center* © 2006. Reprinted with permission from The Bradford Lawton Design Group, www.bradfordlawton.com.)

CONTENT: THE BASIC PROBLEM DEFINED

Using the same object and the same initial drawings as in the previous chapter, do a series of studies in which the object is repeated at least once. In these studies, using the same square format and marker technique as before, focus on how the repetition of all or part of the object can create new shapes in both the positive and negative areas. The same requirement for recognition of the object is there, but because the object will be repeated more than once within the composition, each object within the frame may be used to tell part of the story (Figure 5.3).

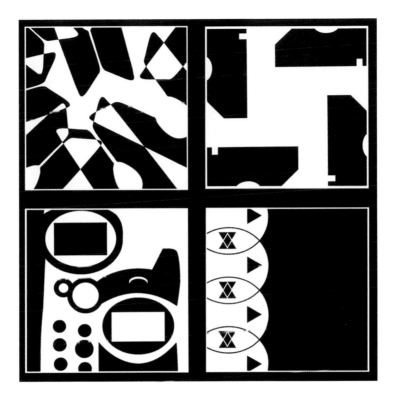

FIGURE 5.3   Examples of student work.   (Top row: left to right: *Repetition—Clothespin* © 2005. Reprinted with permission from Rogerio Molina. *Repetition—Clothespin* © 2005. Reprinted with permission from Julissa Lopez. (Bottom row: left to right: *Repetition—Phone* © 2004. Reprinted with permission from Christina Del Greco. *Repetition—Phone* © 2005. Reprinted with permission from Vanassa Garcia.)

Background

Although this approach to abstraction uses the same design elements as in the previous chapter, this method allows for a different examination of how a designer achieves both variety and unity within a composition. If a design shows an exact repeating pattern, the design becomes too unified and will not engage the viewers' interest. A brick wall exhibits a great deal of unity through the repetition of shape, but other than trying to avoid running into it, most people pay little attention to its design. This fact is not lost on architects and builders who have learned that even small variations in the pattern of bricks can help create interest in the side of a house or building (Figure 5.4).

At the opposite end of the scale, a design in which shapes repeat can still include too much variety. We try to understand what we see partially by seeking visual patterns and then by seeking those things that depart from the pattern.

FIGURE 5.4 Small variations in simple patterns can help create interest in the design.

When a design includes too many elements that are too different from one another, we can no longer see the overall organizing pattern. The resulting composition is uncomfortable to look at, seems chaotic, and is very difficult to "read" as an object or objects. It tends to overwhelm us and become visually static. Figure 5.5 shows two designs that are essentially composed of similar elements. The design on the right achieves a greater degree of compositional unity. Because there are fewer variations, the viewer's eye can take in the composition as a whole. The design on the left is too chaotic and lacks real structure.

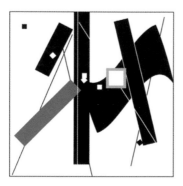

FIGURE 5.5 The design on the right achieves a greater degree of compositional unity than the one on the left.

Conceptual Process

Here are some things to keep in mind as you continue with this project:

- Use the same initial drawing and object.
- Use the same template of 4" × 4" squares and the same technique of marker studies.

- For the initial studies, use both the initial drawing and the simplification studies from the previous chapter.
- Some studies should work with fewer objects, and other studies should work with as many as eight or nine objects. Some studies should show most or all of the object, and others should show only partial objects.
- In evaluating these compositions, pay attention to the negative shapes created by repetition as much as the shapes within the objects themselves.
- Change the scale of the objects both within one frame and from frame to frame.
- Keep in mind that exactly repeating patterns will not hold a viewer's attention for long. Some variation is necessary for interest.
- Too much variety can create visual chaos. What can create unity in a design with too much variety?

You should do a minimum of 35 studies for this phase of the project. This will make you explore multiple possibilities rather than just a few. From those 35, evaluate your work and do 10 refinements. From those 10, choose three to take through the digital production process.

PRODUCTION PROCESS

After you are done with the refinements and have narrowed your designs down to three, scan the drawings and prepare them for use in Illustrator CS4.

Most of the tools that you need to go through the digital production process were covered in Chapter 4. In this chapter, you will learn how to better use some of the tools and options and make your time more efficient.

TUTORIAL	**GROUPING IMAGES**

Because you will be working with multiples of your object in this phase, grouping is an important tool.

Your objects are composed of multiple geometric and organic shapes. Selecting each piece every time and trying to move them together as one unit is tedious. *Grouping* solves this problem. Simply select all the items that you want to be part of a group and with a few keystrokes or mouse clicks, you have a group.

ON THE CD

1. Open the file ch05_double_demo.ai found on your CD-ROM.

There are two layers in this file. One is named Tracing Image and contains the tracing image for this exercise. The layer has been turned into a Template: it is locked, the print option is turned off, and the image is dimmed at 50%. The other layer is named Tracing Layer. This layer houses the shapes that are used to make the phone object.

2. Using the Selection tool, drag a marquee around all the objects on the Artboard or choose Select > All from the main menu.
3. With everything selected, choose Object > Group (PC: Ctrl + G; Mac: Command + G) from the main menu (Figure 5.6).

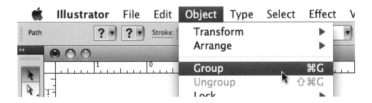

FIGURE 5.6 The location of the Group command in the main menu.

All the objects are now placed within one group and can be selected and moved as one unit (Figure 5.7). If you use the Selection tool (V) to select a part of the group, the entire group will be selected. However, you can use the Direct Selection tool (A) to select and modify objects within the group.

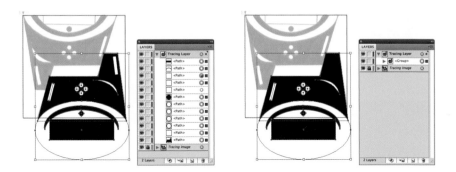

FIGURE 5.7 Several objects can be combined into one single unit that can be rotated, scaled, or moved together.

Isolated Group Mode

Illustrator allows you to enter into groups and modify them using the Selection tools. Simply double-click the group to enter into the Isolated Group Mode. You will know that you are in an Isolated Group because all the objects in your drawing that are not associated with the current group will gray out, and the outer perimeter of the group will turn into a light gray border. While in this mode, you can perform commands and operations like you were working on the objects in regular mode. To exit the selected Isolated Group, either right-click and choose Exit Isolation Mode from the pop-up menu, or double-click outside of the area of the group.

There is a discrepancy in the drawing and the object that has been drawn for you. The screen is black, and it should be white. Better fix it.

4. Choose the Direct Selection tool (A) from the Tools panel and click on the black screen shape within the group to select it (Figure 5.8).

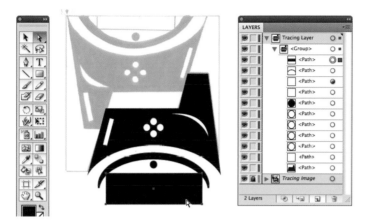

FIGURE 5.8   Use the Direct Selection tool to select the shapes within a group.

5. Change the colors of the shape to the default values using the Default Fill and Stroke command (Shift + X).
6. Click on a black area of the Artboard with the Direct Selection tool to deselect the shape from the group.

TUTORIAL   ROTATING OBJECTS

There are several ways to rotate an image in Illustrator CS4. You have used one method already (in Chapter 4).

If you remember, you used the corner boxes on the selection to rotate the first rectangle in the first design. That is the most straightforward and immediate way to rotate an object.

However, if you want to enter in an exact number of degrees to rotate your object, you can use the Rotate command for that.

1. Select the grouped object with the Selection tool (V).
2. Choose Object > Transform > Rotate from the main menu.
3. In the Angle field of the Rotate dialog box, enter 180. Click on the Preview box to see a preview of the rotation. Click the Copy button instead of OK to make a copy of the shape (Figure 5.9)

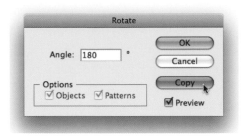

FIGURE 5.9 The Rotate dialog box.

4. Position the new group, as shown in Figure 5.10.
5. Finish the design by adding a 4" × 4" square of white to the background and another 4" × 4" square with no fill and a black stroke as the front border (Figure 5.11).

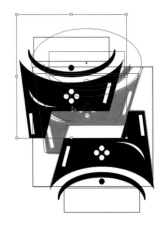

FIGURE 5.10 Position the second group, as shown here.

FIGURE 5.11 The finished design using two shapes.

Now for a Little Trick

Your designs are probably all oriented differently, with objects coming in at weird angles and with weird rotations. Look at the image in Figure 5.12. The phone shapes are all coming toward the center from the corners of the image. Drawing the design on an angle and making it look the way it should might be difficult.

If you notice in the right part of Figure 5.12, the image has been rotated so that the phone shape is straight up and down. That will make it easier to draw (Figure 5.13).

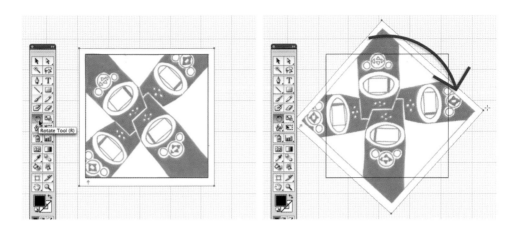

FIGURE 5.12   The image on the left has an object coming into the design from all angles and would otherwise be hard to draw. By rotating the image like the example on the right, the phone shape would be easier to draw and then rotate when completed.

Rather than try to correct the angle of the rotated image, you can simply delete it and replace the image at the correct angle to help guide the rotations (Figure 5.14). With the shape drawn, you can practice rotating the object using the Rotate tool.

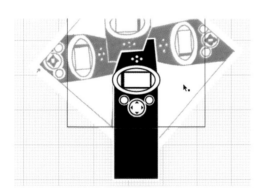

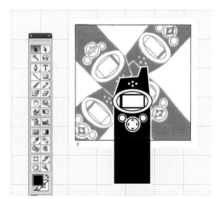

FIGURE 5.13   The phone shape was easier to draw with the image rotated.

FIGURE 5.14   Rather than trying to rotate the image back to its original position, delete the image and replace it.

ON THE CD

1. Open the file ch05_quad_demo.ai found on your CD-ROM.
2. With the Selection tool (V), select the phone group and move the group so that the arrow shapes in the phone design overlap the similar part of the drawing coming out of the lower-right corner of the drawing.
3. Select the Rotate tool (R) from the Tools panel.

The Rotate tool has a lot of power. In Chapter 9, "Design Project 3: Figure Abstraction and Nonobjective Shape," you will learn some advanced uses of this tool, but for now, all you need is the rotating feature of the tool. You must have the object you want to rotate selected before you click on the Rotate tool.

4. Using the Rotate tool, click anywhere on the group, hold down the mouse button, and drag the mouse to the left and right in a circular motion. An outlined preview of the shape will spin around the center point of the object. When you have the correct angle, simply release the mouse button to set the rotation.
5. Copy and paste the phone group to duplicate it.
6. Click on the new group with the Rotate tool and rotate the new group 180 degrees so that its orientation is opposite of the other one. Use the Shift key at the same time to constrain the rotation to 45° angles.

In any case of rotation, holding down the Shift key constrains a rotation to increments of 45°. This can be helpful when trying to get objects to line up opposite each other.

7. Use the Selection tool (V) to move the rotated shape into position, as shown in Figure 5.15.

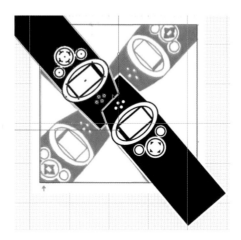

FIGURE 5.15   Position the second phone shape group as shown.

8. Select both phone groups and choose Object > Transform > Rotate from the main menu.
9. In the Rotate dialog box, enter 90 into the Angle field and click the Copy button.
10. Position the third and fourth phone groups so that they line up with the tracing image.

11. Select the third and fourth phone groups, right-click them to open the submenu, and choose Arrange > Send to Back (PC: Ctrl + Shift + [; Mac: Command + Shift + [ ) to send both shapes behind groups one and two (Figure 5.16).

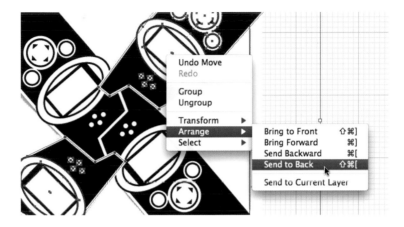

FIGURE 5.16   Right-clicking reveals a pop-up menu with several commands. Choose Arrange > Send to Back to send the third and fourth shapes behind the first two.

12. Finish off the design with a Clipping Mask (Figure 5.17), background, and border the same way you did in the first exercise of this chapter (Figure 5.18).

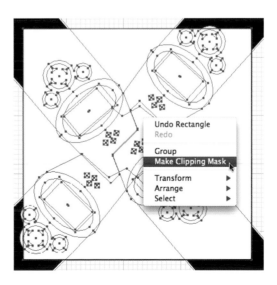

FIGURE 5.17   When all the objects are selected, including the large rectangle shape, Make Clipping Mask becomes an option in the right-click menu.

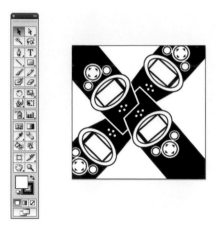

FIGURE 5.18   The final design with four groups.

SUMMARY

With the second phase of this project completed, you have reached the halfway point. You have learned how objects can be simplified by removing the unnecessary parts of the image, and you can create unity through repetition of all or some of the parts of the object.

Look back at the examples in Figure 5.3 and try to find the harmony in the positive and negative shapes of the design. Try to find the rhythm in the repetition of the parts and pieces of the objects. Can you still tell what they are? Can you identify the pieces? Can you feel the peace in the composition? Can you feel the chaos? What works for you?

Simplification and repetition are the stepping-stones for the next phase of the project. Keep in mind everything that you have learned, and it will benefit you in the next step.

DESIGN PROJECT 1 (PART 3): ABSTRACTION USING LINE AND SHAPE

METHOD THREE: LINE AND SHAPE

The methods of abstracting the object covered in Chapters 4 and 5 depended on enclosed and filled shapes as the primary design elements. This chapter deals with a method of abstracting the objects in which closed shapes are combined with shapes implied through the use of line. Using line to imply but not fully enclose shapes also allows for a better integration of positive and negative shapes within the composition. The addition of linear elements also adds another level of variety to the design (Figure 6.1).

FIGURE 6.1   A design that uses linear elements.
(*MCGD* © 2006. Reprinted with permission of Mike Clayton.)

CONTENT: THE BASIC PROBLEM DEFINED

Use the same object and initial drawings as in the previous chapters to do a series of studies in which line is used to imply part of the object. Line should not be used as an outline that completely encloses each shape, nor should it be used to establish value or texture—as in crosshatching or "shading" a shape. The focus of these studies is to explore how both single and repeated lines can create implied shapes that harmonize with the explicitly drawn shapes. Using line in this way will also make you more aware of the integrated relationship between positive and negative shapes (Figure 6.2).

FIGURE 6.2   Student examples.   (Top row: *Line and Shape—Phone* © 2005.
Reprinted with permission from Robin Parker. Bottom row: *Line and Shape—Clothespin* © 2005.
Reprinted with permission from Jeremy Kenisky.)

Background

The two previous methods of abstraction used the manipulation of shape, both positive and negative, to communicate the object in a simplified way. This project is still primarily concerned with shape, but in this case, some of the shapes are implied.

Initially, when asked to use line to create shape, most beginning designers will either draw an "outline" that encloses an unfilled shape—similar to a child's coloring book (Figure 6.3, left), or the designer will use lines to create a pattern or texture within a shape (Figure 6.3, middle). Both of these have a place in creating compositions, but this project will focus on creating implied shapes (Figure 6.3, right). Although less familiar to most students, this is a commonly used device in visual communications (Figure 6.4).

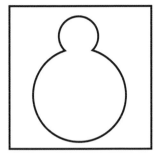  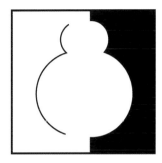

FIGURE 6.3 Beginning designers usually use line to create an outline of the object (left) or make a texture or pattern (middle), when they should use line to create an implied shape (right).

FIGURE 6.4 A logo design using implied line.

The use of line to imply shape can help with the integration of positive and negative shapes into a unified composition. The composition in Figure 6.5 uses similar shapes to achieve some level of unity, but the negative white area on the lower right is a "trapped" shape so it becomes difficult to relate to the black positive shapes and to the remainder of the white space in the composition. Figure 6.6 shows how the same basic shapes can be implied using line. By using line in this way, the negative (white) shapes are more integrated. The gestalt principle of closure allows the viewer to mentally complete some of the shapes.

FIGURE 6.5   The composition completely encloses the shape on the lower right and causes it to look "trapped."

FIGURE 6.6   In this composition, your eye closes off the top of the image and leaves you to imagine the closed area at the lower right.

In addition, the introduction of line adds variety to the overall composition. In the student example shown in Figure 6.7, several line weights are used as contrast to the solid shapes, and the white "negative" shapes are contrasted with the black "positive" shapes to achieve an integrated composition that exhibits both unity and variety.

FIGURE 6.7   Line adds variety to the overall composition.
(*Line and Shape—Phone* © 2005. Reprinted with permission from Robin Parker.)

This project may draw on all the uses of line to create shape, but it should focus primarily on the use of line to create implied shapes.

Look at Figure 6.8. Notice how line and shape are used to imply different meanings. The image on the left uses line to represent the silhouette of a face repeated three times to imply the wings of a swan. The lines, angles, and corners of the house in the center logo imply a sense of space and depth. The combination of shapes and lines in the example on the right frame the negative space when a pen tip is implied. You can use similar practices in your designs as you look at the relationships between the lines and shapes.

FIGURE 6.8   Three examples of logos using line and shape.
(Left to right: *Cosmetic Surgery* © 2006. Reprinted with permission from The Bradford Lawton Design Group, www.bradfordlawton.com. *Van Doesburg* © 2000. Reprinted with permission from Mike Clayton. *Publishing Logo* © 2004. Reprinted with permission from Chrissy Coronado.)

Conceptual Process

Here are some things to keep in mind as you continue on with this project:

- Use the same initial drawing and object.
- Use the same template of 4" × 4" squares and the same technique of marker studies.
- For the initial studies, use both the initial drawing and the simplification studies from Chapter 4. In this phase, you may also repeat the object, but too much repetition will make these too chaotic, so two or three is usually enough.
- Some studies should show most or all of the object, and others should show only part of the object.
- In evaluating these compositions, along with the positive shapes, pay attention to the implied shapes created by line.
- Change the scale of the object both within one frame and from study to study.
- In using line to create an implied shape, consider how the alignments between the ends of the lines work to help unify the design, and consider how using similar angles can also help to create unity and rhythm within the composition (Figure 6.9).

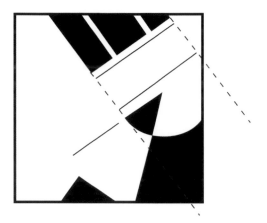

FIGURE 6.9   Consider how the alignments between the ends of the lines work to help unify the design.

PRODUCTION PROCESS

After you are done with the refinements and have narrowed your designs down to three, scan the drawings and prepare them for use in Illustrator CS4.

TUTORIAL	**STROKE OPTIONS**

Up to this point, you have been able to make the stroke of an object thicker, thinner, or set to None. Let's explore the Stroke panel and show you some of the other options that you have when it comes to modifying the stroke of a line or shape.

The Stroke panel can be displayed by choosing Window > Stroke from the main menu. When first opened, only the Weight option is visible. To see the other options, you either have to choose Show Options from the panel menu (Figure 6.10), or you can click on the double triangle by the name.

FIGURE 6.10   The options for the Stroke panel can be opened through the panel's menu.

Changing the Weight

In Figure 6.11, all the lines in the design have been reset to the program's default setting. Using the Weight field of the Stroke panel, you can set the stroke of an object to any number that you enter into that field.

ON THE CD

1. Open the file ch06_strokes_demo.ai located on the CD-ROM.
2. If not visible, view the Stroke panel by choosing Window > Stroke (PC: Ctrl + F10; Mac: Command + F10). It may be nested in with some other panels, but you can pull it from the set by clicking and dragging the tab out of the set. The panel will jump to its own window (Figure 6.11).
3. Open the Stroke option by either choosing Show Options from the panel menu or clicking on the double arrows next to the Stroke tab.
4. Select one of the curves near the center of the design.
5. In the Weight field of the Stroke panel, enter 16 (Figure 6.12). Press the Return/ Enter key to set the change.
6. Starting at the top of the design, the weights of the strokes are 5, 6, 7, 10, 16 (curve), 0, 12, 16 (other curve), 6, and 0 (triangle). Set each of the strokes of the lines accordingly.

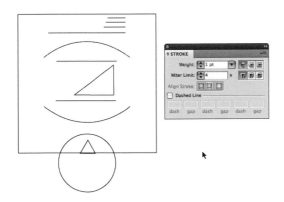

FIGURE 6.11 The Stroke panel contains all of the options for stroke.

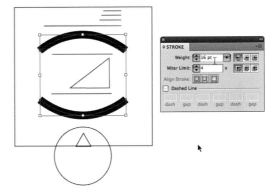

FIGURE 6.12 Enter 16 into the Weight field to set the width of the stroke.

Changing Caps and Joins

A *cap* is the end of an opened line segment, and a *join* is where a straight line (corner point) changes direction. There are three types of caps and three types of joins. Refer to the following steps and figures for caps (Figure 6.13) and on joins (Figure 6.14).

FIGURE 6.13   The three kinds of caps are Butt (top), Round (middle), and Projecting (bottom).

1. Use the Zoom tool (Z) to zoom in on the antenna area of the design near the top right of the design.
2. With the Selection tool (V), click on the top line segment. The weight of this line is 5.

Notice that, by default, the cap is set to a Butt cap (Figure 6.13, top), which has a square end. The line ends right at the end of the segment.

3. With the line still selected, click the Round cap option.

The Round cap extends past the line with a semicircular end. The curve is equal to the half the weight of the line.

4. Now choose the last option: the Projecting cap.

Like the Round cap, a Projecting cap extends one-half the weight of the line making the line longer than the path. If you are going for precision, the Butt cap is the best choice. If you want to give your line a nice, soft, round edge, the Round cap is the best option.

5. Set the cap back to the Butt cap and use the Hand tool (H) to navigate to the lower part of the design around the small triangle. Whereas caps affect the ends of the line, the join affects the corner points (Figure 6.14).

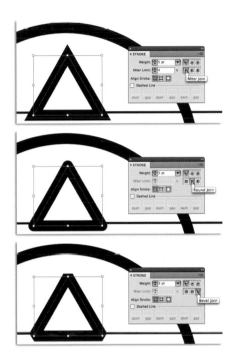

FIGURE 6.14   The three types of joins are Miter (top), Round (middle), and Bevel (bottom).

6. Use the Selection tool (V) to select the triangle shown in Figure 6.14. The default setting for a join is a Miter join (Figure 6.14, top).

This creates a pointed corner to the shape. The miter limit can be anywhere from 1 to 500. The miter limit controls the point at which a pointed (Miter) join converts to a squared-off join (Bevel). The default is set to 4, which means that the corner will not convert from a Miter to a Bevel join until the length of the point is 4 times greater than the stroke weight.

7. With the triangle still selected, choose the Round join option.

Much like the Round cap, the Round join rounds the corners. There is no miter limit associated with this type of join so that field in the Stroke dialog box is disabled.

8. Click on the Bevel join.

A Bevel join creates strokes with squared (beveled) corners. As you can see in the image, beveled joins look odd. There is no miter limit on this option either.

Changing Stroke Alignment

There are three settings for the Align Stroke option: Align Stroke to Center, Align Stroke to Inside, and Align Stroke to Outside. The toggles for this option make the third row of the Strokes panel.

By default, the stroke is always aligned to the center. That means the width of the stroke is always divided in half, with half of the width on the inside of the path and the other half on the outside.

When a stroke is aligned to the inside, the full width of the stroke is on the inside of the path. When it is aligned to the outside, it has the opposite effect.

Look at Figure 6.15. The top panel shows a 6-point stroke aligned to the center of the line. There are 3 points on one side and 3 points on the other. The middle panel shows the stroke aligned to the inside, and the bottom panel shows the stroke aligned to the outside. In the final design, the stroke is aligned to the inside.

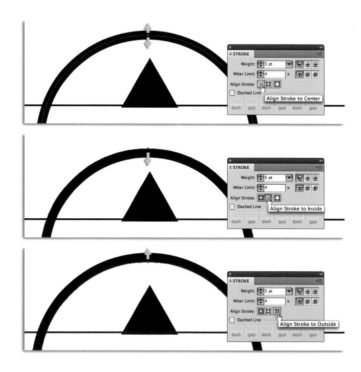

FIGURE 6.15   The three options for Stroke Alignment in Illustrator are
Align to Center (top), Align to Inside (middle), and Align to Outside (bottom).

The lack of stroke alignment once created a real problem with technical drawing (Figure 6.16). In Illustrator CS and earlier, if you wanted to draw a box that was exactly 1-inch wide with a 12-point stroke, you would have 6 points on the inside of the box and 6 on the outside, making your box a little over 1-inch wide (1.16" to be exact). If you wanted a box 1-inch wide, you had to compensate somehow or remove the stroke from the box. Since CS2, you can align the stroke to the inside and maintain the exact measurement you wanted in the first place.

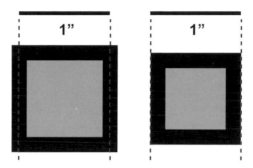

FIGURE 6.16   When the stroke is aligned to the center, the shape is wider than the path (left). With the stroke aligned to the inside, the shape is exactly the width of the path (right).

SUMMARY

The third phase of this abstraction project uses principles from the first two phases as stepping stones to create the forms for the design, but through line and shape, those forms can be interpreted in various ways. Using line, the contour of the shape can be defined without the need for volume. That volume is implied and allows the viewer to finish the shape in his mind. Line should also be used to define shapes within the object but not used as texture of value. Some students feel the need to use lines to create crosshatching, when shape can be used to create a large shape that can be interpreted as value. Consider how alignments between the ends of lines can work together to help unify a design. Use similar angles to help create unity and rhythm in your compositions. Mix line, shape, scale, position, repetition, and implied white space to achieve the best designs.

7

DESIGN PROJECT 1 (PART 4): ABSTRACTION USING TYPE COMBINATION

METHOD FOUR: TYPE COMBINATION

One commonly used method of visually communicating information is combining elements to create a new visual message. Many times, one of the elements used in combination with an image is a letterform. *Letterforms* are familiar and easily recognized, and they offer a large variety of visual styles and shapes that can be used to help the designer express an exact meaning. In using typographic form, the same design concepts of unity, variety, and harmony apply.

Letterforms are used in groups, including a simple combination of letters as initials, and they are frequently combined to form word-marks. Longer groups of letterforms, in phrases or sentences, are used as headlines and titles. Blocks of text create lines and shapes within a page. The selection of the particular style of letterform, and the way in which the combination of forms are placed within the page, greatly affects the way a viewer interprets the message.

Chapter 12, "Design Project 6: Typeface Design," will provide more specific information about type and how type is used in design. Value and color relating to type are also introduced in that chapter. This project specifically explores the combination of a single letterform and the abstraction of the object used in the preceding chapters.

CONTENT: THE BASIC PROBLEM DEFINED

Using the same object as in the previous chapters, combine all or part of the object with a single letterform. The objective is to "fuse" the letterform and the image so that they are completely integrated and create a form that is a synthesis of both into a single new visual unit (Figure 7.1).

FIGURE 7.1   Integrate the object and the letterform.
(*Type Combination* © 2004. Reprinted with permission from Linda Khounnorath.)

This project follows the same general procedures as the previous abstraction problems. Work in black and white within the same 4" square format and explore a wide variety of possible solutions and arrangements in the sketching phases of the project.

For the letterform, use existing typefaces and avoid distorting the proportions of the letter. You may cover up or delete part of the letterform, and scale, reposition, and rotate the forms within the frame. Parts of the letterforms can be cropped, but the letterform should remain identifiable (Figure 7.2).

FIGURE 7.2   Parts of the letterform must remain identifiable.
(*Type Combination* © 2005. Reprinted with permission from Jeremy Kenisky.)

In this project, as with the other object abstractions, it is important to establish compatible shapes between the elements and to use both positive and negative shapes to unify the composition. Variety can be achieved through the use of line, implied shape, value contrast, and scale (Figure 7.3).

FIGURE 7.3   Variety can be achieved by using line, implied shape, and scale.
(*Type Combination* © 2004. Reprinted with permission from Matt Tovar.)

Background

Letterforms are nonobjective shapes to which we attach an arbitrary symbolic meaning. We have to learn the commonly accepted meaning of the shapes of an alphabet. As basic shapes, letterforms are designed using the same principles of design as any other composition.

Understanding Letterforms as Shapes

In seeking to better understand how to create unified but interesting compositions and how to abstract objects, working with existing shapes forces you to examine closely the positive and negative shapes within your original object and within the design of each letterform. Because the basic design of letterforms is already set, you may need to look for different shapes within your object to find the best possible "fit" between your object and a letterform. This exercise helps sharpen your eye for the details of design and lets you explore new ways of exploring line, shape, unity, and variety.

Letters have a specific structure because they are developed as a system more commonly called an *alphabet*. These systems are made up of similar and related shapes to give continuity from letter to letter, which makes reading much easier.

The many different styles of type systems are called *fonts*. This difference in fonts may depend on the time period in history in which they were created, the technology that created them, and the current media and communication demands. Fonts are made up of harmonious shapes that relate to one another in a system with just enough variation of shape to define the individual letters of the alphabet (Figure 7.4). More details about fonts and their history will be outlined in Chapter 12.

FIGURE 7.4 This contemporary alphabet designed with an emphasis on harmony and rectilinear shapes recalls the design of Constructivism. This font was selected as an example because of its obvious adherence to a simple system and clarity of relationships between letters.
(*Van Doesburg Typeface* © 2000. Reprinted with permission from Mike Clayton.)

Letterforms as Communication Design

Each type font has a unique style, and each style communicates differently. Just as each person's tone, choice of words, and emphasis combine to give that person a unique voice and personality, the design differences between typefaces allow you to give each design a different and appropriate visual "voice" for your intended communication.

The distinct style and personality of a typeface is derived from the shapes and shape relationships used within the letterforms. The designer tries to achieve a close relationship of shape and style between the typeface selected for use with a graphic image and the message communicated to ensure consistency and a unified design. Figure 7.5 shows some of the ways in which the lines and shapes of an image and the lines and shapes of letterforms are selected to create a harmonious relationship.

FIGURE 7.5   Forming a relationship between type and images using harmony in both the letterforms and lines and shapes of the stylized figures and objects.
(*Word and Image* © 2003. Reprinted with permission from Patrick Wilkey, www.visiocommunications.com.)

Figure 7.6 shows three examples of the combination of a letter with a simplified image. This blending of type and simplified image shows the abstract design qualities of typographic form and counter form. Notice how the images work well within the letterform's counters and negative spaces. Figure 7.7 shows two examples of the letterform being incorporated into the image. In the logo on the left, the shape of the "H" is implied within the negative space of the perspective form of the I-beam, whereas on the right, the "r" is integrated into the hand replacing the thumb.

FIGURE 7.6   Construction logo drawings. (Left to right: *W Logo* © 2006.
Reprinted with permission of Eric Weidner. *G Logo* © 2006. Reprinted with permission of Jenny Gonzalez.
P Logo © 2006. Reprinted with permission of Robin Parker.)

FIGURE 7.7   Two examples of letterforms integrated into shape(s).
(Left to right: *Heaton Erecting* © 2005. Reprinted with permission from Joseph Blalock.
Rachel's Massage © 2006. Reprinted with permission from The Bradford Lawton Design Group,
www.bradfordlawton.com.)

Anatomy of a Letterform

Designers must be able to recognize and identify the parts of a letterform before they can use them properly. Some of the terminology used to identify these parts is straightforward, and other terminology is abstract. Refer to the diagram in Figure 7.8 for the following terms:

   Ascender: The vertical part of a lowercase letterform that rises above the x-height (b, d, f, h, k, l, t).
   Baseline: The imaginary horizontal line on which all the bases of all letter-forms seem to rest.
   Bowl: The curved part of the letterform that encloses the counter.
   Cap height: The height of a capital letterform measured from the baseline to the cap line.
   Cap line: The imaginary horizontal line to which all capital letters arise.

Counter: The enclosed or partially enclosed area of a letterform. For example, the center of the "e" or "o," or the vertical space between the vertical strokes of the "u" or "n."

Cross bar: The horizontal line that connects the two vertical strokes.

Descender: The vertical part of a lowercase letterform that falls beneath the baseline (p, g, q).

Leg: A horizontal or diagonal stroke that is attached at one end but free on the other.

Serif: The small decorative strokes at the ends of the main strokes.

X-height: The height of a lowercase letter that contains no ascenders or descenders.

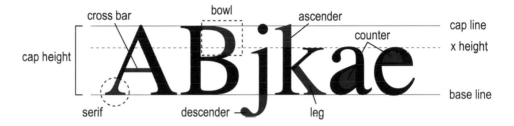

FIGURE 7.8   The anatomy of a letterform.

Conceptual Design Process and Discerning the Interesting Parts of Letterforms

Now that the basic parts of the letter have been identified, you need to differentiate between typefaces. *Typefaces* are groups of letters that share a commonality in stroke, measurement, and style.

Figure 7.9 is a selection of four examples of typefaces. Some typefaces have strokes that are the same throughout the font (Futura), whereas others have variation in the widths of the strokes (Bauer Bodoni). Some have serifs (Garamond), and others do not (Impact). Also in the samples shown, compare the variations in the overall weights and widths of the letterforms.

The letterforms that tend to make the best overall designs for this project are those that are simpler and less decorative. In doing this project, pay particular attention to the counter forms (negative space) of the letters, as these tend to offer many opportunities for combining the image and the letterform (Figure 7.10).

The basic process of exploration through sketches, evaluation, and refinement is the same as in Chapters 4 through 6. In this project, pay particular attention to how well the object and the letterform are synthesized into a unified whole. There should not be a sense that the viewer is seeing two different things but that he or she is seeing one unified image (Figure 7.11).

abcdefghijklmnopqrstuvwxyz 12345

Bauer Bodoni

abcdefghijklmnopqrstuvwxyz 12345

Garamond

abcdefghijklmnopqrstuvwxyz 12345

Futura

abcdefghijklmnopqrstuvwxyz 12345

Impact

FIGURE 7.9   Four examples of typefaces.

FIGURE 7.10   The phone has been placed inside the negative spaces in the letter.
(*Type Combination—Phone with "M"* © 2004. Reprinted with permission from Themah Wilson.)

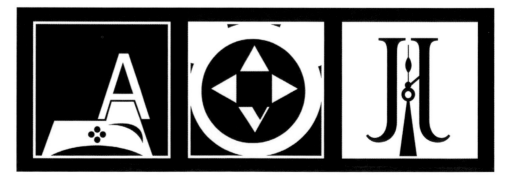

FIGURE 7.11   Student examples.   (Left to right: *Type Combination—Phone with "A"* © 2005. Reprinted with
permission from Robin Parker. *Type Combination—Phone with "V"* © 2005. Reprinted with permission from Robin Parker.
Type Combination—Clothespin with "J" © 2005. Reprinted with permission from Jeremy Kenisky.)

PRODUCTION PROCESS

After you are done with the refinements and have narrowed your designs down to three, scan the drawings and prepare them for use in Illustrator CS4.

TUTORIAL	USING THE TYPE TOOL IN ILLUSTRATOR

The Type tool (T) is one of the most straightforward tools in the program. It allows you to type into the document. To use the Type tool, follow these steps:

1. Launch Illustrator CS4 and create a new document. Name the document "Type Combo." Click OK.
2. Select the Type Tool (T) from the Tools panel, as seen in Figure 7.12.

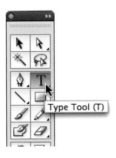

FIGURE 7.12   The Type tool's location in the Tools panel.

3. Click anywhere in the document to set the insertion point for beginning your type. Then type a few characters.
4. With the Type tool, you can select the text as a whole or as individual characters. Simply place the insertion point before the character or characters you would like to select and then click and drag to select them.

At this time, you can change several attributes of the letters. These options are in the Character panel.

5. Open the Character panel by selecting Window > Type > Characters.

With the Character panel in view, the attributes of font choice, point size, and other options are available.

6. You can change the typeface or font using the Font pop-up menu (Figure 7.13).
7. Change the size of the text by clicking on the Font Size pop-up menu in the Character panel (Figure 7.14).

Other options in this panel will be explained further in another chapter.

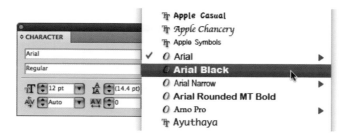

FIGURE 7.13   Select from the fonts you have installed on your computer through this pop-up menu.

FIGURE 7.14   The Font Size pop-up menu with the size set to 12 pt and 36 pt.

Converting Type to Paths: Creating Outlines

When the text is printed or displayed on the screen, the computer reads its font file to understand how to shape, place, and space each character. You may have used a particular font in your document in a computer lab and then returned home, only to open the file and see the characters are all wrong because you used a font that is not installed on your computer at home.

The text that you type in any software depends on the font. A font is a little file used by your operating system. This file holds the character information for all the letters, numbers, punctuation, special characters, and other symbols. Each font is a different file that must be located in its proper place to be used.

Basic text can only have very few modifications. You can change its size, color, and spacing, but you cannot modify it structurally.

The font file that the typeface is dependent on is a collection of vector paths that the computer uses to accurately display and print the font. In Illustrator, you can change the font from being dependent on the font file into compound vector paths based on that information. These paths can be modified in the same way that you have modified points in previous projects.

1. Use the Type tool (T) to place the characters of your design. You can use any font for this exercise.
2. Open the Character panel by selecting Window > Type > Character (PC: Ctrl + T; Mac: Command + T).

3. With the text selected, set the typeface that you want to use. Also set the size of the font to 72 pt.
4. Select the text box using the Selection tool and convert the font to paths by selecting Type > Create Outlines (PC: Ctrl + Shift + O; Mac: Command + Shift + O).

The letters are now converted into compound paths of points and lines. By default, the letters are grouped together. To move them independently, they must be ungrouped (Figure 7.15).

FIGURE 7.15   By default, letters that are converted to paths are grouped.

5. With the letters still selected, choose Object > Ungroup (PC: Ctrl + Shift + G; Mac: Command + Shift + G). These letters/shapes can now be moved independently with the Selection tool (V). As an example, use a capital "A" from the font Capitals (Figure 7.15).

Using the Transform Tools: Reflect and Scale

The Transform tools allow you to modify the appearance of shapes in a variety of ways. You use Scale to make the shape larger or smaller, you use Reflect to flip the shape vertically or horizontally, and you use Rotate to change the angle. If you look closely at the sketch, you can see how each of these commands are used to create the final design. To use the Transform tools, follow these steps:

1. Drag the "A" to the middle of the page so that it will be easy to work with.
2. With the "A" selected, choose the Reflect tool (O) from the Tools panel. It is nested under the Rotate tool (Figure 7.16).

The Reflect tool flips the object across an invisible axis called the *point of origin*. The point of origin is a target-like symbol that appears on the object when a Transform tool is activated. You can move the point of origin by placing the cursor over it and clicking and dragging.

3. Move the point of origin of the "A" shape to the left (Figure 7.17).
4. Place the cursor over the "A" shape and click and drag the cursor to the left, while holding the Shift key.

FIGURE 7.16 The Reflect tool is nested under the Rotate tool.
When a nested tool is selected, it replaces the tool that was there first.
To access that tool again, click and hold the button and select it again.

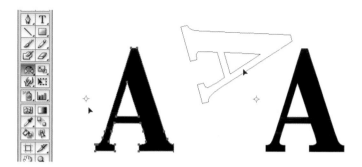

FIGURE 7.17 The Reflect tool flips the shape according to an imaginary axis.
The point of origin is a target-like symbol.

The "A" will begin to rotate around the point of origin, with the shape always pointing toward the point of origin. Holding the Shift key constrains the reflection to 45-degree angles, and the Alt (PC) or Option (Mac) key allows you to drag a copy.

Shapes can be flipped along a specified axis from the Reflect dialog box. To open the dialog box, choose Object > Transform > Reflect (or double-click the Reflect tool).

5. With the "A" shape flipped and still selected, choose the Scale tool (S) from the Tool panel (Figure 7.18).
6. Set the point of origin to the lower-left corner, click on the shape, and drag clockwise to the left while holding the Shift key.

This tool, coupled with the Shift key, scales the shape proportionally. This tool also has a dialog box that you can access by double-clicking the tool in the Tools panel or selecting Object > Transform > Scale.

FIGURE 7.18 The location of the Scale tool in the Tools panel.
Set the point of origin and, using the Shift key, proportionally scale the "A."

The Direct Selection Tool: "Pulling" Points

With the "A" shape as a path, you can distort the letter by moving some of the points within the image. To elongate the left and right stems of the "A," do the following:

1. Select the Direct Selection tool (A) from the Tools panel. Click and drag a marquee around the points in the bottom of the left stem to select them (Figure 7.19).

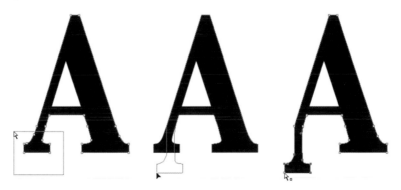

FIGURE 7.19 Drag a marquee around the bottom of the "A" to select the points on the path.
Use preview lines as a guide for moving the points.

2. Notice that the points selected are now solid, and the rest of the points in the path are white. This is a visual clue that you have points selected.
3. With the Direct Selection tool, click and drag the points down about .5 inch.
4. The preview lines show you how the path is going to be changed. Do not release the mouse yet.

5. While dragging down, hold the Shift key to constrain the points' movement horizontally (Figure 7.19). Release the mouse button to place the points.
6. Drag a marquee around the points in the bottom of the right stem to select them (Figure 7.20). Drag them over to the right and down until they match the new baseline set by the other points.

FIGURE 7.20 Drag a marquee around the bottom of the right leg to select the points on the path. Do not use the Shift key when moving these points; instead, trust the preview lines to guide you in keeping the thickness the same.

7. Points can also be moved independently from each other. Using the Shift key, you can select either a single point or multiple points.

Changing Fills and Strokes Using the Tools Panel

The "A" shape has a fill of "black" and a stroke of "none." Fonts, by nature, are filled but contain no stroke. To help you in this exercise, you might want to switch that around and make the fill none and the stroke black. With the "A" shape selected, click on the Swap Fill and Stroke (Shift + X) button in the Tools panel (Figure 7.21).

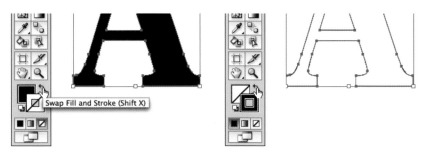

FIGURE 7.21 Use the Swap Fill and Stroke button to quickly change the basic attributes of the shapes.

Using the Transform Tools: Rotate and Scale

For this exercise, you will combine the similar areas of an "A" and a clothespin. The file with the font outline and the shape is supplied for you.

1. Open the file ch07_a_clothespin_demo.ai that is located on the CD-ROM.
2. Move the clothespin shape onto the "A" shape, as pictured in Figure 7.22, and select the Rotate tool (R) from the Tools panel. It might be nested under the Reflect tool because they share the same space in the Tools panel. Do not move the point of origin.

FIGURE 7.22   Move the clothespin over the "A" as shown.

The Rotate tool acts the same way as the Scale and Reflect tools. It also has its own dialog box that you can access by either double-clicking on the tool or selecting Object > Transform > Rotate.

3. With the Shift key pressed, rotate the clothespin shape counter-clockwise, as shown in Figure 7.23.
4. Select the Scale tool (S) and scale the clothespin shape as it appears in Figure 7.23.

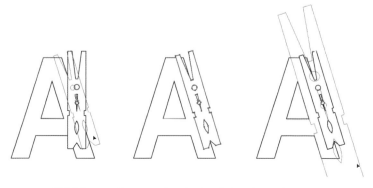

FIGURE 7.23   Rotate and scale the clothespin as shown.

Use the Shift key to keep the proportion of the shape during scaling. Watch the preview lines and use them as a guide for placement.

5. Upon successful scaling, use the Selection tool (V) to move the clothespin shape so that it appears in a place similar to that in Figure 7.24.

FIGURE 7.24   Position the clothespin as shown here.

6. Group the two shapes—the "A" and the clothespin—together using the Group Command (PC: Ctrl + G; Mac: Command + G).

To finish off the design, you need to rotate the image counterclockwise 10 degrees and then change the fill and stroke.

7. With the group selected, open the Rotate dialog box by choosing Object > Transform > Rotate.
8. Enter 10 into the Angle field and click OK (Figure 7.25).

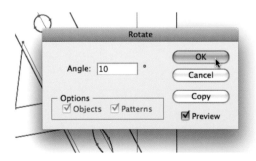

FIGURE 7.25   Rotate the group 10 degrees using the Rotate dialog box.

9. Make a 4" × 4" square that has a black fill and no stroke. Refer to Figure 7.26 for placement.

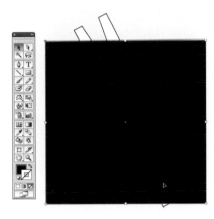

FIGURE 7.26   Place a 4" x 4" square over the design to set the cropping for the Clipping Mask.

10. Select the black square and copy it to the clipboard for later use.
11. Select all the objects and set a Clipping Mask (Figure 7.27).

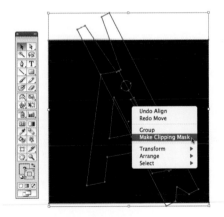

FIGURE 7.27   Select the group and the square and set the Clipping Mask.

12. Paste a copy of the square in the back of the design (Edit > Paste in Back).
13. Use the Direct Selection tool (A) to select the white pieces within the clothes-pin and set their fills to black. Set all the strokes to None (Figure 7.28).

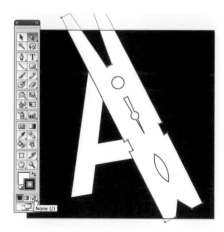

FIGURE 7.28 Clean up the design by filling the shapes within the clothespin appropriately.

Copy and paste the design to another part of the document and invert the fills to get another perspective on the design (Figure 7.29).

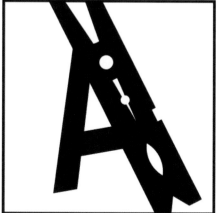

FIGURE 7.29 The final design and its inverse.
(*Type Combination—Clothespin with "A"* © 2005. Reprinted with permission from Jeremy Kenisky.)

SUMMARY

Letterforms are the most common visual elements used to communicate a message. Unfortunately, to most of the public, they are not associated with design. The written word is everywhere, and the visual quality of words is usually ignored. Designers should make a special effort to see the design potential of letterforms.

When you watch television or go to the movies, notice the type used for the titles or credits. Do the shapes and spacing fit the mood of the show? If you go shopping, take a closer look at labels and packaging. Notice the type and the way it is used with other design elements. Is the type appropriate to the contents or cost of the product? Study the type selected for publications. Is it functional and does it visually represent the editorial content or information? This assignment was designed to introduce you to letterforms as design elements and to expand the principles of design to include other nonobjective shapes. Chapter 12, "Design Project 6: Typeface Design," deals with letterforms as design elements and expands the element of type to include value and color.

DESIGN PROJECT 2: USING METHODS OF ABSTRACTION TO CREATE A LOGO

Abstraction Overview

The second project will allow you to explore some ways you can use the things you learned in the previous project to solve a visual communication problem. In this project, you will use abstraction to develop a visual symbol for a business. Such a visual symbol is frequently called a "logo."

In the previous project, you were given an object as the starting point. In this project, you will choose the object to use. Using your selected object, use the Simplification Method and one of the three remaining methods from the previous project.

The four methods of abstracting objects that you have explored are the following (see Figure 8.1):

- **Abstraction Through Simplification**—When using this method, the designer eliminates some visual information to focus attention on the essential qualities or emphasize some particular aspect of the object. Remember to study the object in careful detail, exploring the basic shapes and their relationships within the object. (See Chapter 4 for more details.)

- **Abstraction Through Repetition**—Abstracting an object using repetition allows the designer to repeat all or parts of the object in order to create a more complex design where the composition is unified by the repetition of shape. Repetition does not only mean that the parts are used to create a pattern, but they also can be placed throughout the design in order to allow the negative space to reveal or create other parts of the object. Scale, rotation, and orientation can be used to create rhythm in these patterns. (See Chapter 5.)
- **Abstraction Using Line and Shape**—This method combines closed shapes with shapes implied through the use of line. Using line to imply but not fully enclose shapes also allows for better integration of positive and negative shapes within the composition. Rather than show the object itself, the edge of the object can be implied with a line while a shape can create the rest of the form. (See Chapter 6.)
- **Abstraction Using Type Combination**—In this method, elements are combined to create a new visual message. In this case, the image (or object) is combined with a letterform (or type). The design concepts of unity, variety, and harmony apply. The objective is to "fuse" the letterform and the image so that they create a form that is a synthesis of both and create a single new visual unit. (See Chapter 7.)

FIGURE 8.1   Examples of each method of abstraction.
Left to right: Simplification, Repetition, Line and Shape, and Type Combination.
(*Wire Cutter Abstractions* © 2007. Reprinted with permission from Mauricio Braun.)

CONTENT: THE BASIC PROBLEM DEFINED

Choose an occupation in which someone would use a specific tool or object to complete his or her job. This should be something familiar and not too complex or detailed (Figure 8.2). For example, a carpenter might use a hammer, a saw, or a planer. A chef might use a whisk, a peeler, or a sifter. A mechanic might use a wrench, a car-jack, or a screwdriver. Do not select objects that rely on texture or color because these elements will not be part of this project.

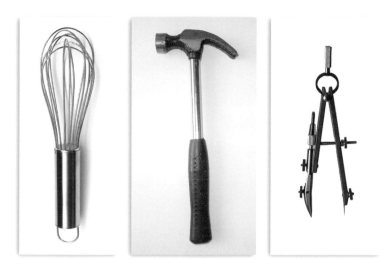

FIGURE 8.2   Objects for this project should be easily associated with a particular occupation and could include objects such as a whisk, a hammer, or a compass.

In the last project, you were limited to using a 4" × 4" square in creating your studies. In this project, you will also use two different size rectangles: a 4" × 6" rectangle and a 4" × 8" rectangle. You may use these either vertically or horizontally.

You will also be required to use type to accompany the final logo. See some examples from students in Figure 8.3.

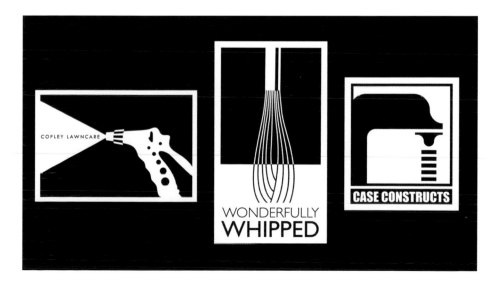

FIGURE 8.3   Examples of student work.
(*Copley Lawncare* © 2007. Reprinted with permission from Kyle Copley. *Wonderfully Whipped* © 2007. Reprinted with permission from Janet McNiel. *Case Constructs* © 2007. Reprinted with permission from Casey Asher.)

Background: From Design to Communication

At some point, students need to begin the shift from purely formal design to design as a means of communication. Although the previous project was concerned only with understanding formal design relationships and with exploring some of the methods of abstracting an object, students need to realize that the ultimate purpose of understanding design is so that they can use visual means to communicate an idea, thought, or feeling.

A logo is a visual symbol that represents a person, group, or organization. Logos need to be able to be recognized quickly and remembered by their intended audience. The selection of the object is very important and needs to be familiar enough that people will know what it is as soon as they see it. A logo must also be highly unified.

The studies in Figure 8.4 were pulled from the repetition and line and shape abstractions of a mechanical pencil. The repetition study on the right communicates faster than the line and shape one on the left. While both are successful studies, the one on the left is easily recognizable as a series of pencil tops with a pencil point inserted for variety.

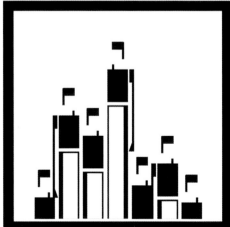

FIGURE 8.4   While they might be good composition, some studies communicate the object better than others. (*Pencil Abstractions* © 2007. Reprinted with permission from Matthew Wells.)

There are many logos that are made up of abstractions like the ones that you completed in the last project. Take a look around you to see if you can identify some of them.

The Picture Frame

In Chapter 1, the *picture frame* was defined as the surface boundaries around a design. The picture frame aids in creating the areas of positive and negative shape (Figure 1.29).

In the first project, you were limited to a 4" × 4" square, or a 1:1 ratio. For this project, you can begin to explore your object using a 4" × 6" rectangle (a 1.5:1 ratio) and a 4" × 8" rectangle (a 2:1 ratio). This modification may better help you communicate the object that you choose.

In this project, composition and content take center stage. The object you choose might require you to explore a more vertical picture frame in order to fully recognize it.

In Figure 8.5, the vertical nature of the hand mixer lends itself to a different format. In the first study, it is hard to make out what the object is. Those familiar with what hand mixers look like might be able to recognize it right away, but others might be able to understand the object better if they see more of it, as shown in the examples in the center or left.

FIGURE 8.5 Examples of studies using the 1:1, 1.5:1, and 2:1 ratios.
(*Hand Mixer Studies* © 2007. Reprinted with permission from Sonia Jimenez.)

In Figure 8.6, the spray nozzle on the left is almost centered in the frame. You can see the water spraying, but not enough to know what is happening.

By doing the same study as the 4" × 6" rectangle, the nozzle can be moved to the right and allow the spray to balance the left of the design without shifting the focus of the design.

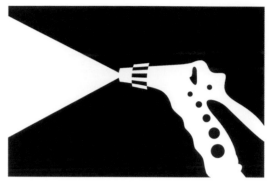

FIGURE 8.6 Adding a few inches to the width of the area allows for better communication of the action happening in the study. (*Spray Nozzle Studies* © 2007. Reprinted with permission from Kyle Copley.)

Being allowed to use other dimensions for your studies will open up many more possibilities as you work through this project. Remember these new sizes can be vertical or horizontal.

Selecting a Typeface for the Logo

The last addition to this project is the use of type in naming the company that accompanies the logo.

In Chapter 7, letterforms were defined as nonobjective shapes to which we attach an arbitrary symbolic meaning. These letterforms make up an alphabet, and the different styles of alphabets are called *typefaces* or *fonts*.

Each type font has a unique style and communicates a certain emotion or feeling. In this project, you must select a font that complements your logo without distracting from it. By choosing the correct type, harmony can be achieved between the type and the image.

In Figure 8.3, you can see several examples of type that were chosen to accompany the studies to create the logo. Each student chose a typeface that had similar characteristics to the object and to the occupation it represented.

Choosing the right type font can be tricky. In Figure 8.7, you can plainly see that the first two choices (Lucidia Calligraphy and Engravers) do not relate well to the geometric quality and even thickness used in the shapes and lines in the object. The third example (Geometric Slabserif) does have the same characteristics and quality as the study and works well in the final design.

Experiment. Take the time to really look at the options and the placement of the type as it works with the logo and the message (see Figure 8.8). Should the type go underneath the logo or to the side? Should the type be all on the same line or multiple lines? Should the type be sentence case or all caps?

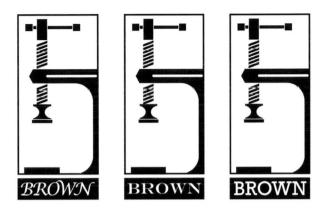

FIGURE 8.7   The type fonts for the first and second example are too decorative for the C-clamp study. The third font choice works quite well.

(*Logo Studios—Brown* © 2007. Reprinted with permission from John Brown.)

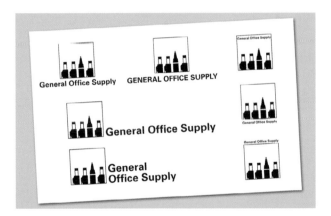

FIGURE 8.8   Experiment with the placement of the type.

More Information About Type

Refer to Chapters 7 and 12 for more information on type and type design.

Conceptual Process

Using the information from the previous four chapters and with the parameters of the problem defined, you can repeat the conceptual process used before as a guide for this project. The following are the steps that you must take to complete this process.

Selecting the Object and Creating the Initial Drawings

Draw your object four or five times with the goal of improving the drawing each time (Figure 8.9). Do not do silhouette drawings. As you do each initial drawing, remember to be careful to observe and improve the overall proportions and shapes within the drawing.

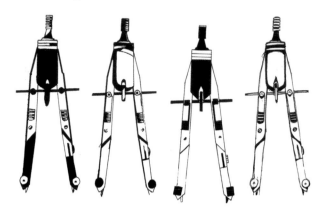

FIGURE 8.9   Sample drawings.
(*Initial drawings—Compass* © 2007. Reprinted with permission from Matthew Wells.)

To study the areas of the drawing, use the same L-shaped cropping frames from the first project.

Create a new template of squares using the following three sizes for the studies: 1) a 4" × 4" square, 2) a 4" × 6" rectangle, and 3) a 4" × 8" rectangle. Use Figure 8.10 as a guide when making your own.

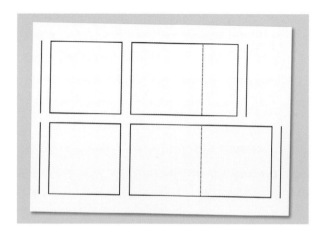

FIGURE 8.10   Create a new template for the new dimensions of the studies.

Place a sheet of tracing paper over the template and draw the boxes that your studies will go into. Remember that you have two more options than just the 4" × 4" square. When you fill in the top sheet, you can replace it and keep working without having to redraw the initial squares.

Creating Studies Using the Simplification Method

As outlined in Chapter 4, the beginning of this process starts with the first steps: simplifying the object. Through these studies, the rest of the methods begin to take shape.

Method One: Simplification

Adjust the cropping frames to show the square or rectangular area of your drawing. As you did in part one of the first project (see Chapter 4), move the frame around the drawing, expanding and contracting the area of the frame until you have isolated what you think would be an interesting composition. Then transfer that composition to one of the shapes on your tracing paper.

Continue to search for and find interesting compositions within the initial drawings. Since you are not working with just a square, be mindful of the rectangular compositions that can be made within the other rectangular shapes. With these added dimensions, you can now explore vertical and horizontal compositions. Remember to fill in the shapes as solids.

You should do at least 25 of these initial compositions.

After you have completed your initial exploratory studies, evaluate them to select those with the strongest overall compositions, the most visual interest, and the best communication for your company, and then refine these. Use the same criteria as outlined in Chapter 4: consider balance, unity through the use of similar shapes, variety to create interest, and recognition of the object. With the addition of the rectangular studies, there are many more possibilities. Try to find the same principles of design within these studies as well.

The refinement drawings should be done within the same format. Based on the drawings that you select from your initial studies, do at least five refinement studies (Figure 8.11). Some of these may be variations from the same initial design study so that you can explore different ways of solving the problems that you see.

 ### *Object Selection: Try More Than One*

In order to explore multiple possibilities for this logo project, you might want to select more than one object for your initial drawing and first studies. Upon completion of the first phase of each object, choose the object that you think best solves the problem. While this might seem like extra work, the results will help you understand the conceptual process and be able to recognize and identify the advantages and disadvantages of each object. This will allow you to determine which idea would be the best solution.

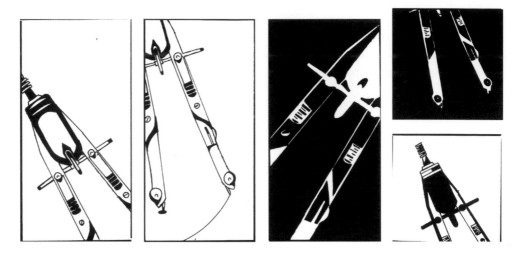

FIGURE 8.11   Refined studies.
(*Compass Studies* © 2007. Reprinted with permission from Matthew Wells.)

Creating Studies Using Your Selected Method

Since you are familiar with some of the methods of abstraction used in the previous project, you may now choose your favorite method for continuing this project. You may choose one (or more) of the methods to complete this project. The remaining methods are:

- Repetition (Chapter 5)
- Line and Shape (Chapter 6)
- Type Combination (Chapter 7)

As outlined in all of the other methods, follow these steps:

- Use the same initial drawing and object.
- Use the same template of squares and rectangles and the same technique of marker studies.
- For the initial studies, use both the initial drawings and the simplification studies from the previous method.
- You should do at least 25 studies for your chosen method.
- Remember to use all three dimensions for your studies. Explore the possibilities of the larger boxes.

Method Two: Repetition

Here are a few notes to help you with the Repetition studies if you choose this method to continue the project:

- Some studies should work with fewer objects, and other studies should work with as many as eight or nine objects. Some studies should show most or all of the object, and others should show only partial objects.
- In evaluating these compositions, pay attention to the negative shapes created by repetition as much as the shapes within the objects themselves.
- Change the scale of the objects both within one frame and from frame to frame.
- Keep in mind that exactly repeating patterns will not hold a viewer's attention for long. Some variation is necessary for interest.
- Too much variety can create visual chaos. What can create unity in a design with too much variety?

Method Three: Line and Shape

If you choose the Line and Shape method, you will need to remember the following information:

- In this phase, you may also repeat the object, but too much repetition will make these images too chaotic, so two or three is usually enough. Some studies should show most or all of the object, and others should show only part of the object.
- In evaluating these compositions, along with the positive shapes, pay attention to the implied shapes created by line.
- Change the scale of the object both within one frame and from study to study.
- In using line to create an implied shape, consider how the alignments between the ends of the lines work to help unify the design and consider how using similar angles can also help to create unity and rhythm within the composition.

Method Four: Type Combination

Here are some things to keep in mind if you choose to use the Type Combination method to create studies for your logo:

- Letterforms that tend to make the best overall design are those that are simpler and less decorative.
- Pay attention to the counter forms (negative space) of the letters. They tend to offer many more opportunities for combining the image with the form.
- Pay particular attention to how well the object and letterform are synthesized into a unified whole.
- You might want to use the same font that the letterform came from when choosing the type for the logo.

Revisions of the Chosen Methods

Once you have completed the studies, select the five most successful studies from each method and revise them. Some of these may be variations of the original studies.

PRODUCTION PROCESS

After you have completed the revisions, choose the most successful study (see Figure 8.12) and proceed to the production process. Scan the final study (or studies if there is more than one you like) and prepare them for use in Illustrator CS4.
  Use the tools and skills that you have learned so far to complete this project.

FIGURE 8.12   Final logo.
(enLine Designs & Concepts © 2007. Reprinted with permission from Matthew Wells.)

SUMMARY

The design process for this project looks a little something like Figure 8.13.

- Choose an occupation and a tool from that occupation.
- Make four to five initial drawings of the object.
- Using your L-shaped cropping frames and your new template, create 25 simplification studies from your initial drawings.
- From those 25 studies choose five and revise them.
- Choose one of the remaining Abstraction methods and create 25 additional studies from your initial drawings and the first studies.
- From those 25 studies, choose five and revise those as well.
- Choose the most successful study and trace it in Illustrator.
- Select a type font that complements your design and set the type in Illustrator.
- Print and mount your logo for your class or your portfolio.

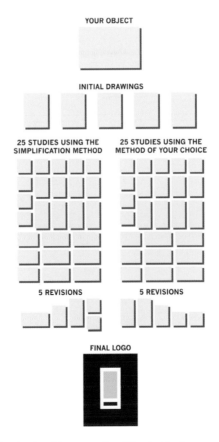

FIGURE 8.13   The Design (Conceptual and Production) process for this project.

9

DESIGN PROJECT 3: FIGURE ABSTRACTION AND NONOBJECTIVE SHAPE

INTRODUCTION AND THE BASIC PROBLEM DEFINED

Design Project 3 consists of five separate sequential designs beginning with a symmetrical, closed form abstraction of a human figure and ending with an open form, asymmetrically balanced nonobjective shape. Details of this project will be discussed in the "Conceptual Process" portion of this chapter. Figures 9.1 to 9.3 are a few examples of this project.

This project incorporates all the design concepts and digital skills you have acquired in the previous projects. It introduces and expands four design principles and explores new digital drawing techniques and procedures. The four principles that will be the focus of this chapter are 1) abstraction, 2) sequence and continuity, 3) discovering the relationship between abstract and nonobjective shapes, and 4) open and closed form.

Background

Before beginning the next project, we should review and examine more closely the principle of abstraction and its relationship with other elements and principles.

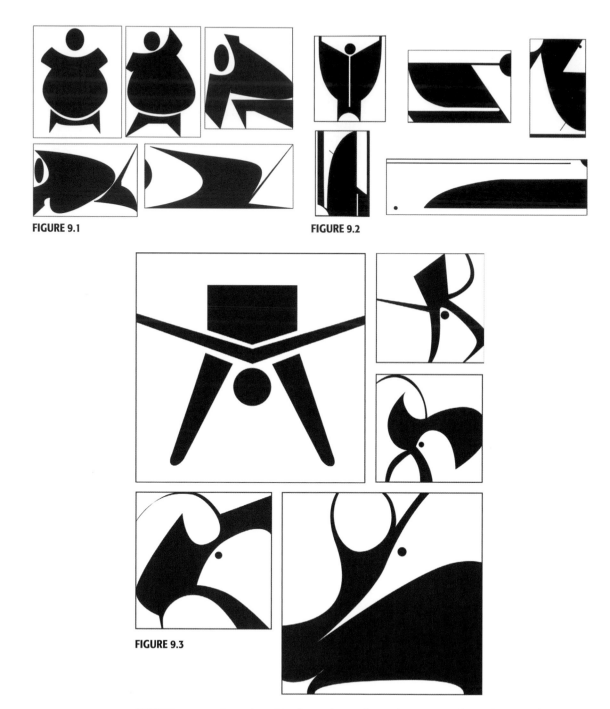

FIGURE 9.1

FIGURE 9.2

FIGURE 9.3

FIGURES 9.1–9.3 Examples of Design Project 3 Figure Abstraction and Nonobjective Shape.
(*Figure Abstraction 1* © 2003. Reprinted with permission from Tiffany Galbaldon. *Figure Abstraction 2* © 2003. Reprinted with permission from Mike Smith. *Figure Abstraction 3* © 2003. Reprinted with permission from Meliza Aaron.)

Abstraction

Abstraction is the process of reducing natural shapes down to their simplest form. As mentioned in Chapter 2, "Principles of Design," abstraction is part of the design process directly related to trademarks and other communication visuals such as posters, packages, and illustrations. Figure 9.4 shows a few examples of abstraction used as trademarks and symbols

FIGURE 9.4 Examples of abstraction.
(Top left: *Ed Net Logo* © 2003, Middle left: *Voice Logo* © 2003,
Bottom left: *Micro Majic Logo*© 2008. Right: *Road Ralley* © 2003.
Reprinted with permission from Patrick Wilkey, http://www.visiocommunications.com.)

Sequence and Continuity

A sequence as it relates to visual design is a series of images organized in a specific order. *Continuity*, also detailed in Chapter 2, is the idea that something is carried over or connected to another element. The project in this chapter consists of a sequence of five images designed with continuity. Sequence and continuity are necessary for understanding animation, motion graphics, corporate identities, layout design, and integration of the many parts associated with architecture and interior design. Figure 9.5 is an example of an animation sequence that combines still photography and computer-generated animation. Figure 9.6 is an example of abstract symbols for a university Web site and an animated sequence of two of these symbols.

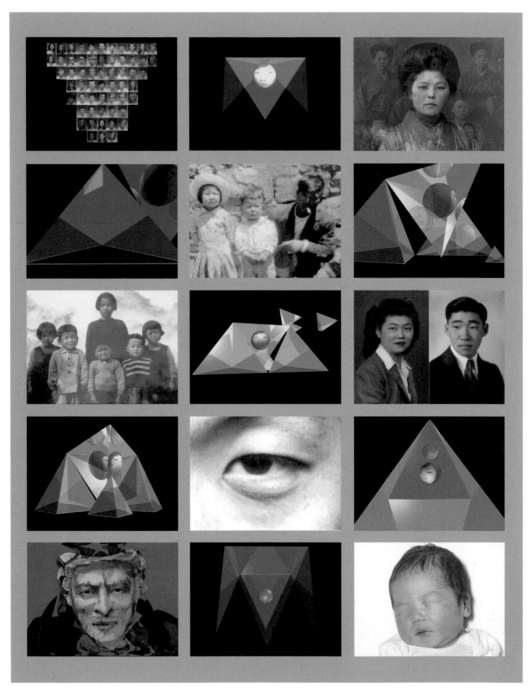

FIGURE 9.5 An animated sequence.

(*Selected frames from "American Sansei" animation* © 2003. Reprinted with permission from Alan Hashimoto.)

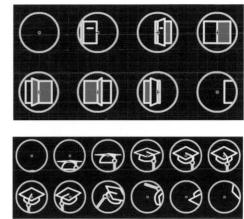

FIGURE 9.6   Abstracted symbols and pictographs.
(*Pictographs* © 2006. Reprinted with permission from Mike Clayton.)

The Relationship Between Abstract and Nonobjective Shapes

Because each of the five images created for this project is designed in sequence with continuity, they naturally establish a relationship between the first abstract figure design and the nonobjective last design. Refer again to Figures 9.1 to 9.3. This process should point out that nonobjective shapes can communicate emotions and information without using a recognizable object.

Closed Form and Open Form

Closed form refers to a composition or design that feels as if an entire scene is in view within a picture frame. There is a feeling of enclosure with a distinct focal point that all the other elements are centered around. Closed form usually suggests a more classic or formal balance. The first of five images that begin this chapter's project should be closed form (refer to Figures 9.1 to 9.3).

Open form is a composition or design that feels as if a scene were cropped and we are viewing only a portion of it. Contrary to closed form, there is a feeling of expansiveness with elements that seem to extend beyond the picture frame. Open form feels less formal and is usually asymmetrically balanced. The last of the five images should be an open form composition. (Refer to Figures 9.1 to 9.3.)

Figure 9.7 is an example of two scenes from an animation that exemplifies closed form located at the left and open form on the right.

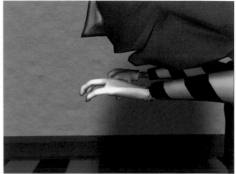

FIGURE 9.7   Open form and closed form.
(Selected frames from the animation *"The Mime"* © 2003. Reprinted with permission from Nathan Tufts.)

Conceptual Process

As a review, Design Project 3 consists of five separate sequential designs to be created, beginning with a symmetrical, closed form abstraction of a human figure and ending with an open form, asymmetrically balanced nonobjective shape.

Design One: Figure Abstraction

This is the most important design because it is the foundation for the other four. More attention will be given to this part of the conceptual process.

Study the characteristics of a human figure. Divide the figure into three to five simple symmetrical shapes and stylize these shapes through the use of unity and variety. Unity may be achieved by making sure the shapes are related in some way. Placing a variety of contrasting shapes and weights next to each other will give the figure interest. The negative space is also being designed so be sure to indicate a picture frame. Through the use of an abstract figure design and diagrams of this design, Figure 9.8 will help illustrate what gives these shapes harmony, variety, and contrast. The design that begins the sequence is located on the left. The image to the right of this design is a diagram that indicates the vertical lines that give the entire design harmony. The next design, third from the left, illustrates harmony through the use of curves, half circles, and circles. Notice how each rounded shape is a different size, which adds to the variety of the design. These curves also give variety to the entire design by contrasting with the straight vertical lines in the previous design on the left. The design on the far right uses a diagonal to add contrast to both the vertical and curved lines.

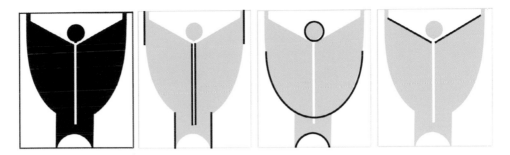

FIGURE 9.8   Abstract shapes that represent a human form and three diagrams of these shapes, detail how the various shapes and their relationships to each other create harmony, variety, and contrast.

Notice how all the shapes are different weights. They also use alternating round shapes contrasted by flat or sharp shapes. Both of these ideas give variety to the entire design.

This next series of images details one way you could begin your first design and points out how variety and unity are achieved throughout the design. These shapes could be drawn traditionally but have been presented here digitally so the shapes are very clear and easy to understand (see Figure 9.9).

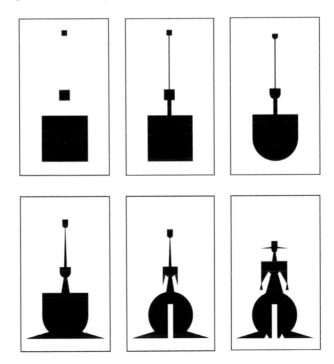

FIGURE 9.9   This series of images details one way you could begin your first design and points out how variety and unity are achieved throughout the design.

Beginning with the design at the upper left, harmonious shapes are balanced throughout this first design by a variety of weights and distances (space) between them. Next, the upper-middle design shows how thin vertical shapes that are different lengths and widths unify these shapes. Unity is maintained by the line direction of the new shapes with different lengths and weights, which establishes variety. The upper-right shape contrasts the flatness of the previous shapes by alternating round sides of each shape for variety. The lengths are slightly adjusted to ensure that all the shapes relate to one another. The lower-left shape adds some diagonals. Each diagonal is different, but they all create shapes that show a firm base to help relieve the tension of the previous round shapes. The lower-middle design reintroduces new vertical shapes to create arms and legs. These verticals are evenly distributed throughout the design, and the shape that creates the legs repeats the flat horizontal and vertical sides to create a relationship with the other horizontal and vertical shapes. The last design adds a few accents that are smaller repeated shapes to maintain harmony throughout the design. Notice how adjustments to the neck shape help it become more related to the other shapes.

The concept of abstracted and stylized figures can be seen in many forms of design. Two examples are illustrated in Figures 9.10 and 9.11. These images are a series of stills taken from computer-generated animations.

In Figure 9.10, notice the variety of weights of shapes that give the figure a feeling of power. The sharpness of all the shapes gives the feeling of protection and aggression. They also help harmonize all the parts of the figure to create unity.

The robot in Figure 9.11 is sleek and feminine. Notice the variety of lengths and weights of shapes that give interest and expression and how they are unified by the similarity of the round shapes found in the head and joints. These shapes are in contrast to the long sharp shapes of the limbs.

FIGURE 9.10 Stylized figure.
(*Character Animation Study* © 2003. Reprinted with permission from Nathan Tufts.)

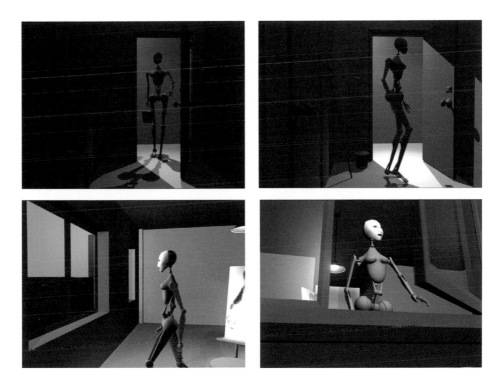

FIGURE 9.11   Selected frames from the animation "The Painter."
(© 2003. Reprinted with permission from Chad Griffiths.)

Designs Two, Three, and Four: Sequential Designs

Each shape in this sequence should have the same amount of change or manipulation from design to design. Starting with a change from design one, the abstract figure, design two would show the same degree of change leading to design three, and design three the same amount of change to design four, which leads to the final design. Each of these designs does not have to resemble a figure because they are merely steps toward the fifth and final design. Each composition should be well thought out and follow the principles of any good design, including unity, variety, and balance.

If the degree of change is similar, the entire project will have continuity and harmony. Through a calculated series of changes, a natural progression of shapes will illustrate an evolution and relationship between an abstract recognizable figure and nonobjective shapes. Review Figures 9.1 to 9.3 and notice the subtle changes between each design. Look again at just the beginning and ending designs. The first design, which is closed form, is significantly different from the final open-form design. This exercise demonstrates how two apparently opposite types of compositions can still be related.

Design Five: Asymmetrical Nonobjective Design

This final design ends the sequence. It should be the result of a logical and well-paced series of designs leading from an abstract human figure to an interesting, unified, and asymmetrically balanced nonobjective composition. Look again at the last design of Figures 9.1 to 9.3. They are similar to Design Project 1 in this book. This last design and possibly designs two, three, and four should follow most of the suggestions in the "Conceptual Process" sections in Design Project 1. The following is a short summary:

- To achieve unity, make sure there are similar angle directions, and parallel vertical and horizontal sides to shapes, curves, and types of shapes.
- To achieve variety, intensify contrast.
- Create good visual hierarchy balanced with unity.
- Keep shapes simple.
- Design within an established "picture frame." Experiment with different proportions.
- Be aware you are designing negative space as you design positive shapes.

All Five Designs: Conceptual Process

For most design solutions, the best way to begin the visualization process is by creating approximations of a design's solutions using a pen or pencil. Many roughs should be explored to make sure all the alternatives have been explored. Narrow down the choices to the ones that best meet the criteria and begin the process of producing an accurate representation of your sketches (Figures 9.12, 9.13, 9.14).

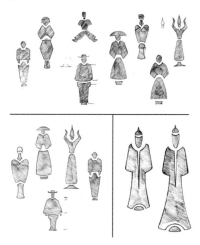

FIGURE 9.12   Begin this project with several thumbnail sketches of design one (five-shape figure). Next, narrow down these thumbnails to just one sketch that will be the starting point for the next four designs.

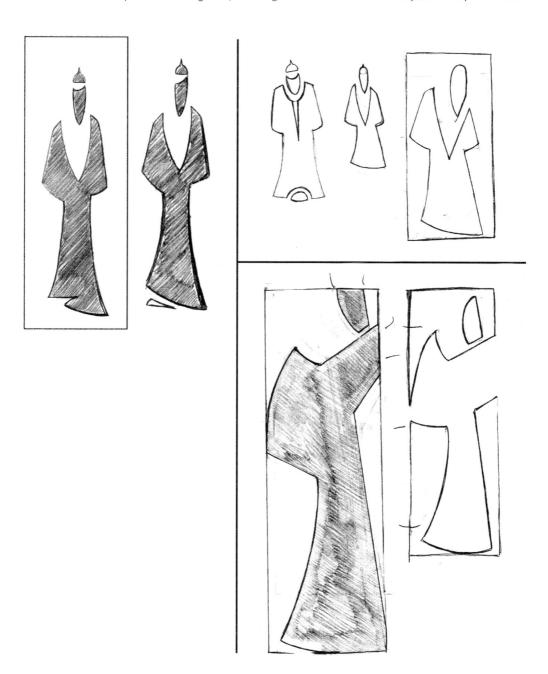

FIGURE 9.13   Create thumbnails for the sequence from abstract figure to nonobjective shape. Narrow these down to the best ones and combine all the designs into one composition.

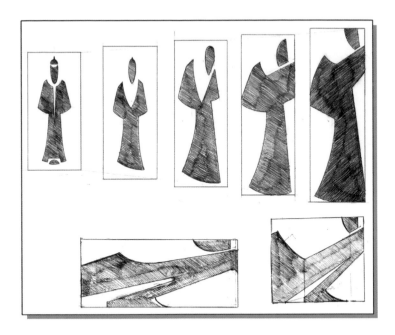

FIGURE 9.14 After all the alternatives have been tested, settle on the best designs and begin the digital production process.

| TUTORIAL | **PRODUCTION PROCESS** |

As in the last project, begin by scanning the sequence of designs. These scans need to be only 72 ppi and grayscale. If all the drawings are on one sheet (as in Figure 9.14), scan the entire sheet. If not, scan the images one at a time, cropping them as needed.

1. After the images are scanned, create a new document and save it as "Figure Abstraction."
2. If the scan you are using is wider than it is tall, you may want to change the orientation of the page in the Layout View. If so, then in the New Document dialog box, set the Orientation of the page to Landscape (Figure 9.15). Changing the Orientation to Landscape rotates the page 90°, making the page display so that the width is longer than the height.

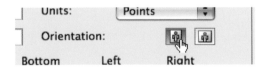

FIGURE 9.15 Because the scan in the example is wider than it is tall, it is best to change the Orientation of the page to Landscape.

The new document is displayed in Landscape mode in the work area. Also displayed is a faint dotted line, with a .5" inset all the way around the page. This is the area of the page that the printer will print. Anything not contained within that boundary will not be printed.

3. You can hide the lines by selecting View > Hide Page Tiling. To show the page tiling if it is hidden, choose View > Show Page Tiling.
4. Place the scan on the work area by selecting File > Place as you have done in previous exercises. This image automatically centers in the document area. If you need to scale the image to fit or import more than one image, do so now and arrange them on the page.
5. With the Layers palette visible, double-click Layer 1 to set its options (Figure 9.16). Name the layer "Drawings" and check the Template box. The layer will be locked, the images dimmed to the specified percentage and the image will not display when printed.

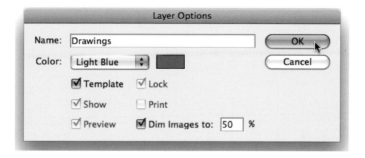

FIGURE 9.16   Set the layer's properties in the Layer Options dialog box.

6. Create a new layer by either clicking on the Create New Layer icon in the Layers palette or choosing New Layer from the pop-up menu.
7. Double-click the new layer and, in the Layer Option dialog box, name the layer "Tracings."
8. View the entire page in the screen by choosing View > Fit in Window (PC: Ctrl + 1; Mac: Command + 1). You can also view the page at actual size by selecting View > Actual Size (PC: Ctrl + 2; Mac: Command + 2).
9. With the Zoom tool (Z), click and drag a marquee around the first step of the figure abstraction drawings, as shown in Figure 9.17. Then release the mouse. The area selected zooms in to fill the screen. If you have gone too far, with the Zoom tool (Z) selected, hold down the Alt key (PC) or Option key (Mac) and the + sign in the cursor will turn into a - sign allowing you to zoom out. Use the aforementioned shortcuts for fitting the page to the window if you need to start over.

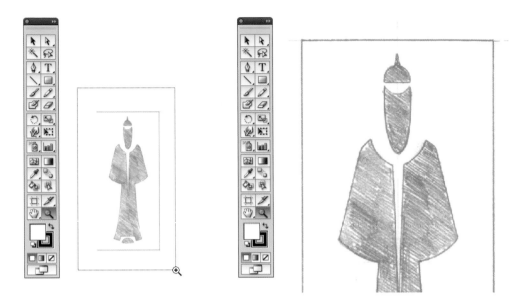

FIGURE 9.17 Use the Zoom tool to zoom in on a specific area.

Trace and Create the First Figure

Using tools and techniques that have been covered previously, trace the drawings to create the designs. There are two different methods for completing this project.

In the description of the project, you were told to create a figure and then draw three intermediary designs before you reach the final nonobjective design. Drawing each step on paper helps to keep a balance and order to what you are doing from start to finish. Visualizing each step helps you to work out the kinks that may occur as you make the transitions from one shape to the next. Then, in Illustrator, all you have to do is trace each of the drawings because you have already completed the real work on paper.

Although it is ideal to work out your designs on paper, you can create the first figure and then use that design to create the variations or steps toward that final design. This allows you to use the computer to create the intermediary steps in the design.

For this first section, we will focus on tracing the drawn images.

Part of the description of the project stated to create a symmetrically balanced figure. Because the figure is symmetrical, it is the same on both sides. Using the tools you have already learned, this will be simple. With a little forethought, you might realize that all you have to do to the initial figure is draw one side and then flip and join it. The following steps will help you in this process.

Using the Pen and Convert Anchor Point Tools

To use the Pen and Convert Anchor Point tools, follow these steps:

1. With the Pen tool (P) selected in the Tools palette, set the fill to None and the stroke to black.
2. View your rulers by selecting View > Show Rulers (PC: Ctrl + R; Mac: Command + R). Drag a vertical guide from the left and place it right in the center of your scan to bisect the symmetrical figure.

In Figure 9.18, for example, the Pen tool (P) was used to draw from the inside of the robe. Then the points were placed and handles were pulled as needed to create the left side of the main shape of the figure. The path should not be closed.

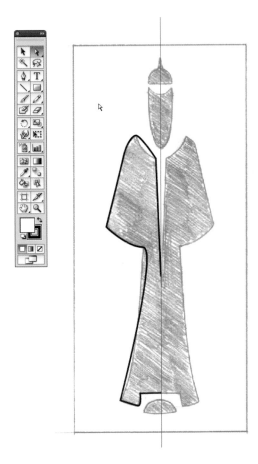

FIGURE 9.18   Use the Pen tool to draw the left side of the robe.

3. Using the Zoom tool (Z), focus on the lower-left corner of the robe. The corner of the robe is a right angle with no handles to pull. It is called a *corner point*. Using the Convert Anchor Point tool (Shift + C), you can change a handles corner point to a point with handles, which is called a *smooth point*.
4. The polygon shape in Figure 9.19 has four corner points. With the Convert Anchor Point tool, click on a corner point and pull out handles to make it a smooth point.

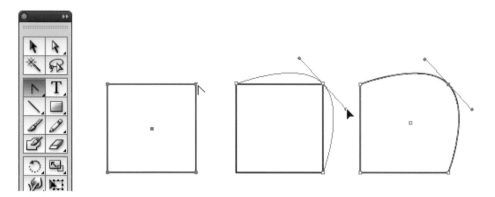

FIGURE 9.19   Using the Convert Anchor Point tool, you can change a corner point to a smooth point.

Likewise, the shape in Figure 9.20 has four smooth points with handles. The Convert Anchor Point tool helps you to remove the handles and make it a corner point.

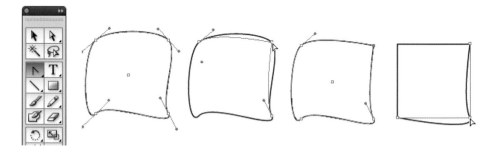

FIGURE 9.20   Using the Convert Anchor Point tool, you can change a smooth point to a corner point.

5. Select the Convert Anchor Point tool (Shift + C), which is part of the Pen tool set. To select the tool, click and hold on the Pen tool until the subset opens. Then select the fourth tool that looks like an open right angle (Figure 9.21). This is the Convert Anchor Point tool.

FIGURE 9.21   The Convert Anchor Point tool is hidden in the Pen tool subset.

6. With the Convert Anchor Point tool selected, click and drag on the corner point to change it to a smooth point with handles (Figure 9.22).

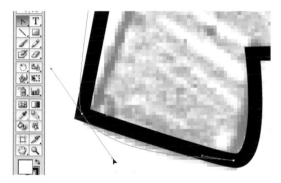

FIGURE 9.22   Use the Convert Anchor Point tool to change the corner point to a smooth point.

7. Using the Direct Select tool (A) in cooperation with its proper modifier key (PC: Alt; Mac: Option), move each of the handles independently to create the correct curve for each line (Figure 9.23).
8. View the page at actual size by selecting View > Actual Size (PC: Ctrl + 1; Mac: Command + 1).

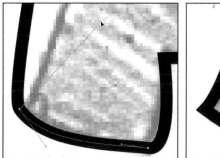 

FIGURE 9.23   Fix the corner of the robe by using the Direct Selection tool to modify the handles independently.

Using the Reflect Tool and Joining Points

Now that the first line segment has been created, you can use the Reflect tool (O) to copy and flip the line. Then you will make the two line segments become one closed path.

1. With the Selection tool (V), select the line that was just created.
2. Select the Reflect tool (O) from the first transform subset under the Rotate tool (Figure 9.24).

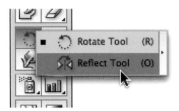

FIGURE 9.24   The location of the Reflect tool.

3. Move the Point of Origin (the target icon) to the center guide by mousing over the target-like symbol, clicking, and dragging (Figure 9.25). This will be the axis at which the line will reflect.

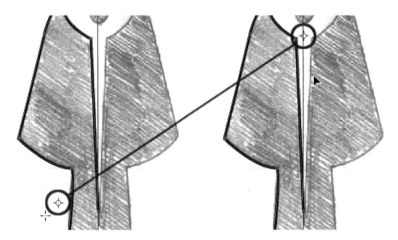

FIGURE 9.25   Move the point of origin to the center guide. This is the axis at which the line will reflect.

4. After the point of origin is placed, move the mouse over to the left of the guide and press and hold the Shift and Alt key (PC) or Shift and Option key (Mac). A double-arrow icon appears. Drag the cursor to the right and the line copies and reflects over the point of origin. Release the mouse, and then the modifier keys. The reflected line appears.

5. As shown in Figure 9.26, use the Direct Selection tool (A) to drag a marquee around the top endpoints at the base of the robe (or any two points that are near each other). The Direct Selection tool allows you to select points within a line. This allows you to select two points even though they are on two different paths.

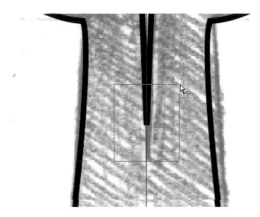

FIGURE 9.26 Select both of the points as shown using the Direct Selection tool.

6. With the two points selected, choose Object > Path > Join (PC: Ctrl + J; Mac: Command + J) from the top.
7. If the Join dialog box appears, there are two options to choose from (Figure 9.27). If you want the new point to be a corner point, click the Corner box. If you want the new point to be a smooth point, check Smooth. In this case, check Corner. Click OK.

FIGURE 9.27 Select Corner from the Join dialog box.

If the dialog box does not appear, then the two points selected were not right on top of each other. A straight line is created to join the paths, and you must manually fix the curves.

8. Using the same steps, select and join the two points at the bottom of the robe as well. This action closes the path.
9. With the Selection tool (V), choose the robe shape and fill it with black.

Using the Pathfinder

The last three shapes that make up this figure are the face, hat, and feet. Using the Pathfinder palette will make quick work of this.

1. If the Pathfinder is not visible, choose Window > Pathfinder.
2. Center the area of the head and hat on the screen using the Zoom tool (Z) or the scroll bars.
3. Select the Ellipse tool (L) from the Tools palette. It may be hidden under the Rectangle tool. Set the fill to None.

Remember the Modifier Keys When Using the Shape Tools

For a bit of quick review, if you hold down the Shift key while drawing a shape, it will be constrained proportionally at a 1:1 ratio. A rectangle will become a square, and an ellipse will become a circle. If you hold down the Alt key (PC) or the Option key (Mac), the shape will draw from the center out. If you hold down both modifier keys, the shape will draw from the center out proportionally.

4. With the Ellipse tool, draw an ellipse for the head. Use the Alt key (PC) or the Option key (Mac) to draw from the center out from the guide to center the shape (Figure 9.28). Draw a second shape, as shown in Figure 9.28, as the "subtraction" area from the first shape.

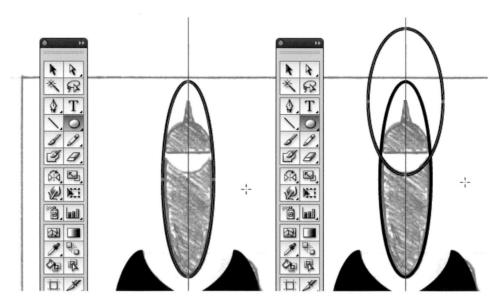

FIGURE 9.28   Draw an ellipse from the center out as shown.
Then draw the second shape as shown on the right.

5. Select both shapes and click on the Subtract button (top row, second button) to subtract the area of the second shape from the first (Figure 9.29). Remember that in CS4, compound shapes are automatically expanded. To disable this automatic expansion, hold down the Alt (PC) or Option (Mac) key when clicking the button in the Pathfinder.

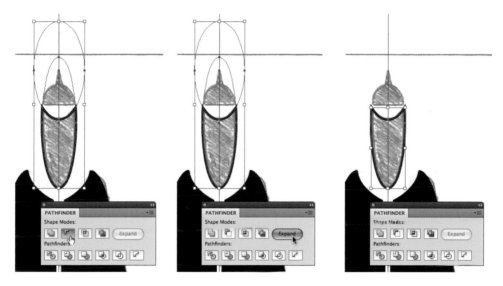

FIGURE 9.29   Use the shape on top to subtract from the area underneath. Fill it with black.

6. Use an ellipse and a rectangle to create the primary shape for the hat. Use the Subtract effect to create the semicircle (Figure 9.30).

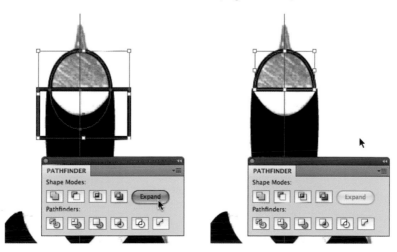

FIGURE 9.30   Draw a circle and then a rectangle as shown to create the basic form of the hat.

7. Select the Polygon tool from the Rectangle tool subset.
8. Click once near the hat shape to open the Polygon dialog box (Figure 9.31). In the dialog box, you can set two options: the radius of the shape and the number of sides. To create a triangle, enter 0.25 in the Radius field and 3 in the Sides field. Click OK.

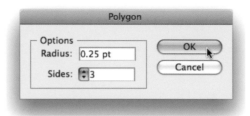

FIGURE 9.31   The Polygon dialog box.

9. Simply resize the triangle to the proper shape. There is no need to hold down the Shift key to keep it proportional because we need it to be a spike for the hat. Once resized, position it over the top of hat so that it overlaps (Figure 9.32).

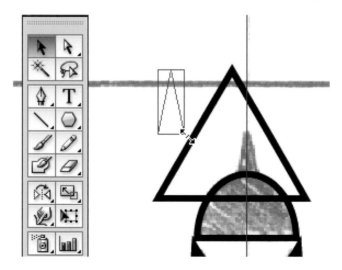

FIGURE 9.32   Scale the triangle accordingly and overlap the shape at the top of the hat.

10. Select both the hat shape and the triangle. Click on the Add button (top row, first button) to add the areas of the shapes together (Figure 9.33). Then fill with black.
11. Select the Hand tool (H) from the Tools palette or hold down the spacebar to temporarily activate it. Click and drag up in the document area to scroll the page down to the feet area.

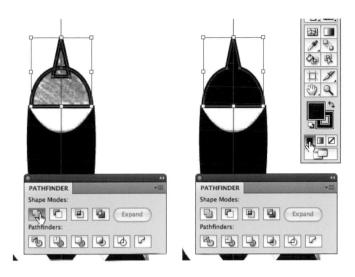

FIGURE 9.33   Add the areas of the two shapes together using the
Pathfinder and fill the resulting shape with black.

12. Draw two ellipses similar to the ones in Figure 9.34. With both shapes selected, click on the Intersect button (top row; third button) to intersect the shape and leave behind the foot shape.

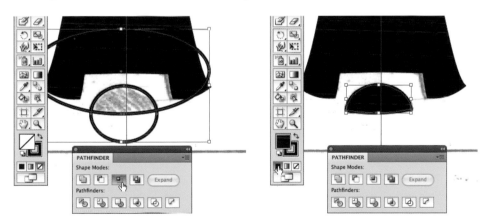

FIGURE 9.34   Use two ellipses and the Intersect button in the Pathfinder
to create the feet shape (left) and fill with black (right).

13. Select View > Actual Size to see the completed first figure.
14. Select all four shapes and set their strokes to None for the best effect.
15. From the top menu, choose File > Print. The result is the figure minus the scanned image and guide (Figure 9.35).
16. Select File > Save to save the current document.

FIGURE 9.35   Print the document to see the completed shapes without the drawing and guides.

Using Group/Ungroup

To finalize the first figure, group the four shapes together:

1. Select all the shapes with the Selection tool (V).
2. Choose Object > Group (PC: Ctrl + G; Mac: Command + G) from the top menu to group the shapes together.
3. Now that the shapes are grouped into one item, use the Select tool (V) to move the group around or the Direct Selection tool (A) to select a shape within the group.

Modify the Figure: Moving Points and Handles

If you want to continue with the project by simply tracing each drawing, go directly to the "Using the Clipping Mask" section following this one. If you want to use the tools within Illustrator to help you experiment with new shapes and steps to your final design, continue with this section. By duplicating the first tracing, you can keep the original intact while experimenting with the copy.

1. With the group selected, choose Edit > Copy (PC: Ctrl + C; Mac: Command + C) to temporarily store the group into the clipboard's memory.
2. Select Edit > Paste (PC: Ctrl + V; Mac: Command + V) to paste a copy of the group into the document. Paste as many copies of the figure as you would like to experiment with.

3. Select the second group and choose Object > Ungroup (PC: Ctrl + Shift + G; Mac: Command + Shift + G) to ungroup the shapes.
4. Using the tools that we have already discussed, modify the points and curves of the shapes so that they create other interesting shapes. Add points, subtract points, or delete unnecessary shapes. In Figure 9.36, there are a few examples of simple variations from the first figure.

FIGURE 9.36   Variations of the first figure created by simply modifying curves and points.

5. When you have achieved an acceptable second step in the figure, group the shapes, copy and paste, and then ungroup them and start on the third step, followed by the fourth, the fifth, and so on until you have created the five figures (Figure 9.37).

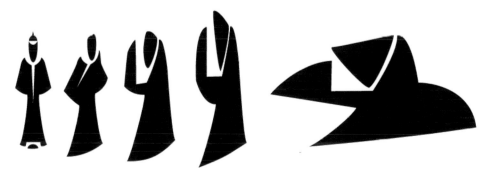

FIGURE 9.37   The final five figures created from experimenting with the tools.

Using the Clipping Mask

Whether you traced all five drawings (Figure 9.38) or created them within the software (Figure 9.37), you will use Clipping Masks (as seen in previous chapters) to crop the shapes.

FIGURE 9.38   The final five figures traced from the drawings.

In the previous chapters, Clipping Masks were used to give the design a better sense of asymmetry and balance. Using them here will also add to the design. In Figure 9.39, the rectangle is used to "crop" the area of the organic shape. Another rectangle is placed over the top of the resulting shape to help enclose or trap the design. The same process will be done with each of the five shapes you created.

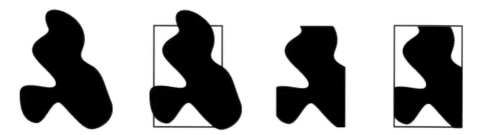

FIGURE 9.39   An example of using the Clipping Mask in Illustrator.

1. Draw a rectangle over the desired shape (Figure 9.40) with the Rectangle tool (M).
2. Copy that rectangle to the clipboard (PC: Ctrl + C; Mac: Command + C) so that it can be applied later as a border to the image.
3. Select the group of shapes and the rectangle.
4. Choose Object > Clipping Mask > Make (PC: Ctrl + 7; Mac: Command + 7) to make the mask.

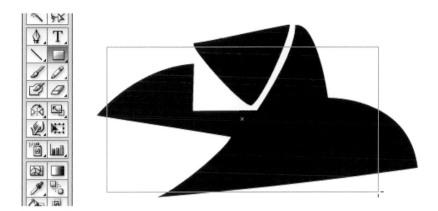

FIGURE 9.40   Draw a rectangle to act as the border and clipped area.

5. From the Edit menu, choose Edit > Paste in Front (PC: Ctrl + F; Mac: Command + F) to paste a copy of the rectangle directly on top of the clipped area. Set the fill to None and the stroke to black.
6. Group the clipped area and the rectangle border by selecting them and choosing Object > Group (PC: Ctrl + G; Mac: Command + G). By grouping them together now, they can be moved easily in later steps. Figure 9.41 shows the final result.

FIGURE 9.41   The final figure abstraction with the Clipping Mask and the border.

7. Repeat this process for all the other shapes. If the shape does not require a Clipping Mask, outlining it with a rectangle will do just fine.
8. Save your progress.

Printing the Final File

To give the best possible presentation, you will need to arrange the five designs on the page before printing them out.

Remember the dotted line border at the beginning of the tutorial that showed you where the printable area of the document was? You can use it as a guide for placing the figures.

1. Turn the Page Tiling Preview back on by choosing View > Show Page Tiling.
2. Arrange the figure abstractions within the dotted line area. Scale them down if necessary to make room for all of them (Figure 9.42).

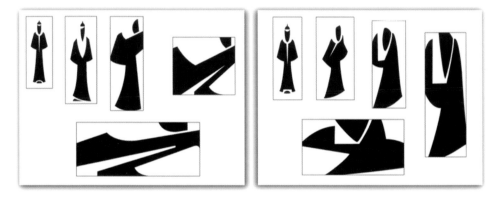

FIGURE 9.42   The final result for each option on the first figure tracing.
(Left: *Figure Abstraction* © 2003. Reprinted with permission from Mark Hyatt.
Right: *Figure Abstraction* © 2003. Reprinted with permission from Mike Clayton.)

3. Choose File > Print to print the page. Because the Print box on the Drawings layer is unchecked, only the contents of the Tracings layer will print.
4. If you want to print one design at a time, simply move the other designs out onto the pasteboard area outside of the Page Tiling Preview and print the one design.
5. Save your file and close it. 🪀

SUMMARY

The fierce competition for audience attention is accelerating every day. The huge amount of visual and textual material being thrown at the viewing public is being delivered through a never-ending supply of new media and formats for electronic communications. Everyone's attention span and tolerance for viewing images and deciphering messages is getting shorter.

Designers must be aware of and incorporate abstraction as a big part of the communication process. Abstraction is the idea of reducing something down to its simplest form. It makes information easier and quicker to read and understand. Trademarks, symbols, posters, packaging, media introduction motion graphics, movie previews, television commercials, Web graphics, music, headlines, titles, and advertising of any kind are just a few examples.

The next time you go to the store, notice how many labels, trademarks, packages, posters, and signs that flash by you in a single short trip. If you are very perceptive and a quick counter, you will see that it could be in the hundreds or thousands.

Other important points of this chapter are the relationships of nonobjective shapes to expressive abstract shapes, continuity and sequence, and open and closed form.

Understanding how to make nonobjective shapes relate to one another in interesting ways is vital to any designer. The remaining projects in this book deal with shapes that do not necessarily represent anything in particular but are designed to create recognizable objects and nonobjective designs that communicate a concept or idea.

Successful use of continuity and sequence can also be easily noticed in music, narrative storytelling, and in motion pictures. Can you think of a movie, novel, or concert you have recently attended where the continuity or sequence was improperly handled? When any work of art is void of continuity, it will seem disjointed and disconnected. If a sequence is not properly put in the correct order, confusion is usually the result. This is the same for visual design.

Open and closed form compositions have very different results, even when the subject matter, values, colors, textures, and shapes are the same. Try to use a closed-form composition as an option for each of the following four projects in this book. Try to use an open-form solution for each project. Notice how differently you have to think when you change from designing closed-form to open-form compositions and visa versa. This may be why most artists and designers have chosen one or the other to create their masterpieces. Which way do you prefer to design? Why?

10

DESIGN PROJECT 4: VALUE

INTRODUCTION

As defined in Chapter 1, value describes light and dark. It is dependent on light, without which value does not exist. Light permits us to see the contrast of values that make up shape and form.

Value and its relationship to shape and design principles is the main topic of this chapter. Design Project 4 is a design exercise that uses the shapes of value found in a photograph. Through the processes of distortion, stylization, and abstraction, the result will be an interesting, harmonious, and unique design. By closely studying the lights and darks of a photograph, you should be able to see the differences in these values and create shapes in which you can apply the lessons learned in previous chapters. A photograph is a logical beginning. It is the most common recorder of visual information and an art form that uses light exclusively. Most photographs deal with realism. Realism is what we see in nature. It is from here we can begin the process of stylization, distortion, and abstraction after the shapes of value are identified.

CONTENT: THE BASIC PROBLEM DEFINED

Similar to previous assignments, an object-oriented program will be used to complete this project. New ideas concerning value, masking, layers, swatches, and other imaging techniques and tools will be introduced. Figure 10.1 shows several examples of this project.

FIGURE 10.1   Examples of the value project.
(Top left: *Value Design* © 2003. Reprinted with permission from Charlotte Pages.
Top center: *Value Design* © 2003. Reprinted with permission from Cantu Logan.
Top right: *Value Design* © 2003. Reprinted with permission from Audrey Gould.
Bottom left: *Value Design* © 2003. Reprinted with permission from Jonathan Harrison.
Bottom center: *Value Design* © 2003. Reprinted with permission from Fon Ulrich.
Bottom right: *Value Design* © 2003. Reprinted with permission from David Cahoon.)

Background

There are many properties of value and its relationship to other elements of design. We will discuss the most basic of these properties before the next project is introduced.

Characteristics of Value

Value was defined in Chapter 1, and the basic characteristics of value and how it is used in visual design were discussed in Chapter 2. The following is a brief review of the characteristics of value as a design element.

- Extreme contrast of values in a design gives a sense of clarity and depth. Similar values may give a sense of subtlety and shallowness.
- When values are very light, the term *high key* is used. Lighter values suggest a brighter, happier mood. Conversely, values that are dark are called *low key*. They usually feel somber and serious.
- Value is also used to describe volume two-dimensionally by imitating the way light reveals a form or an object. The lightest values are in the direct line of light, whereas the darker values are in shadow.

Figure 10.2 is a good example of the variety of characteristics and principles associated with value. You will rarely find such a wide range of value examples in one composition. This colored etching is extremely successful in creating a design that unifies these very different uses of the value into a composition and theme that emphasizes contrast. The skull on the bottom contains values that are highly contrasted. There is a sense of depth and clarity. The bear located at the top feels somber because the values are very close. The shadow area of the skull below is a good example of values that are primarily dark and low key. The value of the bear uses very light values, or high key.

Asymmetrical Balance Using Value

Achieving asymmetrical balance using shape is very literal; the larger the shape, the heavier it will seem. Using an invisible fulcrum or center point, a large shape may be balanced by a smaller shape by moving the fulcrum and shifting the smaller shape closer to the edge and the larger shape closer to the fulcrum or middle of the composition. (Refer to Figure 2.38 in Chapter 2.)

Value can balance compositions asymmetrically through the use of contrast. The more contrast of value between a shape and the background, the more visual weight it will have relative to the size of the shape. This means that both the size and value of a shape should be considered when balancing a design asymmetrically. Figure 10.3 is a simple diagram detailing this concept. The example on the

FIGURE 10.2 A work of art that incorporates almost every characteristic of value.
(*Old Ephraim Cache Valley Legend* © 2008. Reprinted with permission from Adrian Van Suchtelen.)

left shows two shapes that are the same value and same weights. The same shapes are found in the example directly to the right, but the shape at the left is a lighter value. Notice how much heavier the shape at the right feels. The two examples at the right deal with balance and the value of colors. The two red shapes in the example in the middle right are evenly balanced. The example on the right shows how a color that is light in value (yellow) seems to visually weigh less than the red shape of the same size on the right.

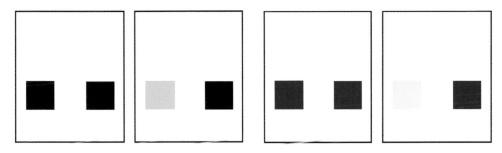

FIGURE 10.3   Both the size and value of a shape should be considered when balancing a design asymmetrically.

Designing with Value

Value becomes visual only when it is used in conjunction with a shape or form. When designing with value, it is obvious that you are also designing with shape. All the principles related to shape apply to compositions that use value. The one principle that requires special attention is that each individual value must be evenly balanced throughout a design in regard to visual hierarchy. This means that if you basically have three values that make up your design, one value must visually weigh more than the other two, and one of the remaining two must visually weigh more than the other. This is an example of visual hierarchy using value. In addition to this idea of hierarchy, each value must be visually balanced throughout the composition. If a value or many values are used only in one area of a composition and not distributed throughout the design, it is similar to using only square shapes on one side of a design and only round shapes on the opposite side. The result is a lack of unity.

To summarize this concept in terms of the universal principles of harmony and variety, values must be used with regard to visual hierarchy for variety and must be evenly balanced throughout the composition for unity. Figures 10.4 and 10.5 are examples of this concept. Notice how each value is evenly distributed throughout the compositions, and each value is used in different visual weights.

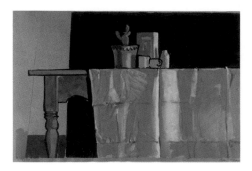
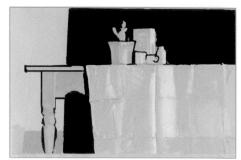

FIGURE 10.4 A painting where the basic values have been separated out and illustrated by darker values to clearly show the distribution. The top-left image is the original painting. The image to the right isolates the darkest values. The bottom-left image isolated the lightest values and shows them against darker shapes. The bottom-right image shows the middle values.
(*Cactus* © 2006. Reprinted with permission from Christopher Terry.)

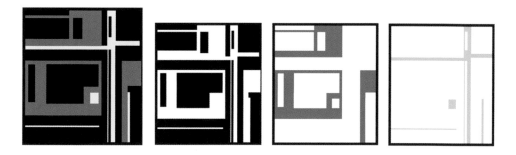

FIGURE 10.5 A nonobjective design that, similar to Figure 10.4, isolates each value to illustrate that successful designs using value should be evenly balanced with each value distributed in a visual hierarchy.
(*Intersection* © 2006. Reprinted with permission from Alan Hashimoto.)

Value and Design Using Photography

The following photographic examples emphasize shape and value as the main focus. Visual hierarchy, unity of shapes, dynamic line direction, and well-defined values are all part of this gallery of well-designed photographs.

Figure 10.6 uses high contrast of values, varied diagonal line directions, and well-placed shapes for drama and dynamics. The design in the center uses strong contrast of value to create shapes that illustrate basic characteristics of good design, similar types of harmonious shapes contrasted by a variety of sizes and weights of shapes. The design on the far right inverts the shapes to show that space or negative shapes are also well designed. This is a good example of a figure/ground relationship.

FIGURE 10.6   Photograph that uses high contrast of values and diagonal line direction.
(*Coke Plant Tower* © 2008. Reprinted with permission from Chris Dunker.)

Figure 10.7 is an example of a photograph that uses the contrasting types of shapes to create variety. By removing the color and concentrating only on value, as illustrated in the center design, we can easily see angular shapes contrasted by circular shapes. The design on the far right is a high-contrast version of this design. By removing most of the value, we can see related shapes that create harmony and shapes that are distinctly different creating variety.

FIGURE 10.7   Photograph that uses value and shape to create an interesting design.
(*Gulf Stream Engine* © 2008. Reprinted with permission from Chris Dunker.)

Figure 10.8 is an example of contrasting shapes that use value. The photograph on the upper left is an example of curvilinear shapes that is emphasized with the high-contrast version below. Notice how light is defining the form. The photograph in the center, with high-contrast version on the far right, uses only rectilinear shapes.

FIGURE 10.8   A photograph that uses primarily curvilinear shapes and a photograph that uses rectilinear shapes.   (Left: *Spider* © 2008. Reprinted with permission from Chris Dunker. Right: *Conveyor Belt Crossing* © 2008. Reprinted with permission from Chris Dunker.)

Value and Depth

Another property of value is its use in creating the illusion of depth or distance. The simple designs in Figure 10.9 illustrate several interesting points related to this idea. The design on the left is made up of shapes that are the same value. The second design on the right shows how contrasting values create the illusion that things are closer. The shapes on the right of the black shape are closer in value to the white background, so they seem to recede. The black background of the design next right shows that the white shape seems closer because it has more contrast than the other two shapes. The right design is an example of value and color. Notice how the darker value color seems closer.

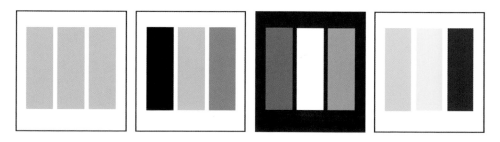

FIGURE 10.9   Simple designs that illustrate the illusion of depth or distance through the use of value.

Figure 10.10 is a colored etching using value to create the illusion of depth. The darker, more contrasted and detailed foliage at the bottom appears much closer. The other areas of foliage seem further away as detail diminishes and values become lighter and more similar to the background.

FIGURE 10.10   Etching that uses value to create the illusion of depth.
(*Fog Along the Bear* © 2008. Reprinted with permission from Adrian Van Suchtelen.)

Conceptual Process

Now that you are more familiar with digital tools and techniques of the production process, and the general conceptual process is not such a mystery, these two ideas will overlap even more. Your familiarity with the computer and related software should help you find more alternative and efficient ways of creating the finished form. Digital techniques will become a natural part of solving visual problems; however, be aware that what is easier isn't always the best. Don't let the computer do all of your thinking. Try to follow the steps involved in the conceptual process outlined in Chapter 3, "Introduction to Content and Form: Problem Solving and the Digital Process," and allow for intuitive problem solving for the most creative results (see Figures 10.11 and 10.12).

The project requirements associated with this chapter are not too involved. Basically, you need to find an appropriate photograph or take one yourself, and create your own asymmetrically balanced composition using designed shapes and three to five values. The subject matter is up to you, and you can use any or all of the tools you've learned up to this point. Remember to balance unity with variety, and use appropriate types of line directions and types of shapes resulting

FIGURE 10.11   A preliminary line drawing and final value project.
(*Value Design* © 2003. Reprinted with permission from Patrick Wilkey, www.visiocommunications.com.)

FIGURE 10.12   A thumbnail, preliminary line drawing and final value project.
(*Lighthouse* © 2002. Reprinted with permission from Mike Clayton.)

in proper hierarchy. The shapes themselves could be nonobjective and combined to create a stylized, an abstract, or a nonobjective design. Review Figure 10.1 for examples of the final compositions and Figures 10.6 to 10.8 and Figure 10.10 to help you select a photograph. The following section on the production process will give you more details concerning the selection and production of the proper images for the successful completion of this project.

PRODUCTION PROCESS (TRADITIONAL AND DIGITAL)

In previous chapters and exercises, step-by-step examples were given to guide you through the process of learning the tools. From this point on, concepts become the emphasis of the examples, so that you might continue with your own work. Take what is being shown here and apply it to your own designs. The steps are the same, but the results may vary.

Preparing Your Project

As has been mentioned previously in this text, a great deal of the actual design can be done on paper before ever touching the mouse. This project is a prime example of that notion.

Figure 10.13 shows an example of the entire process from start to finish. In this case, the designer took a photograph of a stairwell (A), and then created a series of simple drawings (B and C) reflecting the values within the photograph while discarding the unnecessary details in the process. After the line drawing was completed, the designer used a set of markers to create several value studies of the photograph (D). The next step was to scan the original drawing into the computer and create a black-and-white vector line drawing (E). From printouts of the vector line drawing, the designer did a few more marker value studies to limit the number of values as set by the assignment (F and G). Then, using those studies, the designer created the value swatches in the computer and applied them to the shapes (H).

Selecting the Source Material

When choosing the image for this assignment, concentrate on simple images that have high levels of contrast (lights and darks). Flat images will be a little difficult to translate into a portfolio-quality piece.

There is a quick test that you can do to determine whether an image has enough contrast to be successful—squint at it. When you squint, all detail is abandoned and your eyes search the lights and the darks of the image for recognizable shapes. Figure 10.14 shows two examples of blurred images. Can you make out what they are? The one on the left is a lighthouse, and the one on the right is a close-up of a small boy. The first image is easily recognized due to the even balance of lights and darks. The second, however, has too many dark values and too few light values to make the image really "pop" at you.

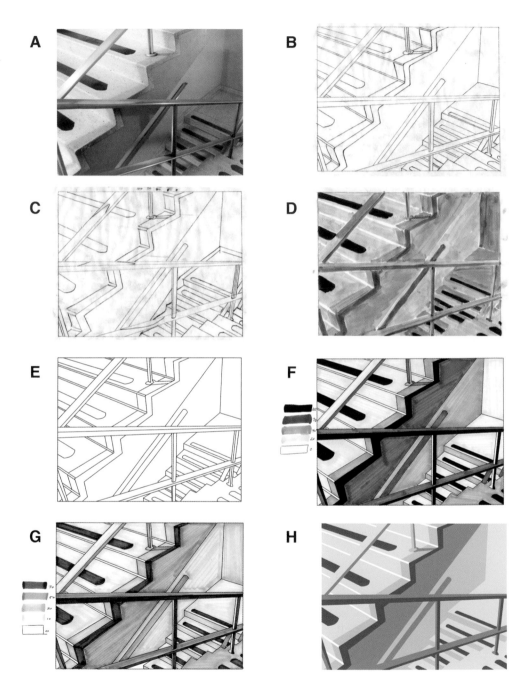

FIGURE 10.13 The entire process for the value assignment from the original photograph to the final value study. (*Staircase Value Process* © 2005. Reprinted with permission of Roberto Miranda.)

FIGURE 10.14   Two blurred images.

Changing the Levels of an Image

There are methods of evening out the tones of images digitally. By using your scanner or any imaging software, you can adjust the levels of gray in an image. Naturally balanced images work the best, but with some tweaking, any image could work.

Some scanners may allow you to change the brightness and contrast as you scan the image into your computer. It is better, however, to scan the image first and then take the image into a program to modify it.

Figure 10.15 is the original scan of the image of the little boy. Below the image is the histogram, which is a visual representation of the levels of gray in the image. There are 256 levels of gray in an 8-bit grayscale image. On the left is 0 (black), and on the right is 255 (white). The height of the lines in between is the number of pixels in the image at that particular level of gray. Notice that a majority of the pixels are concentrated on the left of the graph, which means that the image is too dark. For optimum results, there should be an even number of light and dark pixels.

There is a quick fix in Photoshop that automatically evens out the levels. With the image opened in Photoshop, choose Image > Adjustments > Auto Tone (PC: Ctrl + Shift + L; Mac: Command + Shift + L). The process of using Auto Tone is quite simple. The software determines two points in the image: the lightest area and the darkest area. The lightest area becomes 255 (white) and the darkest area becomes 0 (black). The software then automatically redistributes the amount of pixels evenly throughout the value of the image.

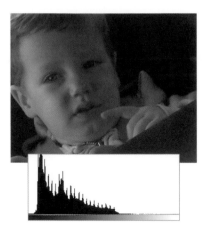

FIGURE 10.15   The original image and its histogram.

In Figure 10.16, on the left is the original image, and on the right is the corrected image with its histogram. Notice how every level of gray is represented in its histogram; this gives the image a good tonal range.

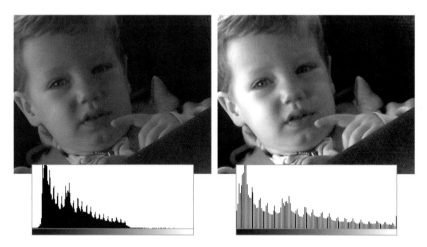

FIGURE 10.16   The before and after images with their respective histograms.

Creating the First Drawing

The first drawing that you create from the source material should be a contour line drawing or a simple shaded drawing. Try to divide the image up by light and dark shapes (Figure 10.17).

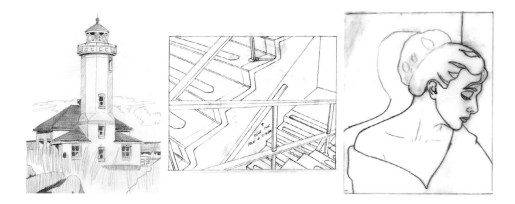

FIGURE 10.17 Simple line and shaded drawings.
(*Lighthouse Drawing* © 2002. Reprinted with permission of Mike Clayton. *Staircase Drawing* © 2005. Reprinted with permission of Roberto Miranda. *Mel Drawing* © 2002. Reprinted with permission of Chad Griffiths.)

Drawing on paper gives you the freedom to express the shapes and gives more leniency in the design.

If you are not confident in your drawing abilities, use tracing paper to create the line drawings. Continually tracing over the image can help when simplifying the drawing. A light table may also be of use.

Creating the Simplified Drawing

With the first drawing done, redraw the image and reduce the number of shapes. Do several drawings until you have broken the image down into its simplest shapes.

Once completed, begin to experiment by filling in the drawings with various shades of gray with dye markers or pencils. If necessary, reduce the number of shapes and values further by repeating this process as many times as necessary. Use tracing paper if you need to. This is the *rough*.

After the rough is complete, tighten up the design into a comp by defining the final shapes and filling them with the shades of gray that will closely resemble the finished values (Figure 10.18).

When you are pleased with the final value drawing, scan the drawing into the computer at 150 to 200 ppi to see the detail in the curves or corners.

FIGURE 10.18   The final value drawing (*Lighthouse Value Study* © 2002. Reprinted with permission of Mike Clayton. *Staircase Value Study* © 2005. Reprinted with permission of Roberto Miranda.)

ON THE CD

TUTORIAL	TRACING THE IMAGE: USING LAYERS AND SUBLAYERS

Begin by creating a new document in Illustrator. Follow the same steps as you have done previously to place the image into the document. For this tutorial, the drawing of the stairwell will be used.

1. Place the tracing image (stairwell_drawing.tif) in the new document.
2. Remember to name the layer you are placing the image on, turn off its Print option, lock the layer, and set its Dim Images To between 30 and 50%. Open the Layer Options dialog box, by either selecting it from the Layers panel option menu or by double-clicking the layer itself.
3. With the tools that you have learned in previous exercises, trace the image to create the various shapes. (Layers have been discussed, but sublayers have yet to be explained. In this example, the stairs in the lower right will be drawn to illustrate the point.)
4. Create a new layer named Mid Stairs. Zoom in on the bottom right area of the drawing. Use the Pen tool to draw the outer shape of the stairs. Set the fill to None and the stroke to black.
5. Click on the gray arrow in front of the layer named Mid Stairs to expand the sublayer. Sublayers are visible when you expand the layer by clicking on the arrow before the layer name, as shown in Figure 10.19. The shape that has been drawn now appears under the Mid Stairs layer and is identified by the name <Path>.

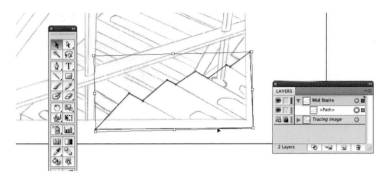

FIGURE 10.19   Layers contain sublayers that hold the individual paths.
The more shapes you draw, the more sublevels are created within that layer.

6. Rename the sublayer by either selecting Options for <Path> from the Layer option menu or by double-clicking on the name <Path>. Change the name to "Mid Stair Shape." Then click OK.
7. Draw the three diagonal tape grips on the stairs.

Naming Sublayers

Notice that as you draw a shape, a new sublayer named <Path> is created for each instance. The finished mid stair area is made up of four shapes. It is confusing to tell which is which without naming them. Naming each individual path is unnecessary in most cases, but it is a good practice to get into if you find yourself having trouble identifying parts of the drawing.

8. Name each <Path> that was created. Identify the shape by clicking on the circle shape to the right of the <Path> name. This highlights the shape in the document (Figure 10.20).

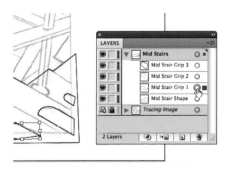

FIGURE 10.20   Clicking on the circle to the right of the
sublayer name selects the shape in the document.

Grouping Sublayers

To group sublayers, follow these steps:

1. Using the Selection tool (A), drag around all the shapes to select them.
2. Select Object > Group (PC: Ctrl + G; Mac: Command + G) to group the objects together. When shapes are grouped together, they are placed into a sublayer called <Group> that can be expanded and collapsed by the arrow in front of the name (Figure 10.21). This <Group> can be renamed.

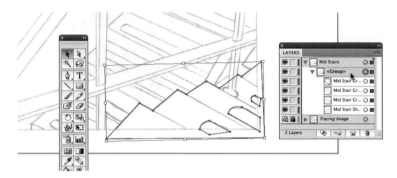

FIGURE 10.21   Grouping objects places the paths into a <Group> sublayer. It is expandable so that the contents may be displayed and selected.

3. Rename the <Group> by double-clicking the name (or selecting Options for <Group> from the Layers Option menu). Name the group "Middle Stairs."

Grouping Retains Layer Information

When <Group>s are ungrouped, the <Path>s are still placed under the layer, with their names and attributes intact.

4. With the group still selected, set the fill color to white.

Changing the Stacking Order of Groups in Layers

Now that the shapes have fills, the next step is easier. As you go through and draw the various shapes for the design, you will, at some point, get the order of the shapes mixed up. The hierarchy of the sublayers is the same as layers. The stacking order goes from top to bottom: whatever is on top is on the top, and whatever is on the bottom is on the bottom. Sublayers can be moved within the sublayers or from one layer to another.

To move a group/sublayer within a layer, follow these steps:

1. Select the group or sublayer that you want to move. (To highlight the object, click on the circle to the right of the name.)
2. Drag the group/sublayer up or down to the new location within the list. A horizontal black line shows where the layer will be placed. Release the mouse to set the new location. The image will change to reflect the modification.

In the example of the group Bottom Stairs, these shapes were drawn after the Mid Stairs so they appear on top in the hierarchy. Because of this, the Mid Stairs group is hidden underneath, blocking them from view.

Organization is key when dealing with overlapping shapes. Because the Mid Stairs were created before the Bottom Stairs, when filled with white, the shapes overlap each other. This is because the Mid Stairs group is underneath the Bottom Stairs group. By moving the Mid Stairs layer above the Bottom Stairs layer in the stacking order, the stairs now appear to have the right depth (Figure 10.22).

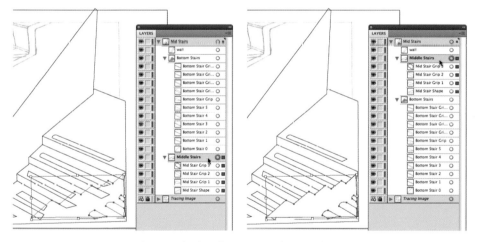

FIGURE 10.22   Layers can be restacked so that imagery that may have been lost or that may have fallen underneath a new part of the drawing can be moved to the top, where it may be seen again.

The Swatches Panel

In the prior exercises, color usage has been limited to black and white. Because this is an exercise in value, shades (percentages) of gray can be used to give depth and variety to the image. In this section, you will learn how to create, delete, and apply color swatches to the shapes.

The Swatches panel holds three types of fills. These three types of colors—color, gradient, and pattern—can either be viewed all at once or by category. In this exercise, color swatches will be used.

There are two views for the Swatches panel, the Thumbnail view and the List view. For the purposes of this exercise, the List view is necessary.

1. Open the Swatches panel by selecting Windows > Swatches.
2. Click on the second button at the bottom of the panel to view only the Color Swatches.
3. Change the view from Thumbnail to List by selecting List view from the panel options menu in the upper-right corner of the panel.

When viewing the colors in the List view, not only is a color swatch visible, but the name of the swatch is also given. This can work to your advantage. The icon to the right of the name indicates that a color is either a process color (four-color triangle) or a spot color (square with a circle).

A process color can only be created by mixing cyan, magenta, yellow, and black (CMYK), such as on a printing press or a four-color printer. A wide variety of colors can be made from combining different percentages of each color on the press. Magazines, posters, and brochures are some examples of items that are printed using process colors.

A spot color is a premixed color that is printed separately from process colors. Mixing the process colors together cannot make all colors. Spot color is used when a precise color is needed, such as when printing a corporate logo. The Pantone Matching System (PMS) is often used as a guide for selecting these colors. Examples of the colors are available in printed form for you to preview and select the correct colors. For this exercise, spot colors will be used.

Creating Swatches

Because we are only working in a grayscale mode, and there are only four shades of gray set in the default swatches, you might need to add some swatches of your own. To create a new color swatch, follow these steps:

1. While holding down the Alt (PC) or Option (Mac) key, click on the Create New Swatch button, which is the second button from the right at the bottom of the Swatches panel (Figure 10.23).
2. The New Swatch dialog box opens (Figure 10.24). In this dialog box, you can set the following attributes. Name the new swatch 15% black. Set the Color Type to Spot Color and the Global Box will automatically be checked.

Swatches and Global Properties

With the Global Box checked, if you come back at any time and change the attributes of the color of this swatch, all the objects that use this swatch will be updated to reflect the changes. If you had the swatch set to 10% black, but wanted to change it to 15%, all objects that were 10% black would appear as 15% black.

FIGURE 10.23   The location of the New Swatch button on the Swatches panel.
Holding down the Alt or Option key automatically opens the dialog box.
If you just click the button, you have to manually open the dialog box.

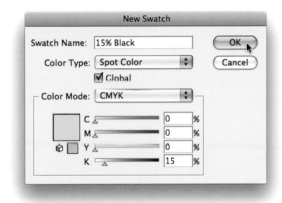

FIGURE 10.24   The New Swatch dialog box.

3. From the Color Mode, select CYMK (or Grayscale). Set the slider on K (black) to 15, or type 15 into the field to the right. Set the three other sliders to 0. Click OK. With the other three colors set to 0, only black will appear in the swatch.

You have now created a new swatch. Repeat the process, as many times as necessary, to create the many other shades of gray you might need.

Deleting Swatches

Many other swatches in this document are not needed. You may choose to delete the unnecessary swatches by selecting the swatch and clicking on the Trash Can icon at the lower-right side of the panel. Be warned that if you delete a swatch, it is gone. There is no "Swatch Reset" in the document. Swatches deleted will only affect the current document, not the system. You may delete multiple swatches using the Shift and Ctrl/Command keys to select the swatches before clicking the button.

You should take the time to delete all the swatches that you aren't going to use and to create ones that you will need. Create a new swatch for each of the following values: 25%, 50%, and 75%. You may restack the swatches like you did with the layers and sublayers earlier in this text.

Applying Swatches

To apply a color swatch to a shape, follow these steps:

1. With the Selection tool, select the Mid Stair shape.
2. In the toolbar, make sure that the Fill Swatch is active (in front of the Stroke).
3. Select the 20% black color swatch.
4. Fill the other shapes according to Figure 10.25.

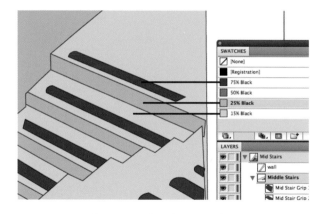

FIGURE 10.25   Using the image, fill in the rest of the shapes appropriately.

5. Select all the shapes in the window and remove the stroke (Figure 10.26).

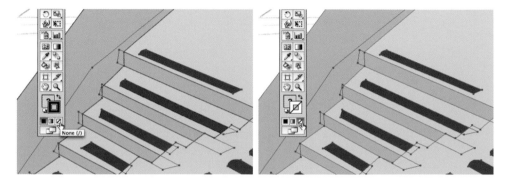

FIGURE 10.26   Set the stroke on all the shapes to None and watch as the values give the design a sense of depth.

Without the stroke, the values in the image become very apparent. You can see the tape on the stairs clearly, but there is a slight problem: the shapes are not dark enough.

Redefining Swatches

To redefine a color swatch, simply double-click the swatch or select Options For in the Swatch panel options menu. Choose the new color attributes and click OK. Unless the Global box is selected for each color and applied beforehand (signified by a small white circle in a gray box next to the process color icon), the color that was changed would not affect the current shapes of that color. When you create a new color swatch, click the Global button. Here's an example:

1. Prior to assigning colors to your design, set all swatches to Global by double-clicking on them and checking the correct box.
2. Assign colors to the shapes, by first selecting the shape and then applying the color.

On the stairwell, the 75% black color looks too dark. Because Global colors were applied to the colors, if the attributes of the 75% black color are changed, all the shapes with 75% black as their color will change.

3. Double-click the 75% black swatch to open the Swatch Options (Figure 10.27).

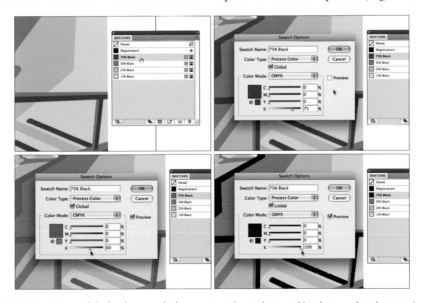

FIGURE 10.27   Using Global colors can help you save time when making large color changes in your design. The 75% black that is being used on the grips and shadows might not be the right value. By going lighter to 60% black (bottom left), the value starts to blend with the 50% black value. At 100% black, there is so much of a change that it becomes overpowering.

4. Check the Preview button. By checking this button, the changes that you make will be previewed in the document.
5. Set the K slider to 60 and press the Tab key. Pressing the Tab key selects the next field, thus invoking the preview. The grips and shadows are way too light and close enough in value to the 50% black shapes that they start to blend together.
6. Set the slider to 100 and press the Tab key. The grips and shadows are so dark that it takes away from the rest of the shapes.
7. Reset the value to the original value of 75.

By using Global colors, color changing becomes less tedious.

Finishing the Design

To polish this design, refer to the previous exercises for details on resizing and cropping. Even though your design might be spread across several layers, create a new layer at the top for the shape that will be the Clipping Mask. But be fore-warned—when the mask is made, all the contents from all the layers jump to the top layer and become bound by the Clipping Mask. An alternative to using a Clipping Mask is using stroke-free white rectangles on the four sides of your design.

SUMMARY

This is the first of four projects that deal with individual research and expression in terms of subject matter and style of designing. Now that you understand the basic principles of design using line, shape, and value, you can begin to experiment with many options and alternatives. As you make your design decisions, a personal style will begin to emerge. A preference for certain subject matter is only a superficial beginning. What types of compositions do you prefer, asymmetrical or symmetrical, closed form or open form? Did you use mostly curvilinear or recti-linear shapes for this project? What is the dominant line direction? Do you have a preference for designs that emphasize unity or variety? Will you be experimenting with low-key values or high-key values for future designs? Given that the next three assignments are fairly individualized, will you be using realistic, stylized, abstract, or nonobjective shapes?

It may be a little early to know exactly what your personal preferences are in terms of design. However, the more images you create, the more your chances become of finding a similarity among your designs that will be evident. As you experiment with design options and become more familiar with the tools, you will discover an individual style. At the end of the last project in this book, look back and see if there are any similarities to your project solutions. Retain what you think is successful and begin to change those things that are not working. In many ways, if you are experimenting with original solutions, your design projects will be a reflection of you.

DESIGN PROJECT 5: COLOR AND COLOR THEORY

INTRODUCTION

Color is the most complex of the elements of design, so it requires an in-depth look and a more detailed discussion than the other elements. This chapter will be an extended discussion on the background and content of color theory, followed by a comprehensive design project that incorporates color theory and its relationship to all of the elements and principles of design.

The general characteristics and properties that are universal in the study of color will be the focus of this chapter. The principles and concepts presented will help you make informed color choices. These design decisions will be balanced with the knowledge of the subjective nature of color. Color in terms of emotional communication requires a vast understanding of the habits and background of the audience. Defining color design problems usually requires a large amount of objective thinking because there can be so many options and exceptions involved in the solution. The information contained in this chapter and the color project later should give you the background and basic training necessary to define and create successful visual designs using color.

CONTENT: BACKGROUND IN COLOR THEORY

Color is the most complex of design elements. It requires a chapter by itself to even begin to understand and define its characteristics. This chapter deals with only the very basics of defining color, exploring color systems, and understanding the many ways color can be used in conjunction with the other elements of design. A general color design project is detailed at the end of this chapter. The following two chapters also use color in their design projects as well.

Defining Color

The two basic systems of color are additive and subtractive. These two systems differ based on the source of the light. If the source is direct, such as light from a spotlight, computer monitor, or television, the system of color mixing is called *additive*. Light is added to create various colors. The three primary colors of an additive system are red, green, and blue. When all three colors overlap, they produce white. When two complementary or opposite colors in an additive system of color overlap, they produce a colorless gray or white.

If the source of the light is reflected or absorbed by the surface of an object, the system of color mixing is called *subtractive*. Objects have no color of their own, only the capability to reflect certain rays of light and absorb others. You can see these different rays of light by putting white light through a prism. A prism breaks white light into the various colors of light we see in a rainbow. A red object absorbs all the rays except for the red ones. Black objects absorb all the rays. White objects reflect all rays of light.

Paintings are good examples of the subtractive system of color mixing. The primary colors of a subtractive system of color are blue, red, and yellow. When all three colors are mixed in equal amounts, they produce a dark or muddy gray. When two opposite or complementary colors are mixed in the subtractive system, the result is a muddy gray contrary to the additive process.

Most of this section will deal with subtractive color, which is the color we are most likely to observe in natural settings. Additive color as it relates to digitally created color and computer monitor displays will be discussed later in this chapter. Figure 11.1 diagrams the basics of the subtractive and additive color-mixing systems. The diagram at the left illustrates how the sun's rays or white light contains a full spectrum of colored rays we cannot see without the use of a device such as a prism. In the subtractive color-mixing system, only the red rays are being reflected from the tomato, and the other rays will be absorbed. If this tomato were green, only the green rays would be reflected. The diagram on the right is showing an example of the additive color-mixing process. Red, green, and blue colored spotlights are mixing together to produce white. Red and green lights are mixing to produce yellow, green and blue are producing cyan, and red and blue are mixing to produce magenta.

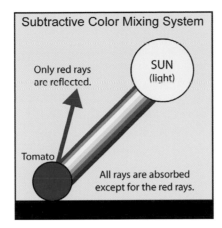
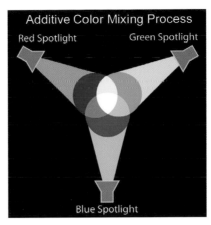

FIGURE 11.1   The basics of the subtractive and additive color-mixing systems.

As a product of light, color will change depending on its environment. During the day, direct sunlight brings out the brightness in the color of outdoor objects. At dawn, with less light coming from the low setting sun, objects will be lit less directly and from one side. The same objects at this time of day will display contrasting light and dark colors. At night, these objects will have little light and color will be muted and may not even be present. A white chicken may appear pale yellow in the early morning light and muted cool gray at night (see Figure 11.2).

FIGURE 11.2   The effects of light on a color image.
(*Venetian Design* © 2003, *Night Venetian Design* © 2003. Reprinted with permission from Anson Call.)

Figure 11.2 is a computer-generated model that is using ambient and atmospheric lighting to duplicate day and night light. There are a few spotlights illuminating some of the areas. Notice how the color changes from warm tones during the day to cool tones at night. Even the spotlights that are a source of the consistent lighting are affected.

Even when the light is the same, color perception changes depending on surrounding colors. A dull color may seem brighter when placed against its opposite or complementary color (see Figure 11.3).

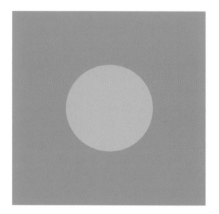
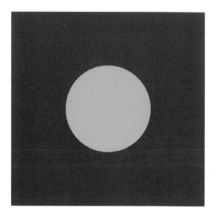

FIGURE 11.3   The example on the left shows two similar colors placed one on top of the other. The example on the right shows one of these colors placed on top of its complement.

An intense color may appear dull when placed against a color that is the same value or intensity (see Figure 11.4).

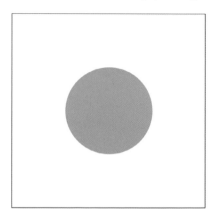

FIGURE 11.4   An example of a color shape placed on a white background is on the left. An example of the same color placed on a color shape that is the same value and intensity is on the right.

A light color will seem brighter when placed against a color that is dark (see Figure 11.5).

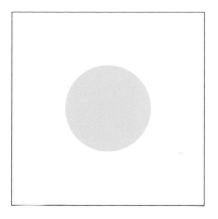 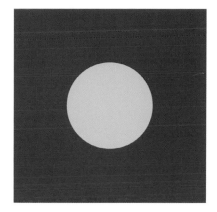

FIGURE 11.5   An example of a light color shape placed on a white background, and an example of the same color shape placed on a darker color shape.

The terms hue and color are often confused with one another. *Hue* describes the different parts of the color spectrum commonly found in a rainbow or reflected through a prism (refer to Figure 11.1). Red, orange, yellow, green, blue, and purple are hues. *Color* also describes these parts of the spectrum, but includes the different colors that may be made from these hues. Chartreuse, lime, and forest are names of colors related to a green hue. Orange is the hue in the colors brown, beige, or tan.

The most common organization displaying and illustrating the relationships between hues is the 12-hue color wheel. It is divided into 3 categories (see Figure 11.6).

- The *primary* colors, red, yellow, and blue, make up all other colors.
- The *secondary* colors are mixtures of two primary colors. Yellow and red make orange, red and blue make purple, and blue and yellow make green.
- The six *tertiary* colors are made from mixing a primary and a secondary color located next to it on the color wheel. Blue-green, yellow-green, yellow-orange, orange-red, red-purple, and blue-purple are the six tertiary colors.

Every color has a *value* based on the lightness and darkness of its hue. When the value of a color is made lighter by adding white, this is called *tinting*. When the color is made darker by adding black, this is called *shading* (see Figure 11.7).

On a color wheel, colors are not shown at the same value. Each color is shown unmixed and pure. At this pure level, yellow is very light in value, and blue is much darker in value (see Figure 11.8).

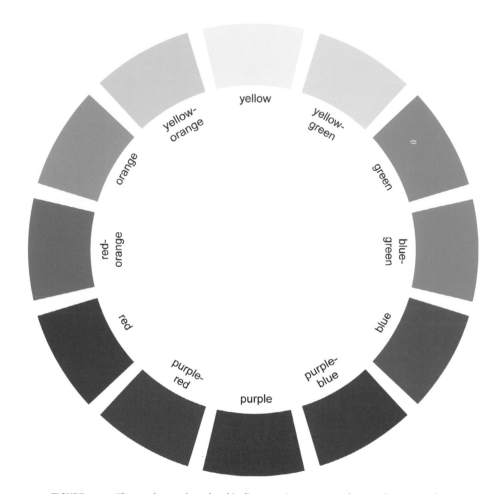

FIGURE 11.6 The 12-hue color wheel indicates primary, secondary, and tertiary colors.

FIGURE 11.7 The shape to the left is a red hue. White is added to this hue to make the shape in the middle a tint. Black is added to the original red hue to create the shape on the right that is a shade.

FIGURE 11.8   The hues, yellow and blue, in their pure state (left). The same hues, yellow and blue, with the color removed leaving only the value of both colors (right).

Value, like color, is influenced by the values that surround it. Most light values will seem brighter on a dark surface and much darker on a light surface (see Figure 11.9).

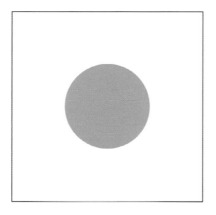 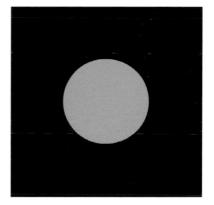

FIGURE 11.9   A light value shape on a white background and the same light value shape on a much darker surface.

Surrounding a color with a black or very dark line will make the color seem richer or clearer. It keeps the color from spreading out and gives the shape a sharp, crisp feeling. By surrounding a color with white or a lighter color, the opposite will happen. The color will seem to spread and seem less crisp (see Figure 11.10).

Intensity or brightness is another property of color. In a pure and unmixed state, a color's brightness is at its full intensity. Intensity is very different from the value of a color. If white is added to a color, it will become lighter in value but lower in intensity. If black is added to a color, it will also become lower in intensity but darker in value. Another way to lower a color's intensity is to add its complement. The *complement* of a color is the color that is positioned directly across from it on a color wheel. For example, yellow is the complement of purple, and red is the complement of green. Adding a color's complement lowers its intensity. If the two complementary colors are added together in equal amounts, the result will be muddy gray. Placing a color next to its complement may heighten the illusion of intensity. This gives the effect that is exactly opposite of mixing two complementary colors. By positioning complementary colors in close proximity to each other, contrast is heightened, and the result is a visual sensation that seems to make each color brighter (see Figure 11.11).

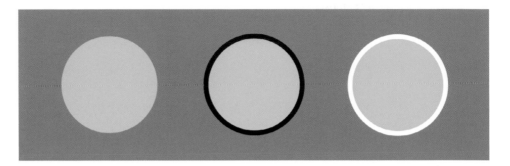

FIGURE 11.10 A color on a neutral background. The same color with a black outline. The same color with a white outline.

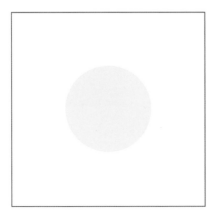 

FIGURE 11.11 Yellow shape on a white background. The same yellow shape on a purple or complementary color background.

Color and Unity

A *color scheme* is a system of colors that creates a visual relationship to add harmony or interest to a design or work of art. Using a traditional color wheel, four basic color schemes may be described.

Monochromatic

One hue and all of its tones and shades make up the monochromatic color scheme. A very harmonious and unified feeling is usually achieved through the use of this color scheme depending on the range of values. The wider the range of values, the more contrast and activity is created. A close range of values usually suggests a more calm feeling. Figure 11.12 shows two examples of designs that use monochromatic color schemes. The example on the left uses a variety of values creating a sense of action. Several diagonal line directions also help give this design a feeling of intense dramatic motion. The values that make up the design of the right are close. The result is a calm and harmonious composition. The variation in the sizes of the objects, diagonal line direction, and contrasting rectilinear and curvilinear shapes adds dynamics to this otherwise calm composition.

FIGURE 11.12 Two examples of monochromatic color schemes. The example on the left uses a wide range of values. The example on the right uses a close range of values.
(Left: *Informatics* © 2003. Reprinted with permission from Alan Hashimoto.
Right: *Studio Window with Bovine Pelvis* © 2008. Reprinted with permission from Adrian Van Suchtelen.)

Analogous

A combination of hues located next to each other on the color wheel create an analogous color scheme. Similar to other color schemes, tones and shades are also included. The feeling expressed by most analogous color schemes is usually harmonious tranquility. Figure 11.13 shows two examples of colored prints that use analogous color schemes. Each composition feels very unified. The print on the left incorporates a wide range of analogous colors that are low in saturation.

Saturation as it refers to color is the purity or intensity of a specific hue. Saturated hues are vivid and intense, while less saturated hues appear more muted and grey. The analogous colors used in the print on the right are more saturated creating a bright and active feeling.

FIGURE 11.13   Two examples of analogous color schemes. The example on the left uses less saturated colors. The example on the right uses high-intensity saturated color.
(Left: *Along the Blacksmith Fork* © 2008. Reprinted with permission from Adrian Van Suchtelen.
Right: *Tulipomania: Fosteriana* © 2008. Reprinted with permission from Adrian Van Suchtelen.)

Complementary

The hues located directly across a color wheel give a lively and active feeling to this color scheme. This feeling of excitement is amplified when these colors are used at full intensity. Figure 11.14 is an example of two compositions that use complementary color schemes. The painting on the left has a variety of colors, but the main tones are green and red. Notice how the red and green are distributed evenly throughout this spontaneous design, making it seem almost symmetrical. The intensity of the two colors is very high, giving energy to the entire painting. The photograph on the right uses distinct areas of complementary colors. This design could seem very subtle and tranquil if not for the contrast of the orange sand and blue sky.

FIGURE 11.14   Example of a painting and a photograph that use a complementary color scheme.
(Left: *Untitled, Lincoln Rhode Island* © 2006. Reprinted with permission from Woody Shephard.
Right: *Sand Dunes, Utah* © 2006. Reprinted with permission from PatrickConePhotography.com.)

Triadic

This color scheme consists of three hues located equal distance from each other on the color wheel. Blue, red, and yellow is the most common example of a triadic color scheme. Triadic color schemes generally give the feeling of dynamic activity. As with a complementary color scheme, a more active feeling is achieved through the use of full intensity hues. Figure 11.15 presents three examples of triadic color schemes. The illustration on the left uses this color scheme effectively to create a very intense graphic symbol with a distinct focal point. The illustration in the center distinctly divides all of the areas of color into specific shapes. Each shape is different in weight, giving variety and more interest to the design. The tonality of this illustration is basically a dark red using yellow as a secondary color and blue as an accent. The painting on the right is made up of a variety of colors; however, the majority of identifiable color is blue, light red, and yellow. Because there is no focal point, the saturated triad color scheme creates a dynamic composition that keeps the viewer's eye moving.

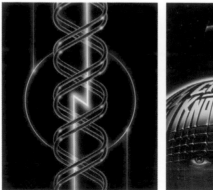

FIGURE 11.15 Three examples of triadic color schemes.
(Left: *Electro DNA* © 2003. Reprinted with permission from Alan Hashimoto.
Center: *Chains of Knowledge* © 2008. Reprinted with permission from Alan Hashimoto.
Right: *Wasatch Fall* © 2008. Reprinted with permission from Woody Shephard.)

Color Unity via Tonality

Color in a composition may feel unified through the use of tonality. *Tonality* is the presence of a dominant hue or color. A variety of colors may make up a composition, but there is a general overall feeling of a particular hue. Figure 11.16 illustrates three examples of tonality. On the left and center are paintings emphasizing earthy warmer tones; one painting emphasizes green and the other brown. There are a variety of colors and values, but the overall feeling is calm and muted. A wide range of colors can be identified in the illustration on the right, but the overall yellow-orange tone dominates. The saturated colors give the opposite feeling than the two paintings on the left. This design does not feel muted or calm.

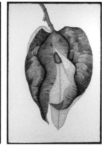

FIGURE 11.16 Tonality examples.
(Left: *Untitled* © 2008. Reprinted with permission from Kathy Puzey. Center: *Sanctuary* © 2008. Reprinted with permission from Kathy Puzey. Right: *Taxi* © 2008. Reprinted with permission from Alan Hashimoto.)

Color and Variety

Similar to the other elements of design, color can give a composition variety and unity. As with all elements of design, variety is accomplished by using contrast. One method that has already been discussed is using complementary or triadic color schemes. Colors that are located further away from each other on the color wheel will have more contrast.

As previously discussed, tonality is the presence of a dominant color or hue. The presence of this dominant element can be contrasted by using other areas of differing hues and colors. This will add interest through variety and establish focal points. These contrasting colors should be used in varying weights and implement the concept of visual hierarchy. As previously discussed, hierarchy is used to organize each area of emphasis so that it does not conflict or take away attention from another area of emphasis. Focal points must be viewed one at a time in stages. One focal point will get the most attention. The viewer's eye will then move to another subtler focal point and from there to another. The careful staging of focal points and areas of emphasis will lead the viewer from one part of a design to the next until the entire design has been viewed in detail.

Figure 11.17 is an example of a variety of colors organized using visual hierarchy. Notice that the dominant color or tone is a brownish yellow-orange, followed by areas of red, then green, with smaller areas of blue, and purple accents. Later, in Figure 11.24, the primary colors related to this illustration are isolated to emphasize the distribution of color.

FIGURE 11.17   A variety of colors are organized using visual hierarchy.
(*Garden Heroics* © 2003. Reprinted with permission from Alan Hashimoto.)

Warm and Cool Colors

A common way that colors may be used to contrast or unify each other is through the use of warm colors and cool colors. The feeling of warmth is associated with past experiences and with images and objects that emit heat or are hot to the touch. The sun and fire are two examples of how we associate colors such as yellow, orange, and red with the feeling of warmth. Warm earth tones are used to emphasize the organic subject matter in Figure 11.18.

FIGURE 11.18   This design uses warm colors. (Left: *Summer Bounty: Tomatoes* © 2008. Reprinted with permission from Adrian Van Suchtelen. Right: *Pine Cone* © 2008. Reprinted with permission from Adrian Van Suchtelen.)

On the other side of the color wheel, colors such as blue-green, blue, and blue-violet tend to give us the feeling of coolness. These colors are associated with blue water or other cool objects and images. Figure 11.19 shows two photographs using cool colors to emphasize the emotional coldness of an empty business lobby and an industrial entrance way.

We generally think of the colors yellow through red-violet as warm colors on the color wheel and yellow-green through violet as cool colors. An interesting illusion created by warm and cool colors is that warm colors tend to come forward and cool colors recede. This idea may be used to create depth or to emphasize one element of a composition over another. An example of this would be a warm figure placed against a cool background. Figure 11.20 shows two examples of creating depth and emphasis using warm colors against cool colors. The illustration on the left uses warm color and light value to bring the mechanical heart forward and push the cool dark background back. The illustration on the right also uses warm color to bring the main object forward. In this case, the saturation and darker value of the tomato is used to separate it from the less saturated lighter cool background.

FIGURE 11.19   This design uses cool colors.   (Left: *Beijing Lobby* © 2008. Reprinted with permission from Chris Dunker. Right: *Blue Door* © 2008. Reprinted with permission from Chris Dunker.)

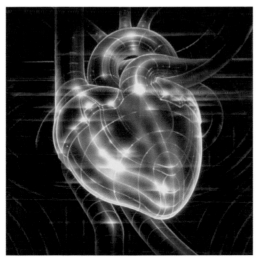 

FIGURE 11.20   This composition uses warm colors to bring a shape forward and cool colors in the background.   (Left: *Mechanical Heart* © 2006. Reprinted with permission from Alan Hashimoto. Right: *One Ton Tomato* © 2006. Reprinted with permission from Alan Hashimoto.)

Color Discord

Discordant colors are color combinations that have no identifiable relationship with each other. Color discord is the opposite of color harmony. These combinations make maximum use of contrasting and contradictory colors to intentionally catch the eye and surprise the viewer. Discordant colors are located far apart on a color wheel but do not combine to make a triadic or complementary color scheme. Discord is best achieved when colors are close to the same value. This increases the chance that true colors will be observed and discord will be more obvious. The two designs in Figure 11.21 are examples of color discord. No obvious color scheme other than color discord seems to fit either of these designs. The illustration on the left has a purple tonality, but the other bright colors do not have a particular relationship to the purple. The example on the right uses extremely saturated colors creating discord. Saturated color discord, coupled with shapes that have little or no visual hierarchy or focal point, creates a very active composition because all design elements command equal attention at the same time.

FIGURE 11.21   Designs that demonstrate color discord.   (Left: *Spring Romance* © 2003. Reprinted with permission from Alan Hashimoto. Right: *Fall Hollow* © 2008. Reprinted with permission from Woody Shephard.)

Color and Design

All the design principles that relate to value (as discussed in Chapter 10) also relate to color. The following is a summary of the design principles that both color and value have in common.

The more contrast of value between a shape and the background, the more visual weight it will have relative to the size of the shape. This rule also applies to contrast of color. The more visual contrast between colors, the more visual weight it will have. In Figure 11.22, the example on the left shows two shapes that are the same color and same weight. The same shapes are found in the example directly to the right, but the shape at the left is a lighter value. Notice how much heavier the shape at the right feels. The two examples at the right deal with balance and the contrast of colors. The second design from the right is an example of contrast of value and color and will make the visual weight appear heavier. The complement of purple is yellow. Notice how the yellow shape has more visual weight than the red shape. In the example on the right, the color of the background is changed to a complement of red, which makes the yellow shape feel lighter and the red shape heavier.

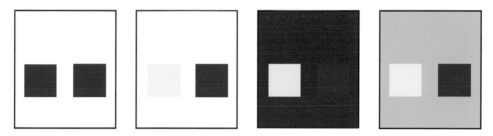

FIGURE 11.22   The more contrast of value between a shape and the background, the more visual weight it will have relative to the size of the shape. The more visual contrast between colors, the more visual weight the design will have.

You can also apply the idea of contrast to the sense of depth. Contrasting or complementary colors will seem closer, and unified or analogous colors will seem farther away. Take another look at Figure 11.22. The more the contrast, the closer the shape will seem. Figure 11.23 illustrates two designs that use color and value to create depth. The painting on the left uses saturated color to bring shapes forward against a less saturated background. The illustration on the right uses more saturated color and darker values to bring shapes forward. The gradual reduction of size relationships, value, and saturation create a sense of depth, as shapes appear to move to the background.

FIGURE 11.23   Two examples of designs that create depth through the use of value and color.
(Left: *Beaver Mountain* © 2008. Reprinted with permission from Woody Shephard. Right: *Lawn Monster* © 2003. Reprinted with permission from Alan Hashimoto.)

Colors should be balanced throughout the composition for unity and designed with variation using visual hierarchy. Figures 11.24, 11.25, and 11.26 are examples.

Figure 11.24 shows colors separated out from an illustration for printing. This process individually isolates each color, pointing out the balanced distribution of color and the variation in weights of colors to achieve good visual hierarchy. Notice that yellow is used more than the other colors, and red is second. Without looking at the original illustration, you can tell by the weights of these colors that the tone will be yellow-orange.

FIGURE 11.24   An illustration and isolated colors pointing out the balanced distribution of color and the variation in weights of colors to achieve good visual hierarchy.
(*Garden Heroics* © 2006. Reprinted with permission from Alan Hashimoto.)

Figure 11.25 is an example of asymmetrical balance using color. The color red is weighted far to the right of the design above or weighted to the left in the design below. Balance is achieved through the proper placement of red accents and other smaller red shapes located on the other side of the fulcrum or imaginary center of the design. The color black is also used in lesser amounts to help balance both compositions.

FIGURE 11.25   Asymmetrical balance using color.
(Two Designs from: *About Me* © 2006. Reprinted with permission from Jiong Li.)

Figure 11.26 is an example that uses value and color to create a dynamic composition. The painted print on the left uses diagonal line direction and the use of warm color and light values surrounded by cool color and dark values. The photograph on the right is an uncommon use of a complementary color scheme to create an unexpected and interesting design. Usually, saturated warm color comes forward and cool colors recede. In this design, attention is given to both the strong contrast in values and the saturated color in the foreground and background. Simultaneously, both the background and foreground fight for attention. The result is an interesting design that is very surreal and dynamic.

FIGURE 11.26   A colored print and photograph that use value and color to create dynamic compositions.   (Left: *Fire on the Mountain* © 2008. Reprinted with permission from Adrian Van Suchtelen. Right: *Erin Fire* © 2008. Reprinted with permission from Chris Dunker.)

CONTENT: BASIC PROBLEM DEFINED

Color preference is very subjective. Everyone has his or her own favorite color. Everyone has his or her favorite color scheme, too. To complete the following project, you may use any color or colors as long as there is some relationship that exists between them.

Using the information from the "Color Theory" section, create an interesting color design focusing on shape. Design Project 5 combines at least three color elements from three different sources and through the processes of stylization, distortion, and abstraction, a color object-oriented design will be created. This assignment has been designed this way for several reasons:

- The three elements (figure, inanimate object, environment) are very different types of shapes. The figure is curvilinear, the inanimate object will most likely be more rectilinear, and the environment may consist of either type of shape or both.
- Using different types of images for the original source material will be more of a visualization challenge and help you understand the different types of printing, resolutions, and digital input devices. The designer cannot rely on a single image that could be directly traced, which gives all the credit to the original designer.

- Making this a stylization, distortion, or abstraction project gives you more freedom to explore beyond realism. The emotional quality of the shapes and colors will be more evident. The focus is placed on the basic principles of design rather than subject matter.
- Arbitrary color allows you to explore a variety of color schemes and color combinations. Because the design can be nonrepresentational, there should be more freedom in choosing colors.

All of these requirements should help you create an interesting and unique design.

Conceptual Process

The following is a specific series of steps and requirements for this color project:

1. Select a theme or central idea that involves designing at least three of these elements into one composition: human figure or animal, inanimate object (machine, building, and so on), environment or shapes and objects related to a particular place or setting.
2. Research visual reference materials such as magazines, books, life drawings, or photographs.
3. Select at least three reference materials that can be combined to create one composition. These original visual references will be called *source material*. They can be color or black and white.
4. Visualize the source material together as one composition. Crop, distort, and manipulate any or all of these visuals into a harmonious design with variety. Each source reference does not have to be in proportion or to scale in relationship to one another. For instance, the environment may be cropped to show a small portion of it or expanded and exaggerated to be more vertical or horizontal. Elements such as trees, mountains, or buildings may be deleted, multiplied, or exaggerated. The figure or animal may be larger or smaller in scale to the environment. You may combine several figures or animals into one organic form or crop into just the face or head. The inanimate object can be handled the same way.
5. Use as many figures or inanimate objects as you like. The object of this exercise is to explore a variety of shapes and to visualize and design separate elements into one composition.
6. To visualize all of these elements together, view all the reference material at once and create thumbnail sketches combining all of the material. This is the quickest way to visualize a variety of options and to analyze the relationships between separate elements. You can study the position, proportion, and scale of each visual in advance. Make changes early to save time and energy.

7. A more restrictive and less imaginative way to visualize elements together would be to scan each source material and combine them in Photoshop. Because the source material is from separate sources, it may look unrelated. Some manipulation is needed to insure all of the elements from source material fit together properly. Using the tools available in the paint program, manipulate and distort each element to help create a more harmonious design. One drawback to visualizing this way is the tendency to stick too closely to the original source material, which may cause the design to lack cohesiveness and individuality.

8. After you can visualize the source material together either as a thumbnail sketch or a Photoshop collage, the shapes and values can be analyzed. If you are designing with color source material that does not feel harmonious, or the material is in black and white or grayscale, don't worry about it. Just concentrate on the shapes and values. The color can be added or fixed later. Trace the outline of all the shapes you can define and add other lines to help harmonize your design and give it variety.

9. Simplify and organize elements into interesting and harmonious shapes similar to the value assignment.

10. Choose to make your design a stylization or an abstraction.

11. Experiment with various picture frame proportions.

12. Experiment with different values and color schemes. The color and values should reflect the mood and style of your theme.

Figures 11.27 and 11.28 are examples of this project.

FIGURE 11.27   The design on the left uses curvilinear nonobjective shapes and an analogous color scheme. The stylized design on the right also uses curvilinear shapes. The saturated complementary colors create a sense of intensity.
(Left: *Color Design* © 2003. Reprinted with permission from Richard Hopper.
Right: *Color Design* © 2003. Reprinted with permission from Erica Herrerea.)

FIGURE 11.28   The stylized design on the left uses curvilinear shapes.
The variety of colors is harmonized by similar values. The example on the right is using
a complementary color scheme and curvilinear shapes. Gradients are used
throughout this design to give it variety and the illusion of form.
(Left: *Color Design* © 2003. Reprinted with permission from Rudy Anderson.
Right: *Chronicles of Narnia, Aslan* © 2003. Reprinted with permission from Phillip Kesler.)

TUTORIAL

PRODUCTION PROCESS

Following the steps as outlined in the previous project, gather your research and begin the process of sketching out thumbnail drawings (Figure 11.29). Create a tightened drawing of the lines to be traced and proceed to scan the drawings. Trace the designs in Illustrator and create a composite placement. Upon completion of the line work, make sure that you have only used closed paths. This will help you color the objects more efficiently.

Mixing Colors

In the value exercise, you worked exclusively with grayscale tones to add emphasis to the values of the design. The same method is used here for drawing, but you are allowed to use color in your design.

By limiting you to the K slider (in the value exercise), all you could use was a monochromatic color scheme of gray. The percentage number typed into the field was the percentage of black used in that shade.

FIGURE 11.29   The process of using research, thumbnails, roughs, comps, and a finish can be applied to this project as well. (*Central Park [Design Process]* © 2006. Reprinted with permission from Mike Clayton.)

There are several methods of "mixing" color based on the kind of computer system and software you use. These different methods of selecting colors are known as *color modes*.

The different color modes can be found in the Color panel Option menu (Figure 11.30). Two color modes we will discuss are CMYK (subtractive) and RGB (additive).

FIGURE 11.30   There are several color modes within Illustrator.
They can be selected from the Option menu of the Color panel.

CMYK

Cyan, magenta, and yellow, along with black (also known as the *Key plate*), are mixed to create colors for the image when printed on a press or with a four-color printer. By using different percentages of C, M, Y, and K, thousands of colors can be reproduced. Independently moving each slider or typing the number into the proper field sets these values.

For example, to create the color red, you would mix 100% of M and100% of Y (Figure 11.31). C and K are not necessary, so they have values of 0%.

FIGURE 11.31   The CMYK values of the color red.

Mixing 30% of C and 15% of M, with Y and K set to 0%, would make a cool light blue.

To achieve the color white, all percentages would be set to 0, whereas black is created when K is set to 100%.

RGB

To create images for the Web to be viewed primarily on monitors, RGB colors are used. Unlike CMYK, RGB uses different levels of the color (numbered between 0 and 255) to create the color.

With a level set to 0, the color is absent; with a level set to 255, the color is at full strength. Because RGB is additive, all levels set to 0 would create black—the absence of light—and all levels set to 255 would create white—the full intensity of light (Figure 11.32).

If the red were at a level of 255 with green and blue at 0, the red would be at full intensity, creating red. Likewise, with a red of 250, a green of 245, and a blue of 35, yellow is created.

FIGURE 11.32   The RGB values of black (left) and white (right).

Mixing and Adding Colors to the Swatches Panel

ON THE CD

With a clean Swatches panel, you will create the colors necessary for your design. For this example, we have taken a detail of the duck (ch11_duck.ai) from the Central Park composition, found on the CD-ROM.

An analogous color scheme that includes hues from blue to yellow has been chosen, and these colors have been arbitrarily used within the design. In this particular exercise, the green duck (a light value) will stand out from the water (a dark value). Using various tints and shades of these colors will help bring the design to life. Because your project will ultimately be output to a color printer, the CMYK color mode will be used.

To mix and add colors, follow these steps:

ON THE CD

1. Open the file ch11_duck.ai found on the CD-ROM.
2. If the Swatches panel is not visible, select it from the Windows menu.
3. Set the view of the Swatches panel to List View (Figure 11.33).

FIGURE 11.33   Change the view of the Swatches panel to List View.

4. If the Color panel is not visible, select it from the Windows menu.
5. Set the color mode to CMYK from the Color panel Options menu.
6. To create the bluish water, set the sliders in the Color panel to the following: C = 85; M = 60; Y = 0; K = 20.

The cyan and magenta mix together in even percentages to create a deep blue. Black is added to darken the color.

7. Click on the New Swatch button in the Swatches panel to add the new color swatch. Double-click the new swatch to open the Swatch Option dialog box (Figure 11.34).

FIGURE 11.34   Click the New Swatch button to add a new swatch to the list.

8. In the dialog box that appears, name the swatch "Water." Make sure that the Color Type is Process Color. Also make sure the Global property box is not checked. Click OK (Figure 11.35).

The newly named swatch now appears in the Swatches panel.

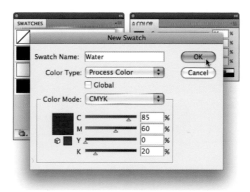

FIGURE 11.35   Name the swatch and set the proper items.

9. Using the Selection tool, select the large rectangle in the background. Its fill color is white, as are the fill colors of the other shapes in this file.
10. With the rectangle selected, make sure that the Fill swatch in the Tools panel is in the foreground.
11. Click on the Water color in the Swatches panel to set the color of this rectangle (Figure 11.36).

The color of the water is too dark. Trying to get a sense of the color from the little swatch is very difficult, so apply the color to a larger shape to see if the color is the right one. In this case, the blue is too dark.

FIGURE 11.36 Set the color of the background rectangle by first selecting it and then choosing the color from the Swatches list.

12. With the rectangle still selected, drag the color slider for K from 20% to 0% (Figure 11.37).

FIGURE 11.37 Change the level of black from 20% to 0% to lighten the blue color.

The color of the rectangle lightened slightly. If a shape is selected when you modify the color in the Color panel, that change is reflected in the selected object.

This might change the color of the shape, but it does not change the Water swatch in the Swatches panel.

13. Double-click the Water swatch to open its Options dialog box.
14. Change the K slider from 20% to 0%. Click OK.

The swatch has now been updated to reflect the new color. Now turn your attention to the green color of the duck.

15. Deselect the rectangle by clicking anywhere outside of it or by selecting Select > Deselect from the top menu.
16. To create the basic green color, set the sliders in the Color panel to the following: C = 63; M = 0; Y = 100; K = 0.

    The cyan and yellow mix to create the green color.

17. To test the color, drag the Fill swatch from the Color panel to the center shape of the duck. The shape takes on the color of the swatch (Figure 11.38).

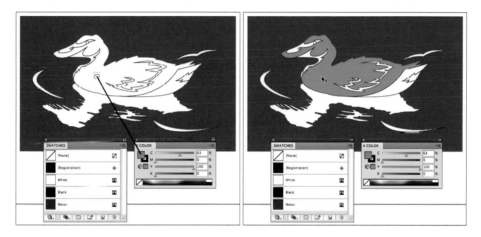

FIGURE 11.38   Test the color by dragging and dropping it onto the center duck shape (left).
The shape takes on the color of the swatch (right).

18. Add the swatch to the Swatches panel by dragging the Fill swatch from the Color panel to the Swatches panel (Figure 11.39).

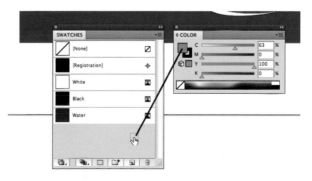

FIGURE 11.39   You can also add swatches to the Swatches panel
by dragging and dropping them onto the Swatches panel.

Dragging and dropping the Fill swatch is another way to add swatches to the Swatches panel.

19. Name the swatch "Medium Green."
20. Create the following colors and add them to the Swatches panel:
    • Light Yellow: C = 0; M = 0; Y = 33; K = 0
    • Dark Green: C = 65; M = 40; Y = 100; K = 25
    • Darkest Green: C = 75; M = 55; Y = 80; K = 70
21. Add the Light Yellow swatch to the top shape near the eye of the duck, as well as its wing shape, and the rest of the colors as shown in Figure 11.40.

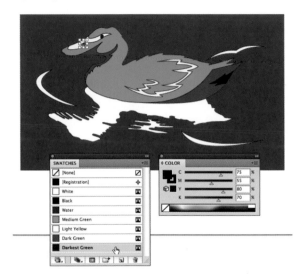

FIGURE 11.40   Use this image as a guide for coloring the rest of the shapes.

22. Remove the black stroke from all the shapes by selecting them all and setting their stroke to None.

Looking at the green and yellow shapes on the blue background (without strokes) makes the duck stand out. The values of the colors work well together. To add subtle movement to the duck, you need to create a darker blue color and apply it to the shadow and ripple shapes.

23. Create a second blue color called "Darker Water" with these settings: C = 85; M = 75; Y = 0; K = 20.

By adding black to the color, the darkness of the blue will stand out from the similar blue color of the water.

24. Apply the new color to the shadows and ripples around the duck.

The water around the duck stands out more now that the shapes are darker in value. The other duck in the design will have the same values but different colors (Figure 11.41).

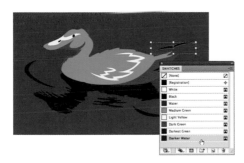 

FIGURE 11.41   The final colored duck (left). A variety of ducks colored similarly in value (right).

Using Gradients

Gradients can be used when you want one color to blend into another. For example, the sky is not simply blue; instead, it gets darker as you reach the horizon. Gradients can give emphasis to key parts of your design. They can bring attention to a concept or simply add a twist of something different. There can be more than one color in a gradient; however, the basic gradient contains two colors. The two kinds of gradients are linear and radial.

A *linear gradient* contains two colors that blend into each other along a straight line. In Figure 11.42, the yellow blends into the red to create an orange color in the middle. The yellow is known as the *start color*, and the red is the *end color*. The diamond in the middle is the *midpoint*, where the colors meet. Each of the gradient sliders can be moved to modify the gradient.

FIGURE 11.42   A normal two-color gradient.

Figure 11.43 shows the end color moved in to the left, making the right side of the rectangle solid red and allowing the gradient to happen in only half the area. The midpoint is still halfway between the start color and end color.

FIGURE 11.43 By decreasing the distance between the ends, the transition of the gradient becomes tighter (left). The midpoint Gradient Slider can control the distance of the blend between two colors (right).

In Figure 11.43 (right), the midpoint has been moved to the right. This determines where the gradient will blend the two colors. The transition from yellow to the intermediate color is 80% of the total distance, giving the red only 20% of the distance to change.

A radial gradient also contains at least two colors, but the start color is in the middle of the gradient and the end color on the edges (Figure 11.44). The midpoint works in much the same way, controlling the point when the blend occurs.

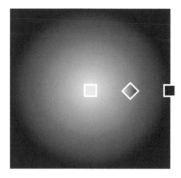

FIGURE 11.44 A basic radial gradient.

Creating a Gradient

To create a gradient, follow these steps:

ON THE CD

1. Open the file ch11_ducksinwater.ai, found on the CD-ROM icon. This file contains the line drawing for the background of the design. All the shapes have a black stroke and a white fill. All the objects are on the same layer for easy selection.
2. Open the following panels from the Window menu: Swatches and Gradient.
3. Select the rectangle area, as shown in Figure 11.45, with the Selection tool.
4. From the Type pop-up menu in the Gradient panel, choose Linear (Figure 11.46).

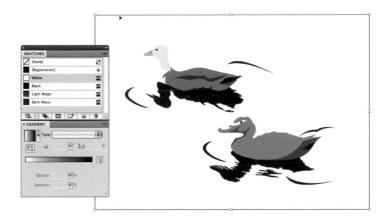

FIGURE 11.45   Select the large rectangle.

FIGURE 11.46   Choose Linear from the Gradient Type pop-up menu.

Automatically a black to white gradient fills the shape. Illustrator, by default, fills the shape with the last gradient created or selected.

5. From the Swatches panel, drag and drop the color Light Water onto the box below the start color in the Gradient panel (Figure 11.47).

There is no other way to add a color to the gradient. You must predefine the color and place it in the Swatches panels or drag it from the Fill swatch from the Color panel.

6. From the Swatches panel, drag and drop the color Dark Water onto the box below the end color in the Gradient panel.

By default the gradient has an angle of 0°, resulting in the gradient moving from left to right across the screen.

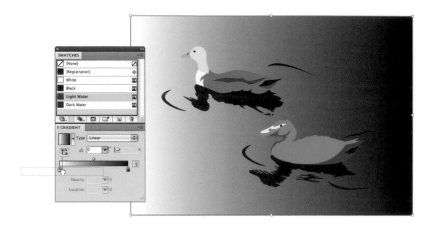

FIGURE 11.47   Drag the color swatch onto the box beneath the start point slider.

7. Type -90 in the Angle field to rotate the gradient clockwise 90° so that the dark color is on the bottom.
8. Drag the Gradient Slider for the midpoint to the left until the Location reads 40% (Figure 11.48).

This action extends the distance of the darker blue on the bottom of the shape. Now the gradient swatch will be added to the Swatches panel for later use.

9. While holding the Alt or Option key, click on the New Swatch button at the bottom of the Swatches panel to add the gradient. Name the swatch "Light to Dark Water." Click OK.

FIGURE 11.48   Move the midpoint slider to the left so the transition of the gradient contains more of the darker color.

Notice that you cannot make any other changes to the swatch in the dialog box. Gradients are rather complicated, so the other options are disabled. If you do not see the swatch appear in the list, make sure that Show All Swatches is checked.

Now, you can experiment and create another gradient for the sky by following these steps:

10. Using the Rectangle tool, draw a rectangle directly above the one you used for water. This will be the sky.
11. With the new rectangle selected, choose Linear from the Type menu of the Gradient Panel.

The shape automatically fills with the last gradient. Changes to this gradient will not be reflected in the swatch or anything using the swatch.

12. Set the start color to White and the end color to Light Water.
13. Set the Angle to 90°, the End Color Gradient Slider to 75%, and the Midpoint Gradient Slider to 50% (Figure 11.49).

This helps to make the blue color gather at the top of the rectangle and gives white more room to blend.

FIGURE 11.49 Modifying the Gradient Sliders brings a new dimension to ordinary gradients.

14. To add this gradient to the Swatches panel, simply drag the Fill swatch from the Gradient panel to the Swatches panel. Name the swatch "White to Light Water."

Although no radial gradients were used in this design, the process is still the same, except you would select Radial from the Type pop-up menu in the Gradient panel.

SUMMARY

Observe color in your daily routine and pay special attention to the conditions of the day or night, whether the light is natural or artificial, and the direction from which the light is coming. Notice how this light affects the objects and textures around you. How do the changes in kinds of light, light source, and light direction affect how you feel?

Look at the color of designed environments such as sports arenas, theaters, parks, lobbies, shopping malls, and even your classroom. How does each affect your mood? Do you think the lighting is appropriate for the activity that is taking place?

Take a look at your clothing choices. Is there a particular color or color scheme that seems to suit you? What kind of image does your choice of color give? How do the colors you wear affect your mood?

The next two chapters will deal with projects using color concepts presented in this chapter. You should be able to make color choices appropriate to the visual feeling you want to communicate. Studying the characteristics and properties of color should help you formulate plans for color schemes that will heighten the impact of your original art and designs.

12

DESIGN PROJECT 6: TYPEFACE DESIGN

INTRODUCTION

Letterforms were introduced as an important design element in Chapter 7, "Design Project 1 (Part 4): Abstraction Using Type Combination." This concept is taken a step further in this chapter with a brief historic classification of type and a section on hierarchy of visual information. You will design a poster exploring a typeface of your choice to incorporate these new ideas. You'll create this poster in color using letterforms and lines of type as shapes. The emotional and communicative quality of a typeface will be researched and captured using the digital techniques and concepts you have learned up to this point. Other digital tools and procedures will be introduced, but the exact process of creating the final design will be up to you.

CONTENT: BACKGROUND

The following concepts will be discussed in this section to give you the necessary information to begin Design Project 6:

- Historic Classification of Typography
- Type Styles
- Visual and Information Hierarchy
- Type as an Element of Design

Historic Classification of Type

The project associated with this chapter deals with the research and selection of a typeface that will be used as the main design element in the creation of a poster communicating the essence of that typeface. A typeface is the name given to the specific letterform design system of an alphabet. To begin the process of selecting a typeface, this section will examine the basic characteristics of typefaces and explore the main categories they are grouped under. Hundreds of books are dedicated to type and type design. Each book contains many classification methods. The intent of this book is not to give you an in-depth look at typography, but to explore type as an example of shape and an element of design. Type is one of the most universal abstract systems of design that visually communicates on a regular basis. The shapes of type reflect the structure and forms of history and culture, which is why it is one of the many topics included in this book. The following information will introduce the basics of type classification. There will be enough material covered to complete the project, but more information and research would be necessary for a thorough understanding of typography and its many uses.

There are a number of ways to group typefaces. The most logical way is to group typefaces according to their function and the period in history in which they were created. By looking at history, we can see how technical advancements and printed mass communications have influenced the design of typefaces. The reading habits of a particular culture at a certain period of time also influenced the way type was organized and distributed. These and many other factors associated with technology and communications can help us understand the similarities and differences that make up the various historic classifications of type. This section covers only the basic categories.

Of the many typeface categories, the most general classifications of typefaces are serif and sans serif. If you were to go one step further, the following five classifications might be enough to narrow down type choices to a more manageable number. Old Style, Transitional, Modern, Slab Serif, and Sans Serif are the five most familiar historic classifications of typefaces. There are many more, but these five will fill the basic requirements for selecting type for this chapter's project. Figures 12.1 to 12.4 compare and contrast characteristics of five selected typefaces, serving as examples of each of the five historic classifications of typefaces.

In Figure 12.1, the dotted line indicates the x-height. The line at the bottom of each letter is the baseline. Notice how much smaller the Old Style typeface x-height is in comparison to the other typefaces, especially the Sans Serif typeface.

Stress is the diagonal slant of the typeface illustrated by the dashed line going through the middle of each "c" in Figure 12.2.

Stroke is the degree of difference between thick and thin parts of a typeface. Notice how the modern typeface Bodoni has an extreme contrast of stroke, and the stroke of the sans serif typeface Univers shows no contrast (Figure 12.3).

FIGURE 12.1   The differing x-heights in each classification.

FIGURE 12.2   Differing stress.

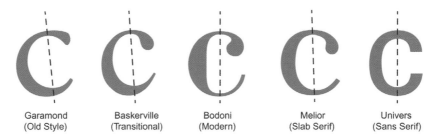

FIGURE 12.3   The contrast in stroke between the two diagonal parts of the letter "A."

The *bracket* is the area that joins the serif to the stroke in Garamond, Baskerville, and Melior (Figure 12.4). This area is shown in dark gray shading. Notice how Bodoni is not bracketed and Univers has no serifs at all.

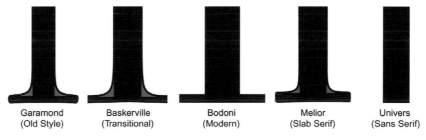

FIGURE 12.4   How typestyles compare and differ in relationship to serifs or lack of serifs.

Old Style Typefaces

Understanding that printing techniques and paper were very crude in the early 1600s, this first typestyle had very little contrast between the strokes of letters, and the brackets were very heavy. The stress or diagonal slant to Old Style letters is extreme (see Figure 12.5). *Old Style typefaces* generally feel more "human" and less "machined." Figure 12.5 shows four examples of Old Style typefaces.

Old Style Typefaces

Garamond

ABCDEFGHIJKLMNOPQRSTUVWXYZ
abcdefghijklmnopqrstuvwxyz

Palatino

ABCDEFGHIJKLMNOPQRSTUVWXYZ
abcdefghijklmnopqrstuvwxyz

Caslon 224

ABCDEFGHIJKLMNOPQRSTUVWXYZ
abcdefghijklmnopqrstuvwxyz

Weiss

ABCDEFGHIJKLMNOPQRSTUVWXYZ
abcdefghijklmnopqrstuvwxyz

FIGURE 12.5   Four examples of Old Style typefaces.

Transitional Typefaces

As the name implies, *Transitional typefaces* bridge the gap between Old Style and Modern typefaces. They have more refined serifs and more contrast in stroke than Old Style, but retain and sometimes accentuate heavy bracketing. When compared to Modern typefaces, Transitional typefaces do not have as much contrast in stroke. Transitional typefaces also have more stress. The changes observed from Old Style to Transitional can be attributed to the advancement in technology from the 1600s to the 1750s. The contrast in stroke, less diagonal stress, and more refined serifs and other features make Transitional typefaces feel a bit more machined but still retain some humanist qualities. Figure 12.6 shows four examples of Transitional typefaces.

Transitional Typefaces

Baskerville

ABCDEFGHIJKLMNOPQRSTUVWXYZ
abcdefghijklmnopqrstuvwxyz

Times Roman

ABCDEFGHIJKLMNOPQRSTUVWXYZ
abcdefghijklmnopqrstuvwxyz

Stone Serif

ABCDEFGHIJKLMNOPQRSTUVWXYZ
abcdefghijklmnopqrstuvwxyz

Perpetua

ABCDEFGHIJKLMNOPQRSTUVWXYZ
abcdefghijklmnopqrstuvwxyz

FIGURE 12.6   Four examples of Transitional typefaces.

Modern Typefaces

Contrary to what this name implies, *Modern typefaces* are not modern by our timetable. At the end of the eighteenth century, these typefaces were modern and a very radical change from previous letterforms. Modern dimensions and characteristics are very exact and mechanical. They have little, if any, bracketing with an extreme contrast in the stroke and no noticeable stress. Giambattista Bodoni was the most influential designer at this time. Many contemporary typefaces are reinterpretations of his original work. Figure 12.7 shows four examples of Modern typefaces.

Modern Typefaces

Bodoni

ABCDEFGHIJKLMNOPQRSTUVWXYZ
abcdefghijklmnopqrstuvwxyz

Modern

ABCDEFGHIJKLMNOPQRSTUVWXYZ
abcdefghijklmnopqrstuvwxyz

Fenice

ABCDEFGHIJKLMNOPQRSTUVWXYZ
abcdefghijklmnopqrstuvwxyz

Bernard Modern

ABCDEFGHIJKLMNOPQRSTUVWXYZ
abcdefghijklmnopqrstuvwxyz

FIGURE 12.7   Four examples of Modern typefaces.

Slab Serif Typefaces

Also referred to as *Egyptian* and *Square Serif, Slab Serif* typefaces are characterized by their blocky serifs and consistent stroke. They were first used sometime around the late nineteenth century and early twentieth century for their clarity of shape, which came in handy for crudely printed advertising and newspapers. These early Slab Serif typefaces used no bracketing and had no contrast in stroke. Later, a more sophisticated group of typefaces called *Clarendons* was introduced. They were a return to more contrast in stroke and minimal use of brackets but still incorporated the flat rectangle serif. Slab Serif typefaces used today consist of both the Clarendons and the designs of the nonbracketed, consistent stroke of the early Slab Serif typefaces, many of which resemble Sans Serif typefaces with simple rectangle serifs added on. Figure 12.8 shows four examples of Slab Serif typefaces.

Slab Serif Typefaces

Lubalin Graph

ABCDEFGHIJKLMNOPQRSTUVWXYZ
abcdefghijklmnopqrstuvwxyz

Rockwell

ABCDEFGHIJKLMNOPQRSTUVWXYZ
abcdefghijklmnopqrstuvwxyz

New Century Schoolbook

ABCDEFGHIJKLMNOPQRSTUVWXYZ
abcdefghijklmnopqrstuvwxyz

Melior

ABCDEFGHIJKLMNOPQRSTUVWXYZ
abcdefghijklmnopqrstuvwxyz

FIGURE 12.8 Four examples of Slab Serif typefaces. Notice the differences in serifs of the top two typefaces without brackets and the lower two Clarendons.

Sans Serif Typefaces

Sans Serif typefaces have been around since the early nineteenth century, but they were not popular until the Bauhaus and Art Deco movements made widespread use of them a hundred years later. Because of the lack of serifs, Sans Serif typefaces have the tendency to read vertically, not the traditional horizontal reading direction we are all used to. They were not used extensively for text until the middle of the twentieth century. Adding more leading or space between shorter lines of type helped with the readability of Sans Serif typefaces. This new trend and the contemporary look of these streamlined typefaces have aided in their popularity. Sans Serif typefaces consist of simple machined shapes that have no extra flourishes. They appear uniform in almost every way. These design features make them suitable for the contemporary look of today's society and attitudes toward digital design. Figure 12.9 shows four examples of Sans Serif typefaces.

Sans Serif Typefaces

Univers

ABCDEFGHIJKLMNOPQRSTUVWXYZ
abcdefghijklmnopqrstuvwxyz

Helvetica

ABCDEFGHIJKLMNOPQRSTUVWXYZ
abcdefghijklmnopqrstuvwxyz

Gill Sans

ABCDEFGHIJKLMNOPQRSTUVWXYZ
abcdefghijklmnopqrstuvwxyz

Franklin Gothic

ABCDEFGHIJKLMNOPQRSTUVWXYZ
abcdefghijklmnopqrstuvwxyz

FIGURE 12.9   Four examples of Sans Serif typefaces.

Type Styles

Type style usually refers to the variety of weights or widths of the letters in a specific typeface. Many names are given to the same weight or width of a letterform. For this chapter, we will be concerned with the most basic or common terms. The most important point is that typefaces are created in many different variations that emphasize a particular feeling but do not destroy the continuity or original integrity of the letterforms. The following is a description of the most common type styles (see Figure 12.10).

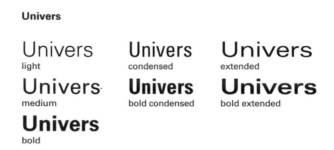

FIGURE 12.10 Common typestyles or variations of the typeface Univers.

Medium

Medium is often referred to as *regular, book,* or *normal.* It can sometimes be relatively heavier than these other variations, depending on how many different weights are included with a particular typeface. The most basic or standard weight of a typeface can usually be described as medium.

Light

Light may sometimes be called *thin.* It is the lighter, thinner version of the medium typeface.

Bold

Bold is a general term for a heavier variation of the medium typeface. Depending on the degree of the heaviness of weight, other terms such as *demi-bold, semi-bold, heavy, extrabold, ultra,* or *black* may be used.

Condensed

Also referred to as *compressed* or *narrow, condensed* is the narrow version of a type-face that gives letterforms the appearance of a vertical line direction.

Extended

Extended or *expanded* version of a typeface is wider than the standard medium typeface. Because of the emphasis on width, a horizontal line direction is created by each letterform.

Visual and Information Hierarchy

Visual hierarchy was discussed in Chapter 2, "Principles of Design," as organizing elements so that they do not conflict or take away attention from another element. Individual lines, shapes, values, and colors must be viewed one at a time in stages from the most important to the least important. The careful staging of elements based on visual hierarchy will lead the viewer from one part of a design to the next until the entire design has been viewed in detail.

This same concept may apply to visual information. Using hierarchy, the most important information should be observed and read first. The less important information should follow.

Figure 12.11 is an example of alternative title designs for a book cover. Beginning with the design on the upper left, the basic information is designed in a way that divides the words logically and lines them up to create a harmonious relationship. The second design on the upper row does the same using a different typeface, which gives the title a lighter feeling. The next design to the right combines both typefaces to add contrast and variety, while keeping the two lines of type vertically lined up to create harmony. The visual hierarchy in these three titles is achieved only because, as an English speaking and reading culture, we tend to read from the top to the bottom and from left to right. Hierarchy is achieved because we read the top first.

FIGURE 12.11   Eight examples of title designs for a book cover.

What if we wanted to make sure viewers would know this was a book on design, and that the fact that it is "visual" or "fundamental" was secondary? The design on the top row right would be one way we could emphasize this. The design to the left on the second row is an example of how we could emphasize the idea of "visual design" over "fundamentals." The design just right of it would do the same only in another typeface. The third design from the left is an example of how the type could be designed to emphasize "design," make "visual" secondary, and show "fundamentals" last. This design also creates contrast among all of the words and unifies the entire title by repeating the same typeface on the top and bottom.

The design on the lower right introduces contrast in the typefaces and builds a firm base of heavier type that forces the viewer to read down an angled slope. The larger "V" in "visual" creates a focal point that brings the viewer's eye back to the top to repeat this process.

Figure 12.12 shows six book cover layouts that use one of the titles created in Figure 12.11. The top row progressively adds new information to the title. The phrase "A Digital Approach" is placed just below the title as a description and is related by lining it up vertically with the last line of the title. Because this line is not as important and reflects a different idea, it is designed with less weight and placed away from the main title. The middle example on the top row adds the name of the publisher and author. This type identifies people behind the book but not the subject of the book. A light related typeface is used on top and below the title to create unity. This information is not as important to the viewer and is on the bottom of the list of information hierarchy. Notice that the publisher is listed on the top. The publisher is obviously much more important than the author. Thin rules (horizontal lines) help keep the loose letters from floating apart and add another unifying device to the entire design. The cover designs on the bottom row begin at the left with type that is the same cool color. Everything relates, and the contrast of the light blue with the black adds some dynamics. The cover in the middle uses red to create a focal point that emphasizes the most important point of the book, "Design Fundamentals." The design on the far right uses the same information but a completely different color scheme. The colors are divided between the types in a similar way as the middle design. The black is replaced by a cream color, the red is replaced by purple, and the light blue is replaced by dark blue. Notice how the feeling of the overall design has changed.

FIGURE 12.12   Six book cover layouts that use one of the titles created in Figure 12.11.

Type as an Element of Design Summary

In previous chapters, the fact that type is an element of design and subject to all the principles of design is well established. The following is a summary of concepts you should be familiar with before you begin the project related to this chapter:

- Letters should be designed as shapes.
- Words are made up of letters, which are individual shapes combined to form a pattern that makes the word a shape with the letters forming the pattern.
- Lines of type or sentences are made of letters and words. Together, they make patterns that make up paragraphs that become shapes. The value of this shape is dependent on the typeface and how close the lines of type are placed together.
- Shapes in patterns (repeating shapes) are not necessarily seen as individual shapes but more like implied texture. These repeated shapes are visualized together and make up a larger shape (for example, a paragraph that forms a shape).
- Designing by using pattern is much like design using value or color. The same or similar pattern should not be restricted to one area of the composition but created so it feels like part of the entire design. You wouldn't use a red or a dark value in just one corner of a design. Pattern should give the design unity. At the same time, patterned shapes should have variety. They should not be the same size. Each patterned shape should be used in unequal amounts just as the value or color is. There should be large areas of pattern, medium areas of patterned shapes, and smaller (accents) patterned shapes. They should be distributed so there is good hierarchy (variety) and good harmony (unity).

Figures 12.13 and 12.14 are examples of designs that use type as a shape.

The two designs in Figure 12.13 were created for a series of educational software packages dealing with mathematics. Notice how the numbers and type are designed the same as any shape. There is harmony and continuity between the two designs, and variety and contrast in color. They both use analogous color schemes but contrast in the fact that one uses warm colors and the other uses cool colors. The illusion of depth is created through the application of lighter and darker values and higher and lower intensity of colors. These compositions are very rectilinear and structured.

Figure 12.14 show six screen captures of a Web site. Similar to Figure 12.13, they use type as a shape and combine other shapes and colors to create depth and interest; however, this is where the similarity ends. These six designs emphasize drastically different design principles. The designs in Figure 12.13 are very structured and geometric with few negative shapes or spaces. Harmonious color fills the entire design. The designs in Figure 12.14 seem very spontaneous and unstructured. Large areas of space are left open, and smaller areas of positive shapes are filled with a variety of shapes and lines. High contrast of colors and values dominates most of the composition. Simply put, Figure 12.13 puts more emphasis on harmony, and Figure 12.14 emphasizes variety.

FIGURE 12.13 Two software package designs that harmoniously combine type and shape.
(*One* © 2006. Reprinted with permission from Alan Hashimoto.
Two © 2006. Reprinted with permission from Alan Hashimoto.)

FIGURE 12.14 This Web site uses type as expressive shapes.
(*Chaos* © 2006. Reprinted with permission from Jiong Li.)

CONTENT: THE BASIC PROBLEM DEFINED

Research and select a typeface. Letters, words, and a small amount of information dealing with the typeface will be designed as a single composition demonstrating the design principles of unity, variety, focal point, balance, abstraction, distortion, rhythm, repetition, and visual hierarchy using the design elements of nonobjective positive/negative shapes, line, value, color, and pattern. Next, follow the suggestions and steps listed below.

1. Study closely the visual characteristics of typefaces you find interesting.
2. Research their origin and find contemporary and classic examples of their usage.
3. Try to get a feeling for the typeface as individual letters, words, and text.
4. Look carefully at both lowercase and uppercase letters. Examine the unique quality of each letter and how they differ from other typefaces.
5. Using the selected typeface, design into one composition at least one letter, one word, and one short paragraph or line of type detailing some aspect of the typeface such as a visual description, appropriate usage, or history. These are just the minimum amount of elements that will make up the design. Parts of letters, multiple letters, repeated words, descriptive sentences, and multiple paragraphs can be used if they are appropriately designed into the entire composition.
6. You can use visuals other than type, but they must not dominate the design or receive more attention than the type. A background image used as a texture is an appropriate example.
7. Nonobjective lines, shapes, and textures that resemble but do not dominate the composition can be used but are not encouraged. This project is about using type as a design element. You should not have to rely too heavily on shapes other than those found in your selected typeface to create this design project.
8. This design must reflect the feeling, style, time period, and, most importantly, the visual design aesthetics of the font.
9. The principles of design are very important to this project in particular, because of the nonobjective nature of type. There is no recognizable subject matter used to communicate a specific meaning or feeling. This will place more emphasis on the communicative quality of how shapes, lines, value, and color are selected and organized.
10. Follow the same procedures as in the Value and Color projects. Use thumbnail sketches or a Photoshop collage to visualize options and alternatives. Experiment with a variety of picture frames, line directions, and value and color schemes.

The following are a few details and reminders concerning the elements and principles of design that should be considered in conjunction with the previous information:

Harmony: Be sure all lines, shapes, values, and colors are designed together and feel related visually and thematically.

Classic letterforms have passed the test of time. Their shapes should not be manipulated and their various parts could be cropped and used to unify the letters, words, and text that make up this design project.

Variety and Hierarchy: Be sure to have enough contrast to make this design interesting. Round or curved shapes next to sharp or angular shapes, and large and thick shapes next to small and thin shapes are just a few examples of how letterform shapes can be designed to create variety.

There are at least three elements required for this project: letter, name of the typeface (word), and text. To achieve successful visual hierarchy, each shape should be different sizes or weights. More contrast will create more drama and dynamic relationships.

Negative Space: Many letterforms include negative space as part of their design. Uppercase A, B, D, O, P, Q, and R, and lowercase a, b, d, e, g, o, p, and q have obvious enclosed negative space that should be considered when designing larger letters into this project. Other letters such as uppercase C, E, F, G, H, J, K, M, N, S, U, V, W, X, Y, and Z and lowercase c, f, h, j, k, m, n, s, u, v, w, x, y, and z do not have enclosed negative shapes, but negative shapes are created through implied lines closing off partially enclosed shapes.

Implied Line

When designing with lines of type, remember the concept of implied line and the idea that lines of type create shapes and values through implied visual grouping of similar elements. The more distance between letters and lines of type, the lighter in value the shape they create will seem.

Color, Value, and Depth: The illusion of depth can be achieved by using the following principles dealing with value and color:

- Darker values have a tendency to recede, and lighter values seem to come forward.
- Cool colors recede, and warm colors come forward.
- Shapes with more contrast in value and color appear to come forward and put more distance between foreground and background. Conversely, shapes with less contrast seem to fall into the background, and the depth between shapes seems to be very close.

Transparency and Translucency: Transparency is when a shape or object can be seen right through another object or shape, which makes the portion of the shape or object in the foreground almost invisible. Translucency is when a shape or object can be seen through another object or shape, which makes it possible for the shape or object in the foreground to be seen at the same time.

Figures 12.15 to 12.18 are examples of the finished project.

 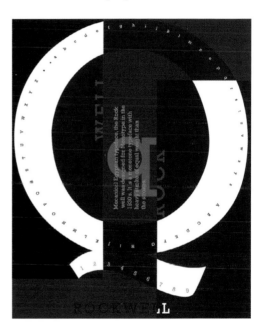

FIGURE 12.15   Finished typeface design projects.
(Left design: *Avenir Typeface Design* © 2006. Reprinted with permission from Trevor Harrison.
Right design: *Rockwell Typeface Design* © 2006. Reprinted with permission from Fon Ulrich.)

Figure 12.17 is an example of an alternative type poster project. This project is basically the same as the font poster, except a modular or grid system is created to help emphasize the principle of unity. The design on the left is an example of a type poster with special attention given to hierarchy and relationships between the alignment of type elements. The design on the right points these relationships out more clearly through the use of red lines.

Figure 12.18 is another example of an alternative type poster project. The theme of the poster focuses on the specifics of the letter. Historical information and letterforms are used as design elements. Similar to the other type poster projects, unity and variety are emphasized.

FIGURE 12.16 Finished typeface design projects.

(Left design: *Courier Typeface Design* © 2006. Reprinted with permission from Audrey Gould.
Right design: *Myriad Typeface Design* © 2006. Reprinted with permission from Tawnya Tate.)

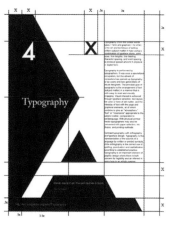

FIGURE 12.17 Type poster emphasizing the alignment of shapes.

(*Type Poster* © 2006. Reprinted with permission from Carlos Lucio.)

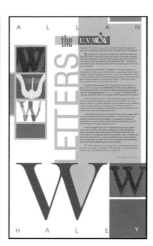

FIGURE 12.18   The "Letter" type poster project.
(Left. *Type Poster* © 2006. Reprinted with permission from Robert Duke. Center: *Type Poster* © 2006. Reprinted with permission from Robin Parker. Right: *Type Poster* © 2003. Reprinted with permission from Jenny Gonzalez.)

TUTORIAL   **PRODUCTION PROCESS**

Fonts and Your Operating System

Before we begin, you may need to know some technical information about fonts. A *font* is a file that your computer uses to create the type on your screen and your printer. There are several different types of font files. The two most common file types are True Type and PostScript fonts.

True Type fonts were created by Apple Computer as a means of allowing a typeface to be displayed at any size on-screen and when printed to a laser printer. This font allows designers a high degree of control over how the pixels are displayed. It is the most common format of font for the Macintosh and Windows operating systems. These font files have the extension .ttf (for example, Helvetica.ttf). The font itself is not cross-platform. For example, True Type fonts purchased for a Macintosh computer will not work on a Windows computer.

PostScript fonts were invented by Adobe. They basically do the same thing as True Type fonts, but are handled with more power and accuracy. However, more than one file is necessary when using a PostScript font; one for the screen information and another for the printer information.

For PostScript fonts to be displayed correctly on your machine, an application called *Adobe Type Manager* (ATM) is needed. A copy of ATM Light is available for free via download from the Adobe Web site (www.adobe.com). PostScript font support is built in to Mac OS X and Windows XP, 2000, and higher. ATM Light is needed for all other versions of the earlier Mac OS systems, even when running in OS X Classic Mode (OS 9.2 or earlier).

Microsoft and Adobe joined forces in 1996 to begin developing a new format called *Open Type*. This font type has cross-platform capabilities so that the font works on both Macintosh and Windows operating systems. These fonts use expanded character sets and layout features to give the designer greater and more precise typographic control. As of the publishing of this book, there are more than 10,000 fonts available in this format with more being added almost daily.

In Mac OS X, fonts are stored in the Font Folder within the Library Folder on the main hard drive. Fonts can be stored within a user's account (Home > Library > Fonts) and will be made available only to that user.

In Windows XP, fonts are stored by default on the same hard drive as the system software in the Fonts Folder within the WINDOWS folder (C:\WINDOWS\Fonts).

The location of the fonts on your computer is particular to each operating system. Consult your computer handbook for the location of the Fonts Folder within your operating system. Remember that if you use a particular font that is unique to your computer, and you try to open your file on a machine that does not have the right font, a warning dialog box will open and ask you to choose an alternative font.

Character and Paragraph Panels

Basically, all the attributes of fonts can be controlled with two panels: the Character panel (Window > Type > Character; PC: Ctrl + T; Mac: Command + T) and the Paragraph panel (Window > Type > Paragraph; PC: Ctrl + M; Mac: Command + M). Normally, both panels are docked together in the same set. To bring a specific panel to the front, click its tab within the set. Click and drag the tab out of the set to separate the panels for use at the same time. In Figure 12.19, the panels are shown separately.

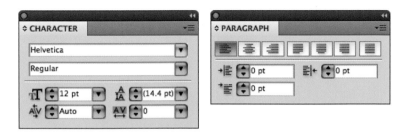

FIGURE 12.19 The Character and Paragraph panels.

The Character Panel

The Character panel contains the attributes for individual characters. Five options can be set from this panel. These options affect the characters and how they relate to each other individually. The following is a breakdown of this panel row by row:

Font: Use the arrow at the right of these fields to open the pop-up menu and choose the typeface for the selected text. The *fonts* are listed alphabetically, and some font sets contain their own variations in submenus. Scroll through the list until you find the font you want (Figure 12.20).

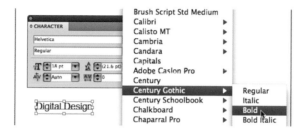

FIGURE 12.20   Choose the typeface from the pop-up menu to change the selected text.

Font Size: A character's *size* is measured in points (72 points = 1 inch); the larger the number, the larger the size of the character. A font is measured from its baseline to capline. Enter the number manually in the field or select a size from the pop-up menu (Figure 12.21).

FIGURE 12.21   Change the size of the font by either entering a number in the field or selecting it from the pop-up menu.

Leading: *Leading* is the vertical space between the lines of text in a paragraph. Leading is measured from baseline to baseline. By default, Illustrator (as well as other programs) automatically sets the leading according to the font size selected. Enter the number manually in the field or select a size from the pop-up menu (Figure 12.22).

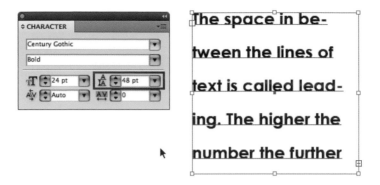

FIGURE 12.22   Leading is the vertical space in between lines of text.

Kerning: Kerning is changing the space in between two characters. This can be adjusted to help make the space between two characters seem more comfortable. The rule of thumb when it comes to kerning is that the space between each letter in the word or title should be able to have the same amount of "sand" poured in each space. Insert the pointer between the two letters to activate this option in the panel. Enter the number manually in the field or use the up and down arrows to move in increments of one (Figure 12.23).

FIGURE 12.23   Too much kerning can make the space between letters feel uncomfortable. Too little distance can cause the opposite to happen.

Tracking: Unlike kerning, tracking is changing the space in between characters over a range of text. Enter the number manually in the field or use the up and down arrows to move in increments of one (Figure 12.24).

FIGURE 12.24   Tracking is changing the space in between more than two letters or a range of text.

The Type Tools

Because the basis of this project is type, the Type tool is an important feature. All six of the type tools are available in the menu under the Type tool icon in the Tools panel. To see all the tools at once, tear away the tools from the Tools panel by holding down the mouse button on the Type tool, dragging over to the tear off tab, and releasing the mouse button (Figure 12.25). A free-floating Type Tools panel is the result.

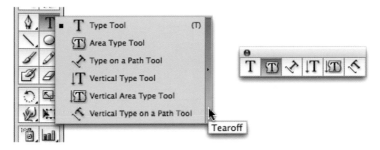

FIGURE 12.25   Click on the tear off tab to make the Type Tools a free-floating panel.

Type Tool

The basic tool in the set is the Type tool, which is used to create horizontal text. Simply click where you want the text to begin and start typing (Figure 12.26). To insert a carriage return, press the Enter (Return) key and begin typing on the next line.

FIGURE 12.26   To place text on the page, click with the Type tool where you would like the text to start, and then type.

If you want to type within a specific area, click and drag out a box in which to place the text. If the text box is not the right size, resize the text box using the Selection tool (Figure 12.27).

If you simply click on the page to set the start of the text, the line will be as long as you make it. Press Enter (PC) or Return (Mac) to drop to the next line.

Resized text that has been created without a predefined text box will stretch and deform unless you hold down the Shift key.

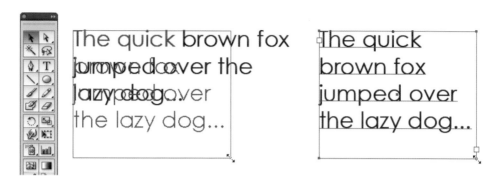

FIGURE 12.27 Resizing the text box dynamically places the text within the text box without distorting it.

If there is more text than will fit in the text box you created, a small box will appear as a visual cue at the right of the last visible line of text. You can select one of the transform handles and resize the text box to the desired size.

Vertical Type Tool

To create vertical columns of text, use the Vertical Type tool. It works in much the same way as the Type tool, but types vertically from top to bottom with lines of text from right to left (Figure 12.28). Although not a very practical tool, it does wonders for Asian characters and Matrix-like type effects.

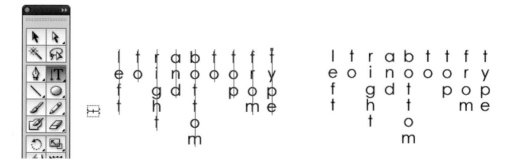

FIGURE 12.28 The Vertical Type tool is not a very practical tool but works best for Asian languages.

Area Type Tools

Although you can create a text box with the Type tool and place the text within this text box, you might want to place text into an odd shape and watch it flow within the space. The Area Type tool is the tool for the job.

Select the Area Type tool and click on any closed simple shape to place the insertion point into the object. Notice as you type that the text flows within the shape, automatically wrapping down to the next line as it reaches the edge (Figure 12.29). The shape can be drawn with the Shape tools or with the Pen tools. The path has to be closed. Illustrator will not allow an open path to be filled with the text. Text within a shape can be edited by using any of the Text tools to place the insertion point.

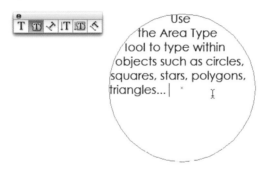

FIGURE 12.29   Using the Area Type tool, text can flow within the shape selected.

You can edit the shape in which the text is contained after the fact by using the Direct Selection and Convert Anchor Point tools (Figure 12.30). The text will automatically fit within the area. The shape in which the text is contained turns invisible when the Type tool is applied to it. The path is still there, but it has no visible stroke or fill.

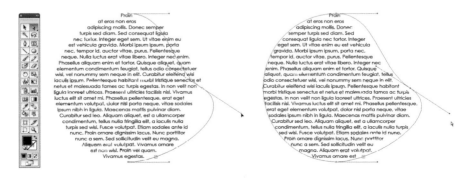

FIGURE 12.30   You can modify the points and curves of a shape with the text inside. The text will automatically reformat to fit the shape.

Keep in mind that legibility is a key issue when using blocks of text. Trying to set type inside of a star (Figure 12.31) may not read correctly. An elliptical shape would work better.

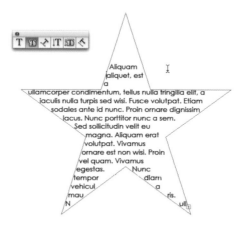

FIGURE 12.31   Placing type within the shape of a star does not read as well as type placed within other shapes.

Path Type Tools

The Path Type tool allows you to type directly onto an open path or a closed simple path (for example, a circle or polygon):

1. Create a new Illustrator Document. Using the Pen tool, draw an open path similar to that in Figure 12.32.

FIGURE 12.32   Create a simple path using the Pen tool.

A wavy line is drawn for this example. The path that you create can be either structured or loose. The path can cross over itself. Take note that sharp corners or sudden curves may distort the text and make it harder to read.

2. With the Path Type tool selected, click on the path near the left to set the insertion point for the text.

The point can be placed anywhere along the path. The stroke of the line the text will attach to becomes None so that it is not seen and does not interfere with the text type.

3. Type a basic phrase such as "The quick brown fox jumped over the sleeping dog." With the Selection tool selected, click outside the type area to deselect the text.

The text is displayed with the path invisible (a blue line acts as a preview). The path and type remain two separate entities but are grouped together. The path may be modified with the Direct Selection and the Convert Anchor tools. Once in a while, the text you type may be too long for the line that you created. Add points to the line or move existing points to lengthen the line.

The text object on the path can be moved up, down, along, or around the path using the brackets that appear at the start, end, and center of the path. The red arrows in Figure 12.33 show you the location of the brackets.

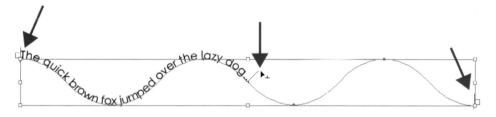

FIGURE 12.33   The start bracket is the vertical line at the beginning of a line of text along a path.

4. With the Selection tool, click the path and type group.

The start bracket, as identified in the top of Figure 12.34, is the starting point of the text along the path. We will use this bracket to move the starting point of this text to the right on the path.

5. Click on the start bracket at the beginning of the line to select it. Drag to the right to move the text along the path (Figure 12.34).

The start bracket can be moved along the path to alter the start point of the text. A colored outline is created to act as a preview of how the position of the text will be altered. Drag the bracket back and forth until you are happy with the results.

6. Click on the center bracket and drag across the path to flip the text along the bottom of the path (Figure 12.35).

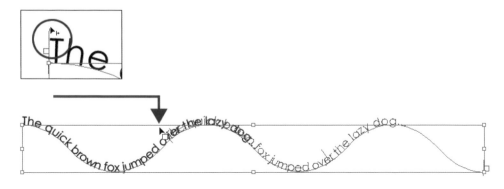

FIGURE 12.34   Move the start or center bracket to reposition the text along the path.

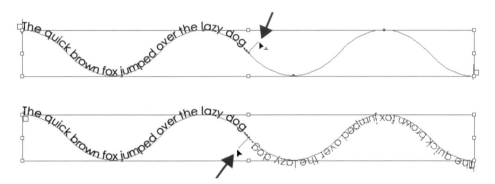

FIGURE 12.35   Drag the center bracket across the path to flip the text.
The text will turn blue to give you a preview.

7. The text can be flipped underneath the path by dragging the center (and the center bracket only) across the path. Drag it back across the path to return the type to its original orientation on the path. The text is only placed when you release the mouse.
8. To keep the text from flipping over the path as you reposition it using the center bracket, press the Ctrl key (PC) or Command key (Mac) to prevent this from happening. You can also choose Type > Type on a Path > Type on a Path, choose Flip, and click OK.

Editing Text on a Path

The text on a path can be edited by selecting the letter, word, or sentence with any of the Type tools. Select the words "brown fox jumped" by highlighting them with the Type tool. With the text highlighted, type "green lizard hopped" (Figure 12.36).

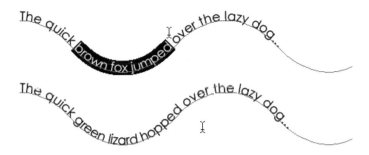

FIGURE 12.36   Highlight the text you want to change (top) and type the new text (bottom).

Editing text is simple. Remember that if your text runs longer than the line, you can edit the path. You can also insert the point anywhere in the text to add new text.

Path Type Tools with Closed Paths and Shapes

The Path Type tool can also be used on closed paths and shapes such as circles, rectangles, polygons, stars, and organic shapes The process is the same as using an open path.

1. With the Ellipse tool, draw a circle with a black stroke and a fill of None.

By using only the stroke, you can really see the line that the text will follow. You can place the Path Type tool on a filled object, but the fill, like the stroke, will disappear when text is applied.

2. Select the Path Type tool, click on the stroke of the circle, and type the phrase again (Figure 12.37).

Wherever you click on the path, this is where the text will start. If you are not happy with the results, change the start point of the line.

3. To move the text around the circle, click on the start or center bracket with the Selection tool and drag it around the outside of the circle.

Drag the start bracket with the Selection tool around the outside of the circle to change its start point. The change will not be made until you release the mouse button.

4. Move the center bracket across the path into the circle to cause the text to flow on the inside of the path (Figure 12.38).

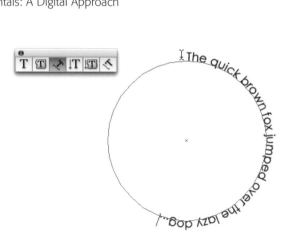

FIGURE 12.37   Type a phrase along the path of the circle.

Drag the center bracket across the path to the inside of the shape to make the text flow along the inside of the path. To return it to the outside, drag back across the line.

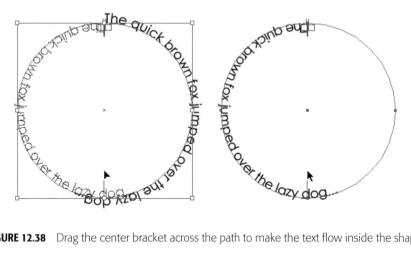

FIGURE 12.38   Drag the center bracket across the path to make the text flow inside the shape.

The initial direction of the type along the path depends on how it was constructed. If the path is drawn from left to right, the text will flow across the top of the path. If the path is drawn from right to left, the text will automatically flow along the bottom of the path.

The path must be a noncompound, nonmasking path. If you use the Pathfinder to merge two shapes together, the path must be expanded to one noncompound path. If a shape is being used as a Clipping Mask, the Path Type tool will not work on that path. Luckily, in Illustrator CS4, shapes that are combined using the Pathfinder are automatically expanded.

5. Draw two circles that overlap each other. Use the Pathfinder to add the shape areas together.
6. Select the Path Type tool and click on the compound path.

If the shapes are still compound, a warning appears. The warning dialog box states that you must click on a noncompound, nonmasking path to create text along a path. These objects still have two paths, which share a portion of the same area. Click OK in the warning box. If you need to, click on the Expand button in the Pathfinder to make the two paths one continuous path.

7. Using the Path Type tool, click on the path to set the insertion point for the text. Type some text onto the path (Figure 12.39).

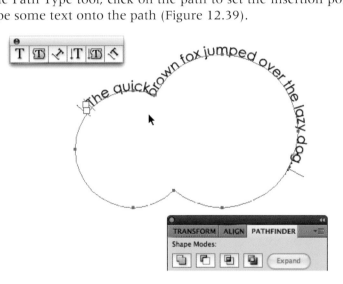

FIGURE 12.39   With the shapes automatically expanded, the Path Type tool will work.

As was mentioned earlier, text that is set along paths with steep and sudden angles and curves may overlap each other, making the type illegible. Add extra spaces into the text to space the characters around these trouble spots, or modify the slope of the path or the angle of the corner.

8. Add extra spaces in between the words that might overlap each other and create illegible type (Figure 12.40).

The Path Type tool will be a great asset to you in this project. Experiment with it and see what you can do. There are some examples in Figure 12.41.

As with the other Type tools, there is a vertical version of the Path Type tool called the *Vertical Path Type tool*. It works the same way as the other vertical tools, typing from top to bottom, right to left.

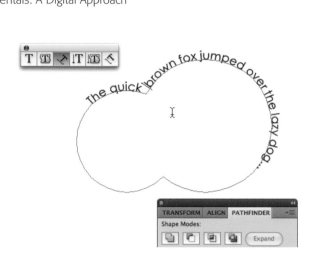

FIGURE 12.40 Add extra spaces in between the text that overlaps.

FIGURE 12.41 Using the Path Type tool.

TUTORIAL

THE PROJECT—A CASE STUDY

Figure 12.42 shows the completed poster for this assignment. The same process that was taken in the other projects was taken here: research, thumbnails, roughs, composites, and finished design.

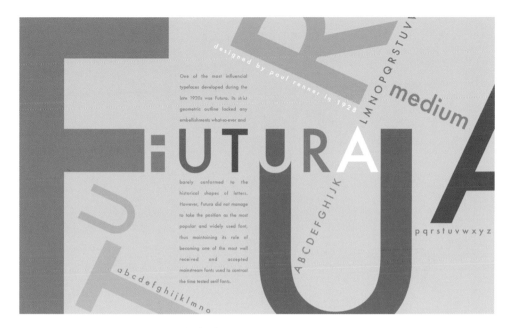

FIGURE 12.42   The final poster design for the Futura Type Poster.
(*Futura Type Poster* © 2003. Reprinted with permission from Mike Clayton.)

Research

The most important step in this process was to research the chosen font, Futura.

In 1928, Paul Renner of Germany developed Futura, which was one of the most prominent sans-serif typefaces created during the Art Deco period. Knowing the designer, his homeland, and the time period is a great place to start.

Look everywhere you can. Do not rely completely on the Internet. Talk to others in your class, and get ideas and inspiration from them.

Thumbnails

From your research, sketch dozens of thumbnails. From those, pick the 10 best ideas and put them together (Figure 12.43). Several of them might look like good ideas at first, but as you pour over the details of the assignment, you'll read that "nonobjective lines, shapes, and textures... can be used but are not encouraged," so throw out all the ideas that do not meet the criteria of the assignment. In the example in Figure 12.43, #1, #3, # 8, and #10 should be omitted.

After carefully reading through the requirements, #9 was chosen because it would yield the most variety.

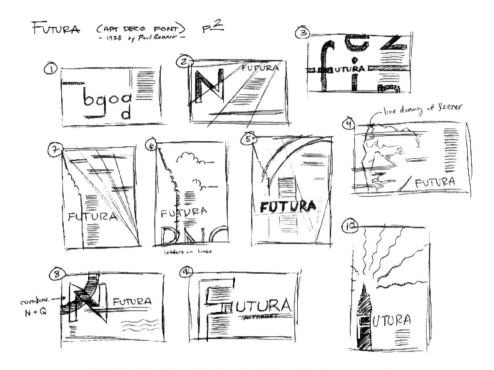

FIGURE 12.43   One of the thumbnail sheets for the poster design.

Roughs

One of the good things about the Type Poster is that it can evolve after it's put into the computer. A mock-up for the rough can be made (using Illustrator) in black and white (Figure 12.44). It's a simple layout using just text, without color, value, or texture.

Looking at the rough, you can begin to decide where to take it. At this stage of the process, print out a couple of the mock-ups and draw on them to gain inspiration. Look at Figure 12.45. To create a sense of unity and variety, the letter from the name of the font was duplicated and letters were reversed out of other letters to create negative shapes and keep the imagery interesting.

At this point, colors need to be researched. For example, by using a picture of a ceramic pot from the 1920s (which was glazed with soft blues, browns, tans, and yellows), eight colors out of the photo were matched and added to the Swatches panel (Figure 12.46) in an Illustrator document. (Refer to Chapter 11 for details on adding colors to your Swatches panel.) This will be the color scheme for the poster.

FIGURE 12.44   The first computer-created rough of the poster.

FIGURE 12.45   This rough is a sketch over a computer printout.

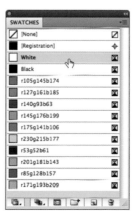

FIGURE 12.46   Color swatches matched from reference material.

Composites

After you have selected colors and have a rough idea, it is time to plot the letters out in Illustrator. Using color as a means of creating visual depth and coupling it with negative shapes created by reversing characters out of each other, the poster begins to come to life (Figure 12.47).

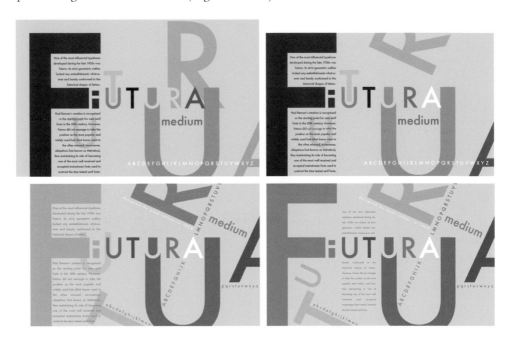

FIGURE 12.47   The first color comp of the poster (top left). We slightly modified the poster by rotating the "R" to the same angle as the left slope of the "A" (top right). More diagonals were added to complement the "R" (bottom left). Relocating the text from within the "F" helped to free up the negative space in the design (bottom right).

The design seems to be very structured with a lot of verticals and horizontals. To create a strong diagonal visual, the large "R" was tilted.

Notice how there is one simple focal point and all of the colors relate. The big dark "F" seems very separate from the rest of the design. The diagonal "R" provides good variety but does not belong unless there are other diagonals. This is obviously not exact.

More diagonals, in the forms of lines of text consisting of the alphabet, can be added. By matching the left slope of the "A," all the diagonals are unified. By changing the colors of the big "F," it becomes subdued and recedes into the background color; however, it still looks visually heavy on the left side.

By moving the text out of the big "F" and aligning the margins of the text to be the total width of the small "U" and "T," the negative space breathes a little easier from not being so cluttered. The little "A" is still the focal point, as are all the elements and colors necessary to make a good basic overall design.

As you apply the design principles contained in this chapter, the project will become a little easier. Use simple transformations (scale, reflect, rotate, etc.) and the Type tools to your benefit.

Frame your image carefully, as was done in the letterform and shape project. Maybe the poster as a whole is not working well, but you like a certain part of it. Pick a part of the poster, crop it, and see if it can be rescued.

Creating Visual Depth Using Value

In Chapter 10, value was discussed in depth. By reducing images to simple shapes and applying gray tones across the image, a sense of depth is created.

Figure 12.48 shows the final color version on top of a grayscale version of the Futura Type Poster. The same principles apply. The darker colors tend to pop up from the light background. The lighter gray letters recede. The contrast in value allows you to focus on what's important.

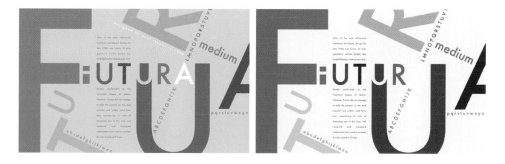

FIGURE 12.48   The color poster (left) and a grayscale value study (right) of the same design help in the identification of unity using value and visual weight and depth.

Color

From the color panel, all but two colors were used (Figure 12.49). The colors are placed evenly throughout the design. The blues on top of the tans help the shapes come forward, as do the darker reds.

It is essential to have a solid color scheme before entering the composition stage. Select the mood for the design. Should you use a panel of loud, vibrant colors; subdued earth tones; cool blues and greens; hot yellows and reds; a complementary color scheme; a split complementary; or a triad scheme?

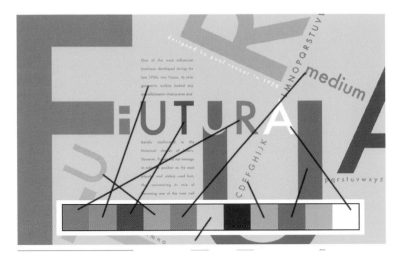

FIGURE 12.49   The color is evenly shared throughout the entire design.

Transparency

Transparency can be used in many ways. You can make objects completely solid or transparent. It can be applied to layers, groups, shapes, type, and so on. You can create special effects with the click of a button.

Access the Transparency panel by selecting Window > Transparency. Simply select the object and use the slider to add a level of transparency to it. The lower the number, the more transparent the object will become.

In Figure 12.50, the blue of the "U" was too strong on the background. Rather than pick another color, its transparency was reduced to 60%. Transparency allows the background color to come through and blends the two together. The same technique was used with the "T."

Try overlapping transparent objects to see how the colors mix. Maybe an interesting shape will appear.

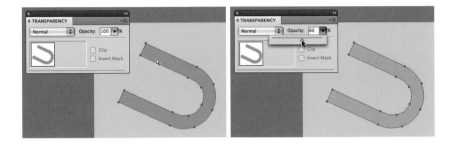

FIGURE 12.50   The transparency of the bluish "U" is set to 60%.

Pattern

Repetitious patterns in design can help the eye follow a set course. Evenly spaced letters of the same basic size, color, or shape can create a pattern. The diagonal alphabet creates a line, even though there are 26 separate parts to that line and two colors. It carries you right through the focal point of the poster.

In Figure 12.51, the letters in Futura help to create a strong horizontal. Although the letters are not the same color or the same shape, they are the same size; this repetition in size helps to create that visual.

FIGURE 12.51   Across the middle of the design, positive and negative shapes help to create a patterned line.

A Quick Review

The Type Poster Project uses a lot of the same techniques and skills from the project on letterform and shape. Here is a brief review of some the tools and options that will be of great benefit to you in this project.

Creating Outlines

Working with a font is one thing, but sometimes it is better to work with an outline of the character. Because this poster project requires only one font selection, after the selection is made, changing the font to outlines (a closed path) is the better road to travel. To convert a font to outlines, follow these steps:

1. Create the text to be converted. Select its typeface and approximate size.

   For this example, the word "FUTURA" and its accompanying font, Futura Medium, were chosen. The font size is between 24 and 36.

2. With the type selected, choose Type > Create Outlines (PC: Ctrl + Shift + O; Mac: Command + Shift + O).

Grouping and Ungrouping

After a word has been converted to outlines, the letters are automatically placed into a group. To select each of these letters individually, they need to be un-grouped:

1. With the text still selected, choose Object > Ungroup (PC: Ctrl + Shift + G; Mac: Command + Shift + G).
2. For practice, with the characters selected, choose Object > Group (PC: Ctrl + G; Mac: Command + G) to regroup the letters.
3. Once again, ungroup the objects.

Using the Contextual Menu

Using the right-button on your mouse and right-clicking in Illustrator CS4, you can access a contextual menu. Within this menu, you can find the previous commands: Create Outlines, Group, and Ungroup.

As you work, you may want to group things together to move them or trans-form them. Remember that the Direct Selection tool can select paths and objects within a group.

Transforming Objects

One of the key components in the type poster is varying the size, angle, and ori-entation of objects to create unity and variety. Using the Transforming tool is crucial to achieving these principles.

1. Select the "F" (or a random letter from your own file) and grab one of the handles. While holding down the Shift key (to keep the object in proportion), drag the handle up and to the left until the character is roughly double in size (Figure 12.52).

FIGURE 12.52   Clicking on the handles with the pointer allows you to scale the object.

Do the same with another letter, like the "U," but this time choose a different handle and go in another direction.

2. With the Selection tool, move another character slightly up from the rest.
3. Mouse over one of the handles until the pointer turns into a curved double-arrow, activating the Rotate operation. Click the mouse and rotate the object to the left or right. Release the mouse button to set the angle (Figure 12.53). Hold down the Shift key, if necessary, to constrain the angle to 45°.

FIGURE 12.53   Rotate the object using the handles.

4. Select another character and choose Object > Transform > Reflect.
5. The Reflect dialog box appears. Click the Vertical button. To see a preview of the change, click Preview. The character reflects along its vertical axis. Click OK.

All these options are available under the Object > Transform menu, the Tools panel, or under Transform in the contextual menu when you right-click on a selected object.

Preparing Your Document

For the other projects in this text, the document size has been kept at the default size of Letter (8 1/2" × 11"). A simple sheet of paper would not be big enough for the purpose of a poster.

Document Size: Tabloid

When creating the document in Illustrator, you can either select from several preformatted sizes or set your own.

For this example, a tabloid-sized sheet of paper was used. Tabloid measures 17" wide × 11" high, or the same size as two sheets of letter-sized placed side by side.

1. Launch Illustrator and create a new document.

2. In the New Document dialog box, set the Artboard Size to Tabloid and the Units to Inches. Set the Orientation to Landscape (Figure 12.54). Click OK.

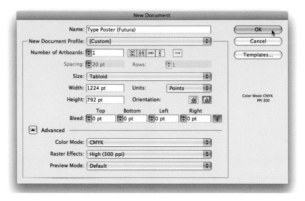

FIGURE 12.54   Set the Artboard size to Tabloid in the New Document dialog box.

You may choose whatever size you want for the dimensions of your poster. Make sure that the size you choose reflects your design. To do so, simply type your measurements into the Width and Height fields of the Artboard Setup portion of the New Document dialog box.

Outputting Your Poster/Design Using Page Tiling

The setup for the document is now complete. With the Rulers turned on, you'll see that the artboard is 17" × 11". The dotted outlines that are enclosed within the space of the artboard represent the size of the paper that is currently selected in the Page Setup portion of the file. The outer line is the actual size of the paper. In this case, the default of Letter is selected. The inside line is the actual printable area of the page. They are also referred to as margins (Figure 12.55).

The entire image does not fit within the printable area of the Page Tile. If printed now, the output would look like something similar to Figure 12.56.

If your printer only prints on standard letter-sized paper, you could move the Page Tile Area around and print out all the pieces that you need and paste them together.

To move the Page Tile Area, locate the Page Tiling tool from underneath the Hand tool in the Tools panel. Use the tool to move the printable area around the page. The pointer is connected to the lower-left corner of the tile area (Figure 12.57). Move the area and print. Then move the area again and print. Repeat this process until the entire area has been printed. The result should be something like Figure 12.57. Trim and mount the pieces to mat board or foam core for stability. This is passable for roughs and comps but not for finished pieces.

FIGURE 12.55   The dotted outlines show the paper's current size and printable area.

FIGURE 12.56   If you were to print, all that would print would be what is in the printable area.

FIGURE 12.57   You can move the printable area around the page with the Page Tile tool (right).
Take the pieces of the design and trim and mount them together (left).

If your printer is capable of printing on tabloid paper, set the printer to print Tabloid in the Page Setup area (File > Page Setup). The printable area should be similar to that shown in Figure 12.58 (left), with the result looking like Figure 12.58 (right).

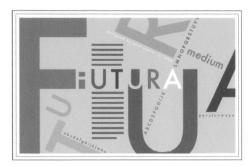 

FIGURE 12.58   With the paper size set to Tabloid, the entire design will fit within the printable area (left). The result of outputting the design on a printer capable of tabloid prints (right).

All printers are different and have their own way of doing things. It would be difficult to try to explain every detail of the printing process because so many variables go into printing. If you have any questions, contact your teacher, local print shop, or service bureau. ♣

SUMMARY

Much of what we know about the history of civilization and the accomplishments of past cultures is through their ability to share ideas, tell stories, and record events. All of society's realities and ideals are preserved and made available through the development of devices and systems to communicate and record this information. Design for communications has always been a reflection of a culture's beliefs, political structure, art, and technological advances. Letterforms are the most widely used visual form of sharing information. This is why this book is concerned with the structure and variations of these designs. Can you look back through history and give examples of the relationship and visual similarities between the transportation design and type designs of that period? How about examples of industrial design and type designs? Can you find examples of interior design or architecture that reflect the shapes, colors, and forms of the more popular typefaces of that period?

If visual information design is directly related to a society's beliefs and technical advancements, what would be the characteristics of a typeface you would create for your present technically advanced social group? What would a typeface of the future look like?

CHAPTER

13

DESIGN PROJECT 7: DIGITAL MONTAGE/COLLAGE

INTRODUCTION

This final project is a culmination of the design theories and content contained in this book. All the elements and principles of design will be incorporated into one composition. Realism, in relationship to other designed shapes such as nonobjective, stylized, and abstract shapes, is encouraged, and theme is used as one of the unifying elements.

Up to this point, only the very basics of Photoshop have been explained and incorporated into projects. This final project will use Photoshop exclusively for the finished design. The basic tools and techniques that make up this powerful program are covered in the "Production Process" section.

Learning the ins and outs of Photoshop and how to create the final project will be very involved. All the elements and principles of design have been discussed, and projects concerning each of these have been completed so there will be fewer new concepts dealing with design theory, less conceptual demands, and more space dedicated to the digital production process.

309

CONTENT: BASIC PROBLEM DEFINED

In this project, you will combine imagery from at least three to five different sources to create a single composition. Photographs, illustrations, typography, and any traditional or digitally created imagery can be used for this project. The design principles of unity, variety, focal point, balance, abstraction, distortion, rhythm, repetition, and visual hierarchy will be demonstrated using the design elements of shapes, line, value, color, pattern, and texture. The final design can use realism or be an abstraction or stylization.

Background Information

In terms of visual design, a montage is a collection of separate images that are designed into one related composition but retain their original identity. All of these individual items form a relationship among each other as one design, but the individual parts are still recognizable.

A collage is a work of art that uses visual materials that were not originally created by the artist for that particular piece. These materials, textures, patterns, and objects retain their own original identity but also become part of a new design that may or may not have the same atmosphere, meaning, or emotional content as the original source from which it is taken.

Both of these types of designs are good examples of Gestalt theory. They are similar in that they combine elements from different sources into one composition, and these elements retain their own integrity while becoming recognizable parts of a whole design. They differ in how the original pieces are gathered or created for the final design. In a montage, the original images are created beforehand with the intention of becoming part of a final design. A collage uses images that existed before the conception of the final design with no intention of becoming part of a larger design. Materials used for collages are often found objects or textures.

This final project can technically be either or both. If photographs or other visuals are created separately with the intention of being used for this project, this is a clear example of a montage. If the materials used are all selected photographs or other visuals not originally intended for this design, it is an example of a collage. The project could contain elements of both. Photographs could be taken and combined with found objects, fabric, or printed material.

Whether your final design is a collage, montage, or both, the most important point is that your design is made up of separate images that retain their own identity but still relate to one another in a single interesting and unified composition. Figures 13.1 to 13.6 are some examples of montage or collage designs. They are also very good examples of the project detailed in this chapter.

The examples in Figure 13.1 are collages. Some of the images are recognizable, but there are many visuals that are not clear. The undefinable or unreadable shapes, color, and textures are meant to act as expressive elements with no specific form of direct communication. These designs do express a personal and interesting message about China. When viewed more formally, the elements and principles of good design seem to be very evident. Lessons learned from previous chapters should help the viewer see harmony and variety between all the shapes, textures, values, and lines. Similar to the type poster assignment, type functions as both shape and pattern. Tonality and open space are design elements that are emphasized. Excellent use of hierarchy in relationship to all of the elements is easy to notice in this very dynamic series of collages.

FIGURE 13.1   Collage examples.
(Top left and top right: *Happiness* © 2006. Below: *Young Revolutionaries* © 2008.
Reprinted with permission from Jiong Li.)

Figure 13.2 contains three examples of collages. The example located at the top is a collage made up of complex organic shapes. such as leaves, birds, and a human face. The simple shape of the perfectly round moon adds contrast to these shapes and makes a distinct recognizable area of interest. The thin geometric lines and circles are not as easy to identify individually but create an interesting subtle pattern. The two designs at the bottom use color schemes that are monochromatic with symmetrical balance. Paying close attention to the values of this design is a must because there is almost no color. There are basically three images being collaged for each of these designs. The hierarchy of shapes and values is emphasized with a harmonious color scheme that gives this design harmony. The use of line to keep these two designs unified was also a good choice.

In Figure 13.3, the design on the left is an example of a montage with collaged elements. The dimensional mannequin heads with globes are very clear; however, the elements in the background, the linear pattern, and the type seem more vague and could be considered more of a collage. The design on the right seems more clearly to be a montage. All of the elements are easy to recognize. These two designs use photographs of very dimensional sculptured images and apply distinctly different types of balance.

FIGURE 13.2   Collage examples.   (Top: *Renaissance Woman* © 2006. Reprinted with permission from Patrick Wilkey, www.visiocommunications.com. Bottom Left: *Self Promotion Illustration for Visio Communications* © 2006. Reprinted with permission from Patrick Wilkey, www.visiocommunications.com. Right: *Self Promotion Illustration for Visio Communications* © 2006. Reprinted with permission from Patrick Wilkey, www.visiocommunications.com.)

All of the examples in Figure 13.4 use layers and transparency to achieve the translucent effect similar to the top example in Figure 13.2, "Renaissance Woman." The design at the top left combines scans of applied textures and faces to create a digital collage. The design on the top right is created using photographs of found leaves and manipulating them using Photoshop. Both of the designs located at the bottom are designed and collaged in the same way as the designs on top. All the compositions use harmonious color schemes that give them a unified and calm feeling.

FIGURE 13.3   Collage and montage examples.
(*Self Promotion Illustration for Visio Communications* © 2006 and *Holiday Promotion for Visio Communications* © 2006 Reprinted with permission from Patrick Wilkey, www.visiocommunications.com.)

FIGURE 13.4   Collages using layers and transparency. (*Leaves* © 2003, *Three Faces* © 2003, *Architecture* © 2006, and *Untitled* © 2006 were reprinted with permission from Jim Godfrey.)

The five examples in Figure 13.5 are montages. Most of the combined imagery is pretty clear. The theme of these designs reflects places in Switzerland. The original images were digitized slides taken with a traditional 35mm camera on location. Monochromatic and analogous color schemes designed with similar intensity of colors give all of these montages a calm feeling. Dramatic use of hierarchy and contrast of values create dynamic interest. The implied brush stroke texture creates an interesting earthy and harmonious composition.

FIGURE 13.5   Montage examples.   (*Morcote* © 2003, *Luzern* © 2003, *Fribourg* © 2003, *Bellinzona* © 2003, *Montreux* © 2003. Reprinted with permission from Robert Winward.)

The three collages in Figure 13.6 make obvious use of Photoshop filters. Numerous filters have been applied to various parts. Filters manipulate, invert, soften, harden, blur, and add special effects and texture to designs. How and when to use filters is a matter of personal choice and is determined by how appropriately the use of a particular filter enhances or influences the communication of the design. Filters and their usage are covered later in this chapter.

FIGURE 13.6   Collages that use Photoshop filters.   (Left: *Remembering Martha* © 2006.
Top right: *Winters* ©2006. Bottom right: *Magics* © 2006. Reprinted with permission from Danielle Fagan.)

Figures 13.1 to 13.6 are good examples of the collage and montage project detailed in the next section.

Conceptual Process and the Project Details

The following is a summary of procedures that are involved in the conceptual process of creating this project. Most of these steps are mentioned in Chapter 11, "Design Project 5: Color and Color Theory."

1. Select several themes that seem interesting. *Theme* is a topic or subject matter that gives meaning and continuity to an entire project.
2. Research these themes and try to find as many different approaches to communicate their content visually.
3. Narrow your choices to one theme and begin collecting and creating images that will support your idea and make your design interesting.
4. Get a feel for the subject matter and try to visualize an appropriate style that will convey your idea.
5. Select and create quality images that can be combined and output at a high resolution (at least 300dpi).

6. In addition to photographs, illustrations, and type, nonobjective shapes, lines, patterns, and textures can be incorporated into the final design.

7. Following are a few details and reminders concerning the elements and principles of design that should be considered in conjunction with previous information:

Combined Elements: Be sure all lines, shapes, values, and colors are effectively combined and feel visually and thematically related.

Letterforms: Classic letterforms have passed the test of time. Their shapes should not be manipulated, but their various parts could be cropped and used to unify the letters, words, and text that make up this design project.

Variety and Hierarchy: Be sure to have enough contrast to make this design interesting. Round or curved shapes next to sharp or angular shapes, large and thick shapes next to small and thin shapes, are just a few examples of how letterform shapes can be designed to create variety.

Color, Value, and Depth: The illusion of depth can be achieved by using the following principles dealing with value and color:

- Darker values have a tendency to recede, and lighter values seem to come forward.
- Cool colors recede, and warm colors come forward.
- Shapes with more contrast in value and color appear to come forward and put more distance between the foreground and background. Conversely, shapes with less contrast seem to fall into the background, and the depth between shapes seems to be very shallow.

Transparency and Translucency: *Transparency* is when a shape or object can be seen right through another object or shape, which makes the portion of the shape or object in the foreground almost invisible. *Translucency* is when a shape or object can be seen through another object or shape, which makes it possible for the shape or object in the foreground to be seen at the same time.

8. Similar to the Value, Color, and Typeface Assignment, the best way to visualize all of these elements together is by viewing all the reference material at once and creating thumbnail sketches combining all the material. This is a quick way to visualize a variety of options and analyze the relationships between separate elements. Position, proportions, and scale of each visual may be studied in relation to each other. Changes may be made early to save time and energy.

9. When the source material can be visualized together as a thumbnail sketch, the shapes and values can be analyzed. You can then research color choices and make decisions.

10. Experiment with various picture frame proportions.

11. Experiment with different values and color schemes.

12. Experiment with a combination of filters and image manipulations.

TUTORIAL

PRODUCTION PROCESS

In preparing for the project, the first step is to pick a topic. The next step is to find material to support your topic. This research is crucial to the success of your project. Material can include images taken with a digital camera (although you can also scan photographs), fabric, textured surface, illustrations, type, and a variety of other things.

From your source materials (Figure 13.7), create thumbnail drawings of the montage. These drawings (like the ones for the color project) can help you compose on paper, instead of wasting time using the computer.

FIGURE 13.7　Source files for the montage.
(*Project images for NYC design* © 2006. Reprinted with permission from Mike Clayton.)

From your thumbnails, create several rough drawings, paying attention to the placement and size of each image (Figure 13.8). When completed, you can begin to scan the images and objects and build them on the computer.

The final result should be close to your original rough drawing (Figure 13.9). You can take liberties in this design later when using the computer. As you begin to put the pixels together, you might see something that does not quite work right. Feel free to fix it.

FIGURE 13.8   Samples from the thumbnails for the montage.
(*NYC Thumbnails* © 2006. Reprinted with permission from Mike Clayton.)

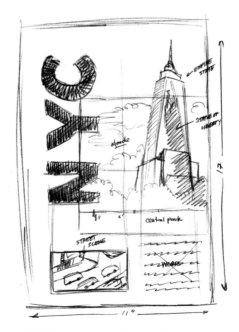

FIGURE 13.9   Rough layout of the montage.
(*NYC Drawing* © 2006. Reprinted with permission from Mike Clayton.)

FIGURE 13.10   The final montage.
(*NYC* © 2006. Reprinted with permission from Mike Clayton.)

Photoshop CS4 will be used to put this montage together (Figure 13.10). Photoshop CS4 is a very robust software application, and this tutorial was created with the intention of introducing you to several tools that will be important in your completion of the project. Be sure to experiment and see what works for you. Feel free to try out and change the settings of the many secondary options and tools.

Document Setup

When creating a new document in Photoshop CS4, there are a few more options to consider than when creating a new document in Illustrator CS4. (Refer to Figure 13.11 for the following steps.)

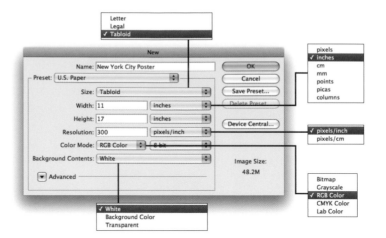

FIGURE 13.11 A breakout diagram of the New document dialog box.

1. Launch Photoshop CS4.
2. From the top menu, choose File > New (PC: Ctrl + N; Mac: Command + N).

This opens the New document dialog box, which is divided into two sections: Image Size and Contents.

3. Name your file accordingly.

It can be changed later when you save the file. It is good practice to name your images up front so that as you work on multiple new images, you won't become confused as to which is which.

4. From the Image Size section, click on the Preset drop-down menu.

This drop-down menu houses several preset file sizes as they relate to standard paper, photograph, screen, video, and metric paper sizes.

5. Select Tabloid.

When the Tabloid option is selected, the Width and Height fields are changed to match the selection. There is not an orientation option in this dialog box, so if you want the Tabloid size to be landscape (horizontal) instead of portrait (vertical), you have to type the dimensions in manually (or rotate the canvas 90° after the file is created).

6. Set Width and Height units to inches.

The default unit of measurement in Photoshop is the pixel. To change the unit of measurement, select the drop-down menu at the right of the Width and Height fields and select inches.

7. Set the Resolution to 300 pixels per inch (ppi).

Resolution is the number of pixels per inch. The higher the resolution, the better the image quality. Photographs printed in magazines can be anywhere from 300 to 2400 ppi. This results in a higher-quality print, but the file sizes are large. Images for the Web and screen presentation only need to be the standard 72 ppi (the same as your screen resolution) and only require a minimal file size.

As you modify the dimensions and resolution of the image in the New document dialog box, the Image Size number at the top of this section changes. This number is an approximation of the size of the file. An image that contains more pixels will result in a larger file size. For example, an image that is 1" × 1" at 144 ppi is four times as large as an image that is the same size but with a resolution of 72 ppi (Figure 13.12).

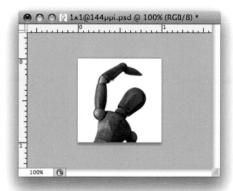 

FIGURE 13.12   The size relationship of two images: 1" x 1" at 72 ppi (right) and 1" x 1" at 144 ppi (left). Notice that the image on the left, according to the total number of pixels, is four times larger than the image on the right.

8. Set the Color Mode to CMYK for images that are going to be printed.

For images that will be displayed on the Web or on-screen in a presentation, RGB is appropriate. Because this project is a poster that will output on a color printer, select CMYK.

9. In the Contents section, choose Transparent.

Your selection in this area affects the background layer in your document (Figure 13.13). If White is selected, the background is filled with white. Background Color fills it with the current color in the Background Swatch. The Transparent option creates a file with one transparent layer (Layer 1).

10. Click OK.

The file that is created is 11" × 17" and has a resolution of 300 ppi. There is no background layer, but there is a transparent first layer. The grey-and-white checkerboard in the background represents transparency.

FIGURE 13.13   The results of the different options from the Contents field: (left-right) White, Background Color, and Transparent.

Saving a New Image

After a new image has been created, you should save it right away. Save your file using the following steps:

1. Choose File > Save As (PC: Ctrl + Shift + N; Mac: Command + Shift + N) from the top menu.

   The Save As dialog box is simple (in spite of all the options).

2. Select the proper file type from the Format drop-down menu (Figure 13.14).

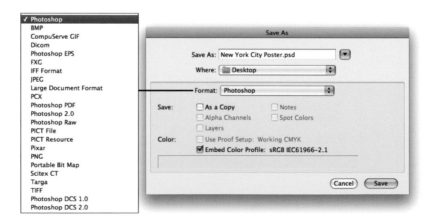

FIGURE 13.14   Breakout view of the Format options in the Save As dialog box.

The file type is very important. The following are some of the more important file types associated with Photoshop CS4:

Photoshop Document (.psd): This is the default option for most users. This file type in no way compresses any information. The individual layers and their properties will be maintained. The file size of this format is large because the file is not compressed in any way.

Photoshop EPS (.eps): The file is saved as an Encapsulated PostScript and can only be printed correctly on PostScript printers. White areas are saved as transparent areas. The vector data (fonts, shapes, etc.) is made available for other applications that the file is imported into. If the file is saved as an EPS and is opened back up into Photoshop, the vector elements will rasterize.

TIFF Format (.tif): This type of file can be used easily in bitmap, page layout, image-editing programs, and on multiple operating systems. Layers can be saved in the TIFF format, but the file size is larger. The option to flatten the layers is given in a prompt if the File Handling subset of the Preferences is set. This file type is excellent for printing.

BMP or Bitmap (.bmp): This native graphics format for Windows users is often used in software for presentations or for use in the operating system itself. This image file type is best used with PowerPoint presentations and some 3D software applications.

PICT File (.pct): The native file format for the Apple Macintosh operating system. They are used on Macs the same way BMPs are used on Windows machines. These images may not display correctly on a PC.

Depending on the file type chosen, the other options in the Save and Color areas of the dialog box may become available.

3. Select the location in which to save the file.

Save the file to your projects folder, hard drive, flash disk, or wherever you store your files.

4. Click the Save button to complete the command.

After you have saved the file once, you can save the file again by using File > Save or the keyboard shortcut (PC: Ctrl + S; Mac: Command + S). Remember to save often. If you want to save the file under a different name occasionally to see the progress you make or to keep an original before changes are made, use the Save A Copy feature, which works in much the same way but does not overwrite the original file.

Color Correction

Most of the images that you scan from photographs or take with digital cameras are not correct color-wise. They tend to be too dark, too light, or have some sort of colorcast (namely bluish or greenish casts). The process of "fixing" the color of an image is called *color correction*.

Although some scanners and cameras have software that corrects the image as it scans or captures the picture, it is better to make these corrections in an editing program such as Photoshop.

The image in Figure 13.15 was taken with a digital camera under normal indoor light. As can be seen on the left side of the image, if the flash is off, this particular camera places a bluish tint over the entire image and washes out the lighter colors. To make the image obtain a truer color and contain a full range of values, some changes must be made to the image.

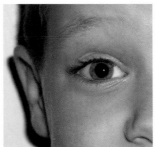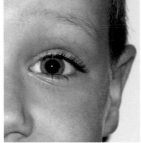

FIGURE 13.15   The left side of the image is untouched. The right side of the image has been color corrected.

Levels

In the value chapter, levels were explained as they pertain to grayscale imagery. When using the Level command on a grayscale image, you are modifying the image's tonal range: the levels of black and white within the image. On a color image, using the Level command adjusts the color balance of the image.

The Levels dialog box allows you to adjust the image by changing the levels of its shadows, midtones, and highlights. This can be achieved manually through the Levels dialog box or automatically by using the Auto Levels command.

Follow these steps to color correct the image:

1. Open the image ch13_face.psd from the Chapter 13 folder on the CD-ROM.

   Notice that the image has a bluish cast over it.

ON THE CD

2. Show the Info panel by selecting Window > Info (Figure 13.16).

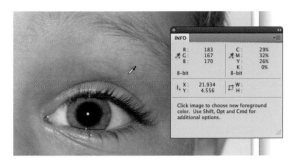

FIGURE 13.16   The Info panel returns the properties of a pixel
(color, placement, etc.) as the cursor passes over it.

The Info panel is divided into four quadrants. The top two quadrants show
information about the color of the pixel. The bottom two show position and
height and width of the current selection.

The upper-left quadrant tracks the actual color values of the pixel that the
current tool is hovering over within the image. By default, it loads the numbers
for red, blue, and green channels in the image. When combined, these three levels produce a color. Remember that "0" means that the pixels are black and that
"255" means they are white. If you mouse over the area in between the eyes, the
software returns the values of 214, 205, and 206 (respectively), or a light gray
color.

3. Open the Levels command by selecting Image > Adjustments > Levels (PC:
   Ctrl + L; Mac: Command + L).

The Levels dialog box looks a little complicated. The Channel options take up
most of the dialog box. There are three major parts of this area (Figure 13.17).

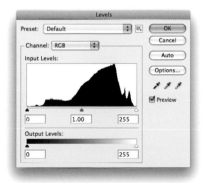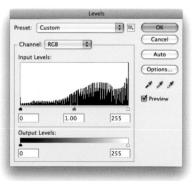

FIGURE 13.17   The Levels dialog box allows you to manually color-correct the image. The histogram
on the left is the uncorrected image, and the one on the right is from the corrected image.

The pop-up menu next to Channel allows you to view the histograms of the channels individually (R, G, and B) or together (RGB). The channels can be modified individually for better control over color correction. To increase the overall redness of an image, select and make changes to that channel.

The Input Levels sliders allow you to manually set the dark and light points of the image. Dragging the sliders resets the points of each Input Level. For example, if you set the Input Level's black triangle to 10, all the pixels to the left of the slider will be remapped to 0 (or black). Likewise, moving the white arrow to the left will cause the pixels to the right to become 255 (or white). The levels in-between will remap the histogram accordingly to help even out the tone of the image. The Input Level's gray arrow sets the midpoint of the levels. Setting it to the right darkens the image by decreasing the percentage of levels between 50% and 255 (white). Alternatively, moving it to the left lightens the image by increasing the number of levels between 50% and 255 (white). You may also input the numbers into the fields (black, gray, and white arrows) to move the sliders.

The Output Levels are modified in the same way, but the results can only be seen when printed. If after printing your image, you notice that the darks are not dark enough, slide the black triangle to the right and remap the output level. Like with the Input Levels, the Output Levels can also be typed into the fields (black and white arrows).

4. Click on the Preview box.

By selecting the Preview box, the changes made to the inputs will be reflected in the image.

The changes will not be made until you click the OK button. To reset the dialog box, press Alt (PC) or Option (Mac) to temporarily change the Cancel button to Reset.

5. Select the White Point eyedropper tool from the right of the dialog box (Figure 13.18).

FIGURE 13.18 The eyedroppers in the Levels dialog box control the (l-r) black point, midtones, and white point.

Using the White Point eyedropper tool from the lower-right corner (under the buttons), you can physically set the White point of the image. Click on the icon to select it.

6. Click on the lightest area of the image, which is around the white part of the eye.

With the tool selected, mouse over the area of the image around the eyes. As you move over the whites of the eyes, the RGB reading in the Info panel will reflect the levels in each. The closer the numbers get to 255, the whiter the area. The average around the eyes is somewhere around R: 215, G: 235, and B: 250. When you are close to those numbers, click to select it. The white point (255) has been set. Notice the image lightens up and the bluish tint begins to drop from the image.

7. Select the Black Point eyedropper tool from the lower-right area of the dialog box. (The Black Point eyedropper is two to the left of the current tool.)
8. Click on the darkest area of the image. In this case, it's the pupil of the eye.

Like the White Point eyedropper, the Black Point eyedropper remaps the black (0) of the level. Clearly the darkest part of the image is the pupil. The numbers for this area should be around R: 25, G: 28, and B: 35. When the darkest part of the image is found, click with the tool to set the black (0) point.

The image really pops from the dull, bluish image that it was before. The eyes have become green and the hair has become brown. The skin tone has improved.

9. Move the grey Input Level slider to the left until it reads 1.20.

Moving the gray Input Slider changes the contrast of the lights and darks of the image, and remaps the midtones to achieve a better continual tone of the image.

10. Click OK to set the change.

Figure 13.19 shows the final color-corrected image. If you are not happy with the change, select Edit > Undo (PC: Ctrl + Z; Mac: Command + Z) to return to the state before the Levels were changed.

11. Undo the Levels Command by selecting Edit > Undo.

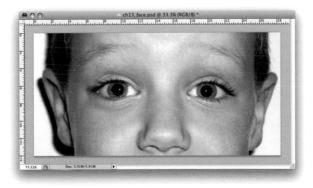

FIGURE 13.19   The final color-corrected image.

Auto Levels

Using Auto Levels allows the computer to recalculate the image by automatically setting the new Black point and White point of the image. To use the auto levels, select Image > Adjustments > Auto Levels (PC: Ctrl + Shift + L; Mac: Command + Shift + L).

The result of the image is pretty good. Tighter control of the color of the image can be achieved through the Levels command. The image that was auto-corrected is a little darker through the midtones. In Figure 13.20, the difference between the auto-corrected version (left) and the manually-corrected version (bottom right) was that the gray Input Slider was controlled to change the contrast to something more to our liking. You can further modify the image by opening the Levels dialog box and moving the gray Input Point to change the contrast of the image.

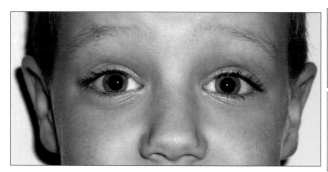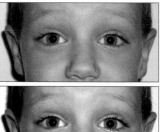

FIGURE 13.20   A comparison of all the images (Auto Levels [left], original [top right], and manually leveled [bottom right]) shows that Auto Levels is not necessarily the best way to go.

Overall, it's better to color-correct the image manually rather than to let the software do it for you automatically.

Color correct all of your images before you begin to create the montage. Although the Level command only affects the current selected layer, it becomes a tedious task to try to do it within the montage. However, you might want to further modify an image after it has been placed within the montage to unify it with the other images and elements.

Combining Images from Separate Files

Because this project is a montage, you will need to combine multiple images into one Photoshop file. The result of combining images is one file with multiple layers. Each of the layers can be moved and edited independently from the original. There are many methods that can be used to accomplish this.

Layer Options

A layer can be moved from one file to another using the Duplicate Layer command from the Options menu in the Layers panel.

ON THE CD

1. From the Chapter 13 folder on the CD-ROM, open files ch13_empty.psd and ch13_sunset.psd.

   To open files, select File > Open and navigate to the Chapter 13 folder on the accompanying CD-ROM. Repeat this command for each file. Because the CD-ROM is a read-only media, copies of the file will be opened. A dialog box may appear prompting that the files are "read only." You will have to save the files to your hard drive to keep them.

2. View the Layers panel by selecting View > Layers.

   The Layers panel may already be viewable. It is almost always coupled with the Channels and Path panels. They will appear as tabs in the panel window.

3. With the ch13_sunset.psd file active (in front), select Duplicate Layer from the Options menu in the Layers panel (Figure 13.21).

   The Options menu is under the arrow in the upper-right corner of the Layers panel. The Duplicate Layer dialog box appears.

FIGURE 13.21   Select Duplicate Layer from the Option menu in the Layers panel.

4. In the As field of the Duplicate Layer dialog box, name the layer "sunset."
5. From the Destination area, choose ch13_empty.psd (Figure 13.22).

From the drop-down menu, choose the destination for the file. The names of all the files that are currently opened will be reflected in this menu. Choose the appropriate file to which you want to duplicate the layer. If you want it to open up into a new image, select New and give the file a name in the field below.

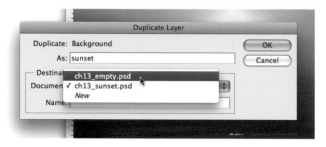

FIGURE 13.22   From the Destination menu, choose the file to which you would like to copy the layer.

6. Click OK.

The background layer is added to the ch13_empty file. The layer is automatically centered in the file and is in its own layer (Figure 13.23).

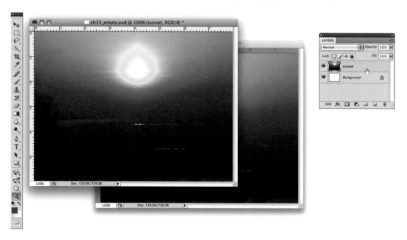

FIGURE 13.23   The resulting placement for the new layer is centered in the destination document.

The Move Tool

Use the following steps to duplicate layers using the Move tool.

1. With the ch13_empty.psd file still active, choose Edit > Undo Duplicate Layer (PC: Ctrl + Z; Mac: Command + Z) to undo the last command.

2. With the ch13_sunset.psd active, select the Move tool (V).

The Move tool is located in the first row, second column of the Tools panel. It is represented by a black triangle with a plus sign to its lower right. Use the V key to toggle to this key. Click on it to select it.

If you mouse over a tool long enough, the name of the tool and the shortcut key will appear; in this case, it is V for the Move Tool. The shortcut key for simple tools will be shown in parentheses after the name of the tool.

3. Click on the image in the window and, while holding down the mouse button, drag the image from ch13_sunset.psd file to the ch13_empty.psd file (Figure 13.24).

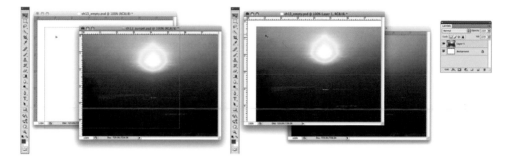

FIGURE 13.24   A preview box shows that a layer is being moved from one file to another. The new layer is placed where it was dropped, not centered as in the previous method.

A rectangular preview box shows you the size of the object being moved from one file to the other. If both files are viewable at the same time (as seen in Figure 13.24), you can drag and drop layers back and forth between them. You can also drag the layer from the Layers panel to the new file. The layer is dropped where you put it, unlike the Duplicate Layer command, which automatically centers the layer. To place the layer in the center of the destination file, use the Shift key as you drag and drop.

4. From the top menu bar, select Edit > Undo Drag Layer to undo the previous command.

This removes the new layer (Layer 1) from the ch13_empty.psd file.

5. As in Step 3, drag the layer from one image to the other while holding down the Shift key. Release the mouse button before the Shift key to place the file in the center.

The new layer (Layer 1) is centered in the destination file.

1, 2, 3: Select All, Copy, and Paste

Images can also be combined using a simple series of select, copy, and paste commands:

1. With the ch13_empty.psd file still active, choose Edit > Undo Drag Layer (PC: Ctrl + Z; Mac: Command + Z) to undo the last command.
2. With the ch13_sunset.psd active, choose Select > All from the top menu.

By choosing Select > All, a marquee is drawn around the entire perimeter of the canvas. This marquee is a box with a dashed line that "marches" around the selection. The area on that layer within the box can now be copied.

3. Select Edit > Copy (PC: Ctrl + C; Mac: Command + C) to copy the image to the clipboard. The area within the marquee is now stored in the clipboard.
4. Bring the ch13_empty.psd file to the front by clicking on its title bar. The Layers panel changes to reflect the active file.
5. Select Edit > Paste (PC: Ctrl + V; Mac: Command + V) to paste the image from the clipboard into the ch13_empty.psd file.

The copied image is pasted into the center of the destination document in its own layer.

Layers

Layers make using Photoshop easier by allowing you to work on individual elements of an image without affecting the others. When there is no part of an image on the layer, the images behind come through. You can combine parts of images on each layer using a variety of different techniques, some of which will be discussed later.

Like in Illustrator, layers in Photoshop can be renamed, reordered, hidden, locked, and made to be transparent.

Renaming Layers

There are two ways you can rename layers in Photoshop.

The first and easiest way to rename a layer is to simply double-click the name of the layer in the Layers panel and type the desired name (Figure 13.25 left).

The second method of changing the name of a layer is to go through the Options menu and choose Layer Properties. The resulting dialog box enables you to not only give the layer a name but also a color label (Figure 13.25 right). These color labels can be useful when creating images that have many layers. Layers with photographs could be one color, effect layers could be another, text layers another, and so on.

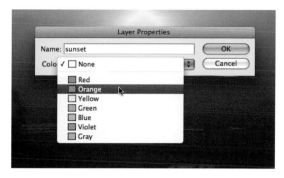

FIGURE 13.25   Renaming a layer is as easy as double-clicking on its name (left). You can also rename the layer in the Layer Properties dialog box and even assign it a color (right).

Changing the Stacking Order of Layers

Like in Illustrator, the hierarchy of layers is the same: the top-most layer appears in front, while the bottom-most layer is in the back. The Background layer (if there is one) is the very back of the layer hierarchy.

To change this order of layers, simply drag the layer in the Layers panel to its new place in the order.

ON THE CD

1. In the Chapter 13 folder on the CD-ROM, open file ch13_layers.psd.
2. Click on the central park layer and drag it in between the times square layer and the sunset layer (Figure 13.26).

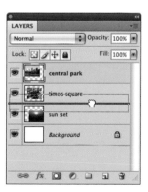

FIGURE 13.26   Drag the layer in between the correct layers to reorder them.

It is that simple. The layer is now between the times square layer and the sunset layer.

Panel Options

Some people complain about the size of the thumbnail image to the left of the layer name, but few know that it can be remedied. There are actually four different sizes for thumbnails: None, Small, Medium, and Large.

To access this option, choose Panel Options from the Options menu in the Layers panel.

Hiding and Showing Layers

Layers can easily be hidden and shown with the click of a button. It may become necessary as you work to hide a particular layer and concentrate on a certain area.

To hide a layer, simply click on the Hide/Show layer (eye) icon to the left of the layer (Figure 13.27). To show it again, click again. If you try to modify the layer while it is hidden, a dialog box will appear telling you that the layer is hidden.

FIGURE 13.27   Hide the layer by clicking on its eye icon. If there is no eye symbol, it is already hidden.

Linking Layers

In Photoshop you can link layers to each other. Linked layers can be moved, copied, pasted, transformed together, and aligned. To link layers, follow these steps.

1. In the Chapter 13 folder on the CD-ROM, open file ch13_layers.psd.
2. Click on the central park layer in the Layer panel to select it. Then hold down the Shift key and select the times square layer. Both layers should be highlighted.
3. From the Options menu in the Layers Panel, choose Link Layers to link the central park layer to the times square layer (Figure 13.28).

FIGURE 13.28   You can link layers together by either choosing Link Layers from the Options menu within the Layer Dialog box (left) or by clicking the Link icon (right).

You can link another layer to the active layer by selecting the first layer that you would like to be linked and Shift-clicking the layer(s) to be linked to the first selected layer. Also, at the bottom of the Layers Panel, click the Link button (the first button) to link the layers.

4. With the Move tool, move the image around within the document window (Figure 13.29).

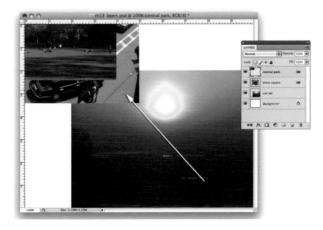

FIGURE 13.29   Linked layers are moved when the active layer is moved, regardless of where it is in the stacking order.

When layers are linked, they can be moved together.

5. Select the times square layer and click the Link icon at the bottom of the panel to unlink it from the central park layer.

To unlink a layer, simply select the layer and then click on the Link icon at the bottom of the panel to clear it. The layers will remain linked until you break the chain.

Locking

Four locks can be placed on layers: locking transparent pixels, locking image pixels, locking position, or locking all of them (Figure 13.30). First, selecting the layer to be locked and then clicking on the desired lock icon at the top of the Layers panel will lock the layer. The following is a description of each lock:

FIGURE 13.30   The four locks: (l-r) Transparent Pixels, Image Pixels, Position, and All.

Lock Transparent Pixels: By checking this box, transparent pixels within that layer cannot be painted on or affected. Only pixels that already contain information (color) are affected. This helps when touching up edges of selections.

Lock Image Pixels: Just the opposite of the previous attribute, this locks the colored pixels so that only the transparent ones can be colored.

Lock Position: This setting keeps the layer from being moved. The layer can be painted and modified in other ways, it just cannot be moved.

Lock All: This setting locks the layer from being affected in any way. You cannot move it, resize it, color it, or change its levels. If a layer is part of a linked group, all the other layers in the chain are affected as well.

Follow these steps to become familiar with locks:

1. Using the ch13_layers.psd file on the CD-ROM, hide all the layers except for the central park layer by clicking on their eye icons.
2. Select the central park layer and click on the first lock button, which is Lock Transparent Pixels.

3. Using the Paint Brush tool (B), paint on the central park layer.

You will not be able to paint on transparent pixels, only on pixels that already contain some color information (Figure 13.31).

FIGURE 13.31   Only pixels that are already colored will be colored when this attribute is locked.

4. Hide the central park layer and show the times square layer.
5. Select the times square layer and click on the second lock button, which is Lock Image Pixels.
6. Use the Paint Brush tool (B) to paint on the layer.

With the Lock Image Pixels button checked, it is not possible to paint on existing pixels. A warning dialog box (Figure 13.32) appears, stating "Could not use the brush tool because the layer is locked."

FIGURE 13.32   A warning dialog box appears to tell you that you cannot complete the operation due to the image being locked.

7. Hide the times square layer and show the sunset layer.
8. Select the sunset layer and click on the third button, which is Lock Position.

9. Using the Move tool, attempt to move the image in the document window. A warning box appears informing you that locked layers cannot be moved.
10. With the sunset layer still active, uncheck the Lock Position button and click on the fourth button to Lock All.

You cannot do anything to the layer. You cannot paint on it, or move it, or edit it in any way. This becomes useful as you begin to get things just the way you like them. If a layer is completely locked, a black lock appears to the right of the name of the layer. If one of the other locks is engaged, a gray lock occupies that space.

Opacity

A layer's opacity governs the degree of transparency a layer has. As a layer becomes more transparent, the layers underneath it begin to come through. This can create some really interesting effects when creating your montage.

There are two forms of opacity in the Layers panel: Layer Opacity and Fill Opacity.

Layer Opacity: Affects the entire layer, including any layer effects (drop shadows, inner glows, etc.) it might have.

Fill Opacity: Only affects those pixels that were originally painted on the layer, not the effects or modes.

Figure 13.33 shows the differences between the two. The top image has a Layer Opacity of 40%, and the drop shadow that is applied to the layer is also affected. However, the bottom image has a Fill Opacity of 40% as well, but only the pixels that were originally drawn on the layer are affected. Look closely at the drop shadows to see the difference. As you create your montage, experiment with these two sliders, and you might be surprised by how powerful they can be. There may be part of an underlying image you would like to have creep through, or you may want to use some line work or type without it being too overpowering in the design. Lower its opacity and see what happens.

Masking

In your montage, there might be just part of one image that you want to include. Instead of erasing (removing pixels) from the image, you can simply block it out and make it transparent. The concept of masking is just that, blocking out parts of the image from view while maintaining the integrity of the image.

Masking is simple. It consists of two parts: the layer and an attached mask (Figure 13.34).

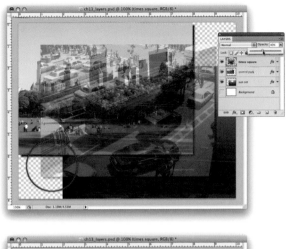

FIGURE 13.33   The differences between using Layer Opacity (top) and Fill Opacity (bottom).

FIGURE 13.34   The original image (left), the mask (middle), and the result of the
mask applied to the image (right).

A *mask* is a grayscale overlay on top of the layer image. The area on the mask that is white is opaque, and whatever is black is transparent. The varying levels of gray result in different opacities of the layer. The closer to black the shade of gray is, the more transparent it becomes.

Adding a Layer Mask

Follow these simple steps to add and modify a Layer Mask to an existing layer:

ON THE CD

1. In the Chapter 13 folder on the CD-ROM, open the file ch13_empire.psd.

   The image is of the Empire State Building (Figure 13.35). You will be eliminating the surrounding buildings and the sky. This can be done with a simple mask. It is first necessary to convert the background to a layer so that a mask can be applied.

FIGURE 13.35   In this exercise, you will mask out the building from the blue sky in the background.

2. Double-click the Background Layer to convert the background to a layer. Give it the name "empire state building" and click OK.

   Like double-clicking a layer to name, a background layer can be converted into a regular layer the same way. The New Layer dialog box appears. There are several options for this layer; however, you only need to name it.

3. With the layer now selected, choose Layer > Layer Mask > Reveal All (Figure 13.36).

FIGURE 13.36   The location of the Reveal All command, which adds a mask to a layer.

The Layer Mask has just been added. In Figure 13.37, the thumbnail for the layer is visible on the left with the mask thumbnail to its right.

FIGURE 13.37   The mask appears as an empty thumbnail next to the layer's preview thumbnail image.

Painting on a Mask Layer

To make areas of the mask transparent and opaque, you must use the Paint tools to apply colors to the mask:

1. Select the mask thumbnail by clicking on the second thumbnail.

To select the mask layer, so that it can be painted on, simply click on the mask thumbnail next to the image thumbnail in the layer.

The Brush

The Brush is used to apply color pixels to a layer, whether it be a normal layer, a Layer Mask, or so on. The color comes from the Foreground Color swatch. To use the Brush tool, follow these steps:

1. From the Tool panel select the Brush tool (B).

The Brush tool is the second icon in the second section of the Tools panel (Figure 13.38). When the Brush is activated (selected), the Options bar changes to its set of attributes. The second drop-down menu houses the brush sizes. There are several types of brushes from which you may choose. Because the images in this montage are 300 ppi, a larger brush will be needed.

FIGURE 13.38   The location of the Brush tool in the Tools panel.

2. Make sure the Options bar appears at the top of the screen (Figure 13.39, under the top menu). If it is not visible, choose Window > Options.

FIGURE 13.39   The Options bar for the Brush tool.

The Options bar will dynamically change according to which tool is selected. These options can be used to make accurate measurements or set specific properties for that tool. The Info panel will also reflect the current measurement for a selected item.

3. From the Options bar, set the brush to the Soft Round 200-pixel brush (Figure 13.40).

FIGURE 13.40   The location of the Soft Round 200 pixel brush is in the Brush Preset Picker in the Options bar.

To select the Soft Round 200 pixel brush, scroll down through the list of brushes until the number beneath the brush is 200.

4. Set the Foreground Color to white and the Background Color to black by clicking on the Default Foreground and Background Colors icon (Figure 13.41, left).

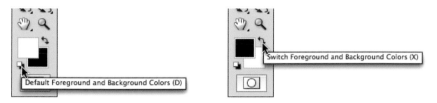

FIGURE 13.41   Click the icon shown to set the default colors to the swatches (left). Click the icon shown to switch the Foreground and Background colors (right).

The Default Foreground and Background Colors icon is to the lower left of the main color swatches in the Tools panel. Clicking on this icon resets the foreground color to white and the background color to black.

5. Set the Foreground color to black by clicking on the Switch Foreground and Background Colors icon (Figure 13.41, right).

The Switch Foreground and Background Colors icon is to the upper right of the main color swatches in the Tools panel. Clicking on this icon switches the foreground color to the background color and vice versa. In this case, black will become the foreground color and white will become the background color.

6. Paint on the sky on the left of the image with black to make it transparent (Figure 13.42, left).

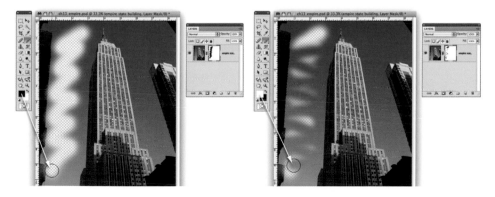

FIGURE 13.42   Paint with black while the mask thumbnail is selected to make pixels on that layer transparent (left). Paint with white to restore the opacity of the pixels (right).

Whatever is painted with black on the mask will become transparent without erasing the pixels. They are merely masked out. If a mistake is made, either undo the brush stroke or paint with white.

7. Click the Switch Foreground and Background Colors icon to switch the colors back, making white the Foreground Color.
8. Paint with white where you painted with black to see the sky restored to the layer (Figure 13.42, right).

Painting on the mask with white reveals the area that may have been covered up with black. Notice that the image returns as you paint over it.

9. From the Swatches panel (Window > Swatches), choose 50% Gray (Figure 13.43) and paint with it on the image.

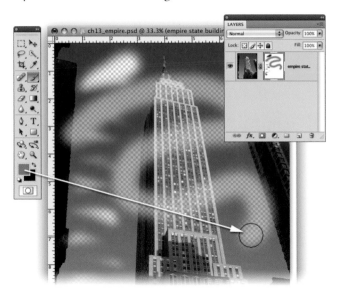

FIGURE 13.43   Painting with different shades of gray results in varying levels of opacity.

Painting with a varying percentage of gray results in a semitransparent image being revealed. Cool effects can be achieved by doing this. You will also notice that if you use a soft brush, the edges of the brush leave behind a gray "halo," allowing the original to show through slightly. To avoid that, choose a hard-edge brush.

Disabling a Mask

To temporarily turn off the effects of the mask of a certain layer, simply disable the mask. From the top menu, choose Layer > Layer Mask > Disable to disable the mask (Figure 13.44).

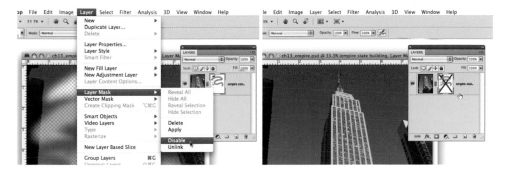

FIGURE 13.44   Disabling the mask allows you see the entire image, without deleting the mask. A giant red "X" covers the thumbnail to signify that it is disabled.

The mask thumbnail is still there, it just has a big red "X" through it, letting you know that it has been disabled. The mask has not been deleted, simply hidden.

To enable the mask, choose Layer > Layer Mask > Enable. The mask is then reapplied to the image. Editing the mask can continue if necessary.

Deleting a Mask

When it comes to removing a Layer Mask from a layer, there are two results that can come of it.

To delete a mask from a layer and leave the layer unaffected, choose Layer > Layer Mask > Delete. This removes the mask and leaves behind the entire image. The area that was once transparent is made opaque, and the mask is discarded.

If you want the Layer Mask to be removed but the layer to take on the transparent properties of the mask, choose Layer > Layer Mask > Apply. The mask is removed, but the pixels that were once transparent are now deleted, leaving only the object on the layer. Those discarded pixels cannot be retrieved.

Discard the current Layer Mask by selecting Layer > Remove Layer Mask > Discard.

Painting on a mask is often not the best way to make a mask. However, using a series of tools to select the areas can make the process easier.

Making Selections

Rather than painting the areas of layer transparent, you can use the Selection tools to select areas of an image and then apply the Layer Mask to that area. There are three major types of tools: Marquee tools, Lasso tools, and the Magic Wand tool.

Marquee Tools

The Marquee tools are used to create selections based on predefined areas: rectangles, ellipses, and single-pixel rows and columns. By default, the selection box is created from its corner. To use the Marquee tools, follow these steps:

1. In the Chapter 13 folder on the CD-ROM, open the file ch13_sunsetselect.psd.
2. Select the Rectangular Marquee tool (M) and simply click and drag a box around the setting sun (Figure 13.45).

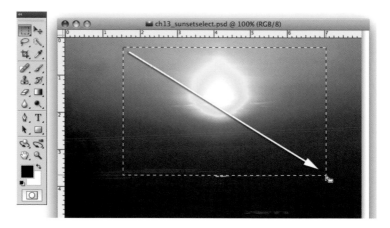

FIGURE 13.45   Use the Rectangular Marquee tool to draw boxes around areas you want to select.

Holding down the mouse button and dragging the mouse creates a selection border around the desired object. Hold down the Shift key during the initial selection to keep it constrained to a square (or a circle if using the Elliptical Marquee tool).

3. Select the Elliptical Marquee tool from the Tools panel by clicking and holding on the Rectangular Marquee tool until the submenu pops up and then choosing the second tool in the menu (Figure 13.46).

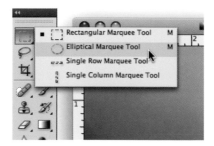

FIGURE 13.46   The Elliptical Marquee tool is hidden under the Rectangular Marquee tool.

The Elliptical Marquee tool lies in a submenu underneath the other marquee tools. Single Row and Single Column are also in that menu.

You can use the keyboard shortcut Shift + M to toggle between the Elliptical and Rectangular Marquee tools.

4. Click and drag from the upper left of the sun (as seen in Figure 13.47) and drag down and to the right until the border surrounds the yellow halo of the sun.

FIGURE 13.47   Start the ellipse from the top-left edge of the plate. By default, the Marquee tools draw from the corner.

The border surrounds the sun on all sides, but according to where you started to drag, the border may not be aligned correctly around the plate. Adding the Alt (PC) or Option (Mac) key to the command makes the tool draw from the center out.

5. With the Elliptical Marquee tool still selected, while holding the Alt or Option key, click in the center of the plate and drag outward (Figure 13.48).

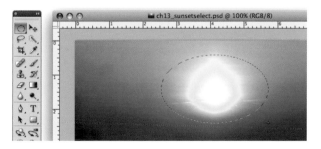

FIGURE 13.48   Using the Alt or Option key allows you to draw from the center out.

This makes selecting the area around the sun a little easier. Keep trying until you get the hang of it. After a selection has been made, you can use the same tool to move the border of the selection (Figure 13.49, left).

If the Move tool (V) is used, the area within the border will be moved (Figure 13.49, right).

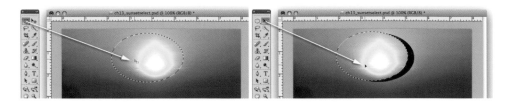

FIGURE 13.49   With the Marquee tool still active, use it to reposition the selection border (left), not the contents (right).

6. Deselect the selection by choosing Select > Deselect (PC: Ctrl + D; Mac: Command + D).

The Single Row and Single Column marquee tools select a one-pixel row or column when used. These tools do not have a wide variety of uses, but they can be used to sample single lines from an image to create a pattern or other element. Experiment with them at your leisure.

Options for the Marquee Tools

When the Marquee tools are selected, the Options bar changes to house the several different settings for this tool (Figure 13.50). The set of four icons on the left controls the relationship between the current selection and the next selection (Figure 13.51).

FIGURE 13.50   The Options bar changes to show the options for the Marquee tools when they are selected.

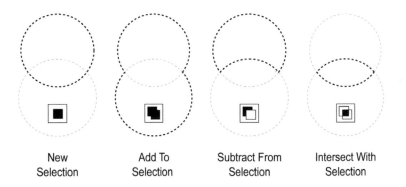

New
Selection

Add To
Selection

Subtract From
Selection

Intersect With
Selection

FIGURE 13.51   There are four different selection options that can be made using the Options bar when using the Marquee tool.

Within the Options bar there are several options that can be set before a selection is made with the Marquee tool.

New Selection: By default, if you draw one border and then draw a second, the first disappears. Each click-and-drag results in a new selection.

Add to Selection: The area of the next selection is added to the current selection.

Subtract from Selection: The area of the next selection is subtracted from the current selection.

Intersect with Selection: The area that the first and second selection share (in which they overlap) is a result of this action.

Feather: When a pixel number is entered into this field, the resulting selection's edges are blurred to give the selection a soft edge (Figure 13.52). When working with high-resolution images, this number needs to be higher than when using this setting for a low-resolution graphic.

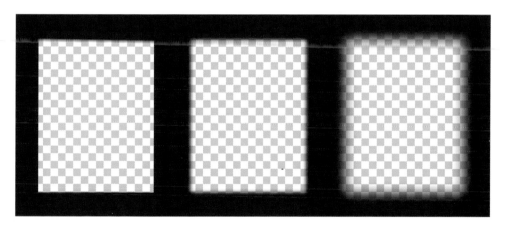

FIGURE 13.52   The Feather option gives a blurred edge to selections that are made.

Anti-Aliased: When this box is checked, the jagged edges of the selection are blurred into the background image to keep from getting a hard line when the selection is moved, deleted, or otherwise modified (Figure 13.53).

Style: This drop-down menu contains the following settings as they relate to this tool:

- **Normal:** Your dragging determines the size of the selection.
- **Fixed Ratio:** This is a set height-to-width ratio. If you want to make a selection based on the proportion of your screen, then 4 would be in the width and 3 in the height, giving you a ratio of 4:3.
- **Fixed Size:** This is an absolute pixel measurement. You specify the border's height and width.

FIGURE 13.53   When the Anti-Aliased button is unchecked, the resulting selections have a hard edge (top) when compared to selections made when it is checked (bottom).

Lasso Tools

There are three Lasso tools to choose from: the Lasso tool, the Polygonal Lasso tool, and the Magnetic Lasso tool (Figure 13.54).

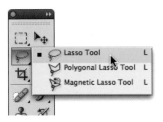

FIGURE 13.54   The Lasso tools.

The Lasso tool is the easiest of the three to use. The tip of the lasso is the icon's hot-point (for example, center). To use the Lasso tool, click and drag around the edge of the object. Whatever is contained within the border is selected (Figure 13.55). Follow these steps:

ON THE CD

1. In the Chapter 13 folder on the CD-ROM, open the file named ch13_empire-lasso.psd and select the Lasso tool from the Tools panel.
2. Place the point of the Lasso tool along the bottom-left edge of the building (Figure 13.56).
3. With the mouse button pressed, drag the lasso up the side of the building.
4. Continue around the building until you come back to the point of origin. Release the mouse button to complete the selection.

FIGURE 13.55   Selections that are made with the Lasso tool are made freehand; the selection is made wherever you draw.

FIGURE 13.56   Place the Lasso tool along the left edge of the plate as shown and then follow along the edges of the object that you would like to select.

You have to be very steady when using the Lasso tool. If at any time you make a mistake, simply click off to the side to delete the selection. It takes patience and a steady hand to master this tool.

The Polygonal Lasso tool works a little differently than the Lasso tool. Whereas the Lasso tool traces using a path, the Polygonal Lasso tool makes selections based on polygons (points and lines). Figure 13.57 shows the tool in action. In this particular image, the Polygonal Lasso will be extremely helpful. The Lasso tool can dynamically change to the Polygonal Lasso tool and back when you hold down the Alt (PC) or Option (Mac) key when using the Lasso tool.

FIGURE 13.57   The Polygonal Lasso tool draws using the point-and-click method for straight lines selections.

You create the path by moving the tool and clicking where you want that particular line to go. Click on the start of the path or double-click to snap the path closed.

The Magnetic Lasso Tool

The Magnetic Lasso tool calculates the difference in the contrast of light and dark pixels by automatically creating a selection between the two (Figure 13.58, right). As the tool travels around the edge of these objects, it automatically places insertion points along the path of the selection. There is no real need to remain accurate as the software does all the work. Follow these steps to use the Magnetic Lasso tool:

FIGURE 13.58   The Magnetic Lasso tool differentiates between the light and dark pixels to create its path.

1. Select the Magnetic Lasso tool (L) from the Tools panel by selecting the third icon under the Lasso tool (Figure 13.58, left).

2. Place the tip of the Magnetic Lasso tool along the same edge of the building and, while holding down the mouse button, move the tool to the right, roughly along the same path as the edge.

Notice how the selection path snaps in-between the dark pixels of the background and the light pixels of the plate. Also notice the inserted points along the path of the selection. Continue to complete the selection by going around the building. As you reach the top part of the building, go slowly. You can click the mouse to set points rather than let them set themselves. Follow along the path between the sky and the tower. When the tip of the tool reaches the first inserted point, a small circle will appear next to the tip (Figure 13.59). This signifies the completion of the path. Double-click the mouse to complete the path.

FIGURE 13.59   When the path is closed, a small circle will appear to the lower right of the tool.

With the path completed, it is replaced with the selection (marching ants) border.

Feathering

A Feather can be set before the selection is made by setting the number in the Options bar, or after the fact by choosing the command from the top menu. You can smooth hard edges that occur at the edges of a selection. The higher the number, the higher the loss of detail. To use the Feather tool, follow these steps:

1. From the top menu, choose Select > Feather. Set the Feather to 5 and click OK.

The Feather dialog box appears. Set the desired number for the feathering in the field and click OK.

2. Hide the selection by choosing View > Extras (PC: Ctrl + H; Mac: Command + H).

This operation hides the border from view. However, the object is still selected.

3. Choose Edit > Cut (PC: Ctrl + X; Mac: Command + X).

The selected area is cut from the document and placed in the clipboard (Figure 13.60). Notice that the edge of the selection is soft, not jagged. This is the result of the feathering.

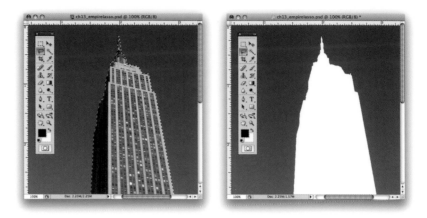

FIGURE 13.60   The selection is removed from the file, leaving behind a soft edge.

4. Undo the last action to restore the cut portion of the image.
5. Choose Select > Deselect to clear the selection.

Magnetic Lasso Options Bar

The options for the Magnetic Lasso tool appear in the Options bar. The three most important options are Width, Edge Contrast, and Frequency (Figure 13.61). The Width option tells the tool how many pixels around the tip it is allowed to select when creating the path. The Edge Contrast is the percentage of light and dark pixels that control the lasso's sensitivity. A high number chooses edges that contrast sharply, whereas a lower number chooses the lower-contrast edges. The Frequency is the number of insertion points the lasso places along the paths. Together, these three options can make selecting objects very easy.

FIGURE 13.61   The Options bar for the Magnetic Lasso tool.

Magic Wand Tool

The Magic Wand tool selects similar colors that are adjacent to the selected pixel. For example, if you click on a light-colored pixel, all the other adjacent consistently light-colored pixels will be selected.

The number of pixels selected is controlled by the Tolerance, which is located in the Options bar (Figure 13.62). The higher the number, the more pixels will be included in the selection. Press the Shift key when clicking to add more pixels to the selection. In Figure 13.62, the selection made from the wand in the image on the left had a Tolerance of 32. Notice how the blue in the sky near the bottom of the image is darker than the rest of the sky. Those pixels fell outside the Tolerance set. With the Tolerance set to 64 in the image on the right, more pixels are selected. You can increase the inclusion of pixels that fall within the tolerance range specified by using Select > Grow.

Finding the Magic Wand Tool

In versions CS3 and CS4 the Magic Wand tool is hidden underneath the Quick Selection tool in the Tools panel. To select the Magic Wand tool, click and hold on the Quick Selection tool until the icon for the Magic Wand tool appears.

The Quick Selection tool allows you to paint a selection using an adjustable round-tip brush. As you "paint" with it, the selection expands to include the similar colors within the selection.

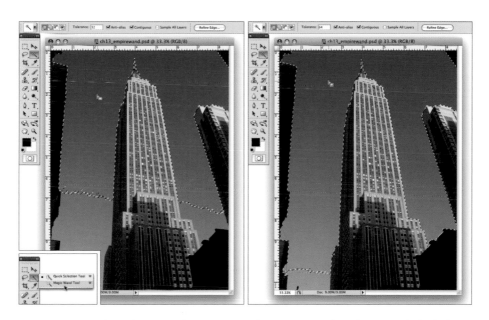

FIGURE 13.62   The Tolerance in these images is different. Notice how the one with the higher Tolerance (right) includes more pixels in the selection.

Using Selections and Masks Together

Earlier in the chapter, a Layer Mask was attached to a layer first and then painted on to create the transparent and opaque areas. Although this is an easy way to do it, there is another way that may be a little more accurate.

Converting a Selection into a Mask

After a selection is made using the Selection tools, it is easy to convert that selection into a mask.

Using the Magic Wand tool makes selecting the building a snap. Making the outside area transparent is even easier.

ON THE CD

1. In the Chapter 13 folder on the CD-ROM, open the file named ch13_empire-wand.psd.
2. Double-click the Background layer to change it to a normal layer.
3. Using the Magic Wand tool (W), set the Tolerance to 32 and click on the sky near the top of the image. About 50% of the sky is selected. Select the rest of the pixels by choosing Select > Grow two times.

Using Grow twice traps those last remaining pixels from the sky while leaving the buildings alone (Figure 13.63, left).

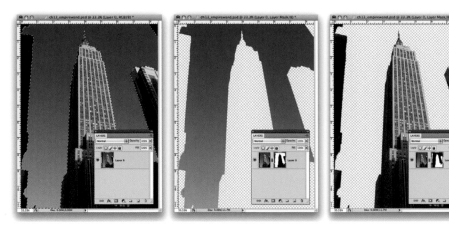

FIGURE 13.63   The selection of the sky (left). The result of the Reveal Selection command (middle). The result of the Hide Selection command (right).

4. With the selection active, choose Layer > Layer Mask > Reveal Selection.

A mask is created. and the area that was outside the selection has been made transparent (Figure 13.63, middle). Now you need to hide the pixels that have been selected.

5. Choose Edit > Undo Add Layer Mask.

The mask that was just created will be removed from the layer, and the selection made with the Wand and Grow commands will become active again.

6. With the selection active, choose Layer > Layer Mask > Hide Selection.

Rather than select the building, as we did with the Lasso Tools, using the Magic Wand made quick work of the sky.

7. Use the Brush tool to clean up the leftover pixels that may have not been selected and also to remove the other buildings on the left and the right. Keep in mind that if you make a mistake in painting the mask, use the Brush with White to bring the pixels back.

If you had chosen Hide Selection instead, the area within the selection would have become transparent (Figure 13.63, right).

Transformation Tools

As in Illustrator, Photoshop has its own set of Transformation tools. Transformations such as Scale and Rotate can either be performed on certain selections or entire layers.

Flipping Layers

Sometimes, objects fit into the design better when they are flipped (reflected across an axis). Layers can be flipped horizontally (left and right) or vertically (top and bottom) (Figure 13.64).

FIGURE 13.64   An image (left) can be flipped horizontally (middle) or vertically (right).

To flip an object, follow these steps:

1. From the Chapter 13 folder on the CD-ROM, open file ch13_transform.psd.

In the file, there are several layers. In this exercise, you will flip the empire state building layer and place it on the right side of the page.

2. Select the empire state building layer to activate the layer.
3. From the top menu, choose Edit > Transform > Flip Horizontally.

The empire state building layer flips across its y-axis. It doesn't matter that it was flipped; there are no visual clues that would even cause suspicion. But beware of flipping images that contain words, symbols, signs, tags, and so on. Things that appear unusual tend to jump out at you first and that could be very bad.

Move the selected layer over to the right side of the document.

Scale

Some images that you prepare will be a little large and may need to be scaled down:

1. Using the same file, unhide the clouds layer and select it.

Show the layer above by clicking on the empty square in the clouds layer. Then select the layer by clicking on it. Make sure you select the thumbnail.

2. From the top menu, choose Edit > Transform > Scale.

There is no shortcut specifically for the Scale command. By choosing it from the Edit menu, a bounding box appears around the contents of the layer. When the box appears, notice that the Tool Box Options appear at the top of the screen.

3. Place the mouse over a corner of the bounding box and, while holding down the Shift key, move the handle inward (Figure 13.65).

The bounding box is larger than the image. Use the Zoom tool (Z) to zoom in and out (hold Alt or Option to toggle it) so that you can see the entire bounding box (Figure 13.66). Holding down the Shift key as you scale the image constrains the height and width of the scale, just as it has in other operations.

4. Scale the image until the measurement in the width and height reads approximately 75% (Figure 13.67).

FIGURE 13.65   Using the Shift key keeps the file proportioned correctly.
The addition of the Alt or Options key will allow you to scale from the center out.

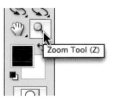

FIGURE 13.66   The location of the Zoom tool in the Tools panel.

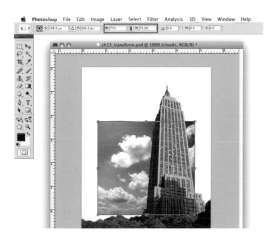

FIGURE 13.67   Use the Info panel or the Options bar to check the current percentage of the scale.

There are two buttons at the end of the Options bar; they are Cancel (Esc) and Commit (PC: Enter; Mac: Return; Figure 13.68).

FIGURE 13.68 The Cancel and Commit buttons are on the far right of the Options bar.

By clicking on the Commit button, the transformation is set. If the change is not what you wanted, click on the Cancel button. Nothing is permanent until either the Cancel or Commit buttons are clicked.

5. Click on the Commit button to set the transformation.

Depending on the speed of your computer's processor and the size of the file, Photoshop renders the transformation, rewriting the pixels in the layer to match the change.

6. Undo the transformation by selecting Edit > Undo Free Transform to reset the image.
7. Choose Edit > Transform > Scale again.

Rather than dragging the handles of the bounding box, the percentage of the Scale can be typed manually into the Options bar.

8. Click on the link symbol in-between the Width and Height fields of the Options bar (Figure 13.69).

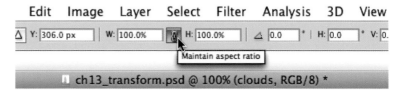

FIGURE 13.69 Click the link symbol to maintain the aspect ratio of the scale.

Clicking this symbol maintains the aspect ratio of the Scale. If you type one number into the width, that same measurement will be reflected in the height field.

9. Type 90 into the width field (Figure 13.70).

By typing exact numbers into this box, you can gauge the size of the image a little better. Change the number over and over again until the size is right.

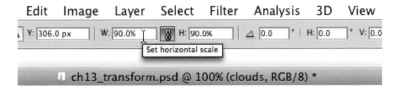

FIGURE 13.70   Set the scale width to 90%. The scale height will match it.

10. Move the image up near the top, behind the contents of the empire state building layer as shown in Figure 13.71.
11. Click on the Commit button to set the new scale.

FIGURE 13.71   Position the image before committing to the transformation.

Rotate

To use the Rotate command, the steps are similar to those for using the Scale command:

1. Select the empire state building layer and choose Edit > Transform > Rotate.
2. Mouse over the lower left handle and click and drag clockwise until the spire on the Empire State Building on the left is pointing straight up (Figure 13.72).
3. Click on the Commit button to set the transform.

You can also type a number into the Angle field of the Options bar to rotate an object.

FIGURE 13.72   Rotate the image so that the spire of the tower is a little more to the right.

There is a really simple shortcut called the Free Transform command (PC: Ctrl + T; Mac: Command + T) that will allow you to do several different transformations at once.

4. Undo the last transform by choosing Edit > Undo Free Transform.
5. From the top menu, choose Edit > Free Transform.

Using the handles, scale the image as usual.

Rotate the image by placing the cursor just outside of one of the handles until the rounded arrow appears, and then click and drag to rotate the object.

You may also type the measurements into the Options bar. Then click on the Commit button to confirm the transformation.

Notice that there was no selection made prior to doing the transformations. If a layer is selected, then the entire contents of the layer are affected. If an area of the layer is selected, it can be transformed separately from the rest of the contents of the layer. That information is "hovering" over existing pixels. However, when the Commit button is clicked, the pixels are placed on top of those pixels.

Continue the process of making selections, applying masks, and transforming the objects to create your montage. Feel free to experiment with all the other tools and menus and see what else you can do with this robust program.

Using Illustrator with Photoshop

Photoshop and Illustrator integrate really well with each other. Earlier in the book, you placed images created from Photoshop into Illustrator to trace. The paths that you create in Illustrator can be used in Photoshop as either vector or bitmap elements. Different methods of integration yield very different results.

There are three simple methods for bringing Illustrator files into Photoshop:

- Open the Illustrator file directly into Photoshop.
- Copy and paste elements from Illustrator to Photoshop.
- Drag and drop elements between both programs.

Opening Illustrator Files Directly with Photoshop

When you open an Illustrator (.ai) file in Photoshop, the resulting image is always a bitmap (pixel-based) version of the artwork and text.

ON THE CD

1. In Photoshop CS4, choose File > Open.
2. Navigate to the Chapter 13 folder. Select liberty.ai from the list (Figure 13.73). Click Open.

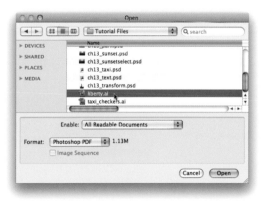

FIGURE 13.73   The Open Dialog box in Photoshop allows you to choose .ai files as well as .psd files.

3. In the Import PDF dialog box (Figure 13.74), give your file a name. Set the Crop To to Bounding Box. Set the Resolution to 300 ppi. Set the Mode to RGB with a Bit Depth of 8 bit and make sure that Anti-aliased is checked. Click OK.

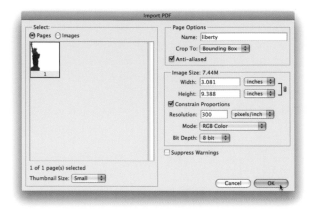

FIGURE 13.74   The Import PDF dialog box allows you to choose
from various settings to control your image.

With these options set, the resulting image will have the dimensions that it had in Illustrator; however, instead of being vector, it is a 300 dpi, RGB, smooth image in a document the same size as its outer dimension (Figure 13.75, left).

FIGURE 13.75   The different result of choosing Bounding Box (left) and Media Box (right)
when setting the Crop To option.

4. Close the file and reopen it. This time set the Crop to Media Box.

With the Crop option set to Media Box, instead of opening in a window as wide and high as the object, the window is the size of the document that it was created in (Figure 13.75, right). In this case, the paths were created on a letter-sized Artboard. When you open an Illustrator file this way, if you set the Crop to Bounding Box, some of the pixels that touch the edge of the file are often missing or look flat. When opened in the Media Box format, there is space around the object for the program to anti-alias the edge pixels.

Copy and Pasting Elements Between the Programs

Another way to move elements from Illustrator to Photoshop is as simple as copying and pasting. This method results in a few different types of layers within Photoshop CS4.

1. Launch both Illustrator CS4 and Photoshop CS4.

2. In Illustrator CS4, open the file named taxi_checkers.ai in the Chapter 13 folder.
3. Select all the shapes on the Artboard by choosing Select > All (PC: Ctrl + A; Mac: Command + A), and copy them to the clipboard by choosing Edit > Copy (PC: Ctrl + C; Mac: Command + C) (Figure 13.76).

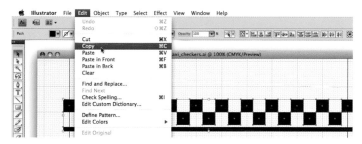

FIGURE 13.76   Copy the shapes from Illustrator to the clipboard.

4. Change over to Photoshop CS4 and open the file ch13_taxi.psd in the Chapter 13 folder.
5. In Photoshop, choose Edit > Paste (PC: Ctrl + V; Mac: Command + V) to place the elements into Photoshop.

    The Paste dialog box will appear with four options (Figure 13.77):

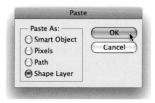

FIGURE 13.77   The Paste dialog box.

Smart Object: The elements are pasted as a special Vector Smart Object, which can be scaled, transformed, and moved without degrading the image. This layer is editable through Illustrator by choosing the Edit Object in the options menu.

Pixels: This option pastes the element as pixels that can be initially scaled, transformed, and moved before it is set and rasterized onto a layer. Scaling and rotating after it has been set can degrade the image.

Path: This option pastes the elements as paths that can be edited by the Pen tools within Photoshop.

Shape Layer: The elements are pasted into a shape layer that contains a path filled with the foreground color.

6. In the Paste dialog box, choose Shape Layer.

The new artwork appears in a layer named Shape 1 (Figure 13.78). By making the artwork a Shape Layer, you can resize and reposition it as many times as you want with no degrading of the image.

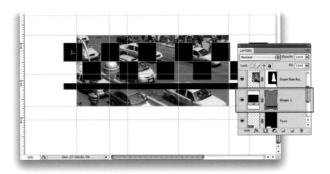

FIGURE 13.78   A new Shape Layer is created with the artwork from Illustrator.

7. Scale the selection to about 40% using the Options bar, move the selection around, and place it as shown in Figure 13.79.

FIGURE 13.79   Scale and position the new artwork as shown.

8. Once it is in position, click the Confirm button in the Options bar or double-click the selection to set it.
9. Double-click the color swatch on the Shapes layer to change the color of the shapes (Figure 13.80).

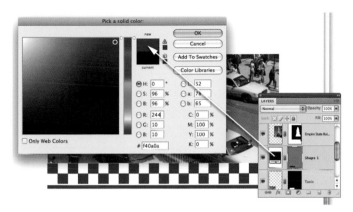

FIGURE 13.80   You can change the color of a Shape Layer by simply double-clicking on the color swatch in the layer.

Dragging and Dropping Elements Between Programs

The shortest distance between two points is a straight line. The one-click method of moving elements back and forth between the two programs is simply dragging and dropping elements between two open windows from the different programs.

1. Revert the ch13_taxi.psd file back to its original state by choosing File > Revert.
2. Position the windows of both the ch13_taxi.psd and the taxi_checkers.ai file so that you can see both of them.

Viewing Two Programs at Once

It is important that you are able to see both windows. This technique is easier to do on the Macintosh operating system because the applications are not confined to their own window, however, these same applications on the PC are.

If you are working on a computer with Windows you will need to scale down the window that your application is in as much as you can so that you can see both programs.

3. In the Illustrator file, select all the shapes and drag them over into the open Photoshop window (Figure 13.81).
4. Resize the new element the same way that you did in the last example.

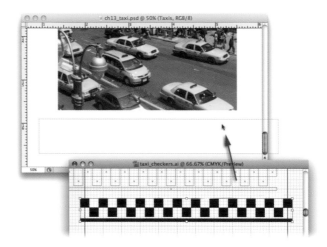

FIGURE 13.81 Drag and drop the artwork from one application to the other.

When you drag and drop elements from Illustrator to Photoshop, it converts the shapes into a single Vector Smart Object (Figure 13.82). Vector Smart Objects are Photoshop layers that can be edited in Illustrator and when saved, the layer in Photoshop is updated. For a Vector Smart Object to be used properly, the edited file must be saved in the same location.

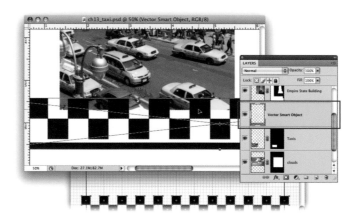

FIGURE 13.82 Paste the contents of the clipboard as a Vector Smart Object.

5. Edit the new Vector Smart Object by either right-clicking on the vector layer and choosing Edit Content or choosing it from the Layer panel's Options menu (Figure 13.83).

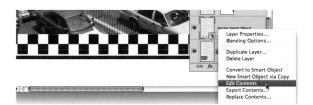

FIGURE 13.83   You can choose Edit Content from the Layer's Option menu or choose it from the right-click submenu.

The artwork opens into its own editable window in Illustrator (Figure 13.84).

FIGURE 13.84   You can edit Vector Smart Objects in Illustrator and then return them to Photoshop.

6. When you are done editing the object in Illustrator, choose File > Save to save the change and update the Photoshop file.

These methods barely scratch the surface of how Photoshop and Illustrator talk with each other. Consult the Help files or your software manual for more information.

Layer Blending Modes

Built into Photoshop are dozens of effects that you can use to enhance color, lines, shape, texture, and pattern. The simplest of these effects are the Blend Modes. To understand the nature of the Blend Modes, some key terms need to be defined:

- The *base color* is the original color on the layer.
- The *blend color* is the color being applied with the layer, painting, or editing tool.
- The *result color* is the color resulting from the base color and the blend color.

At first glance, this might be a little difficult to understand, but with experimentation, you will come to understand how these modes work.

Although there are dozens of Blend Modes, we will concentrate on are the Blend Modes associated with Layer and the Layer panel: Darken, Multiply, Screen, Soft Light, and Hard Light. Study the images in Figure 13.85 as you read the following descriptions.

Darken: This mode looks at the color on the base layer and the blend layer and chooses the darker color. Pixels that are lighter are replaced with the darker ones. There is no real blending, just selection.

Multiply: The base color and the blend color are multiplied. The resulting color will always end up darker. Black plus any color yields black. White plus any color leaves the color unchanged. Lighter colors will have less effect on pixels, whereas darker colors will have more effect.

Screen: The base color and the blend color are multiplied by their inverses. The resulting color will always be lighter. It has the opposite effect of Multiply.

Soft Light: If the blend color being applied is lighter than middle gray (50%), the color appears as if it were dodged (lightened). If the color that is applied is darker than middle gray (50%), then the result is darker.

Hard Light: If the blend color being applied is lighter than middle gray (50%), then the Screen Mode is applied to it. If the color that is applied is darker than middle gray (50%), then the result is the Darken Mode.

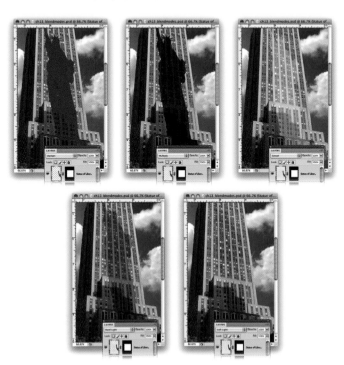

FIGURE 13.85   Blend Modes applied to the shadow layer: (clockwise from top left) Darken, Multiply, Screen, Hard Light, and Soft Light.

The goal here is to have the shadow of the Statue of Liberty blend into the side of the Empire State Building.

1. Open the image ch13_blendmodes.psd from the Chapter 13 folder on the CD-ROM. Resize the window so that you are focused on the building and the shadow.
2. Select the Statue of Liberty Shadow layer and experiment with the Blending Modes (Figure 13.86) and see how the blend layer (Statue of Liberty Shadow) and the base layer (Empire State Building) react in each mode.

FIGURE 13.86   The location of the Blend Modes for layers.

3. Set the Blend Mode of the Statue of Liberty Shadow layer to Multiply.
4. Set the Opacity of the Statue of Liberty Shadow layer to 50% (Figure 13.87).

FIGURE 13.87   Set the Opacity of the shadow layer to 50% to help the shadow become a little more believable.

Figure 13.88 shows the entire step-by-step process of making the shadow blend into the building, the trees, and the park.

Now that the shadow blends in to the side of the building, it still seems to be a little too sharp. Using filters, you can soften the shadow and increase the believability.

FIGURE 13.88 Create and color the shadow layer (left), set the Blend Mode to Multiply (middle), and set the Opacity to 50% (right).

Filters

Filters allow you the power to change the look of your designs, imagery, and photographs. Simple filters help you retouch and clean up scans and photographs. Other filters can change your photographic images into paintings, drawings, relief sculptures, mosaic tiles, and so on. Extreme filters can wildly change the appearance of your work by using blurs, ripples, twists, and other distortions.

All of the filters are located in the Filter menu. (Figure 13.89).

Blur

Blur filters can be applied to an entire image or just a selection. They are widely used to retouch photographs and help remove specks and noise. A blur filter averages the pixels next to hard edges to create a smooth transition between shapes. This is precisely what we need to do with the shadow on the side of the building from the previous exercise.

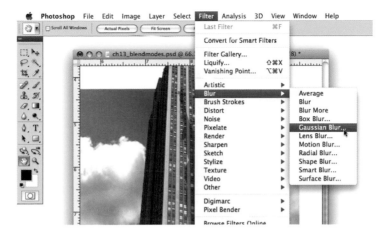

FIGURE 13.89   The Blur filters are located in the Filter menu.

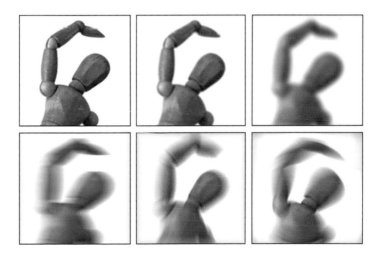

FIGURE 13.90   Blur filters (clockwise from top left): No Blur, Blur More, Gaussian Blur, Radial Blur (Spin), Radial Blur (Zoom), and Motion Blur.

Before you dive into the Blur filters, here is a brief description of some of the Blur filters that are available. Refer to Figure 13.90 as a guide as you read the descriptions.

Blur and Blur More: This simple filter helps eliminate noise where color transitions occur. The normal Blur filter is the weakest of the Blur filters. More Blur is four times stronger. There are no user options with these filters. Simply select the filter to apply it.

Gaussian Blur: This filter is an image-softening effect that uses a Gaussian (or Bell) Curve to generate a hazy effect. This is the most popular of the Blurs because it has user-controlled options.

Motion Blur: This filter creates a blur according to a certain direction (from 360° to -360°) and has an intensity setting that ranges from 1 to 999. It simulates an image of a moving object.

Radial Blur (Zoom or Spin): Simulates a blur of a zooming or spinning camera. The Zoom blur reads along radial lines, whereas the Spin follows concentric lines. There are settings within the filter to control its quality and value. With this filter, you must choose the center of the blur by moving the origin point around the image.

To use the blur tools, follow these steps:

ON THE CD

1. Open the image ch13_filters.psd from the Chapter 13 folder on the CD-ROM. Select the Statue of Liberty Shadow layer.
2. Choose Filter > Gaussian Blur.

The Gaussian Blur dialog box opens. The layer is shown by itself in the preview window against a transparent background so that you can see the full effect of the blur. There is only one slider to control the radius of the blur. Refer to Figure 13.91 for the following few steps.

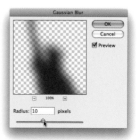

FIGURE 13.91   The Gaussian Blur dialog box with the Radius set to 0.5, 5, and 10.

3. Set the Radius to 0.5 for a slight blur.

The blur is hardly noticeable at the lowest setting.

4. Drag the slider to set the Radius to 5 for a medium blur or 10 for a large blur.

As you drag the slider into the higher numbers, you will see the blur get larger and more distorted. The distortion can be so great that the image becomes unrecognizable.

5. Set the Radius to 2 for the shadow blur (Figure 13.92). Click OK.

FIGURE 13.92   Set the Radius to 2 to get the blur effect that feels comfortable for the image.

With the Gaussian Blur set to a Radius of 2, the shadow loses its hard edge and successfully blends into the building and trees.

Noise

The Noise filters remove or add noise (pixels that have a random color). Noise filters can help create unique textures or remove pixels from trouble spots in an image such as dust and scratches.

There are three important filters in the category:

Add Noise: This filter applies random pixels of varying color levels to an image. The effect is the same as shooting photographs on high-speed film. There are two options for distribution within the dialog box. Uniform distributes the color values using a subtle effect. Gaussian distributes them using a bell-shaped curve to create a more speckled effect. The Monochromatic option applies the filter without changing the color of the image.

Despeckle: This filter finds the edges in the image where considerable color changes happen and blurs everything within the selection except the edges. It removes the noise while keeping the details intact.

Dust & Scratches: This filter reduces the noise by changing unrelated pixels and finding a balance between sharpening the image and hiding the defects that it locates. The Radius and Threshold settings help to control the amount of sharpening and change. It is commonly used to remove the dust and scratches from photographs; thus the name of the filter.

Add Noise Filter

To use the Add Noise Filter, follow these steps:

1. With the file ch13_filters.psd still open and active, select the NYC layer.

A Design Hint

The type and gradient were created in Illustrator and brought over separately into Photoshop. The "NYC" type was rotated and converted into a selection (right-click the thumbnail icon in the layer and choose Select Layer Transparency from the pop-up menu) and then became a mask for the gradient of colors taken from the sunset photograph.

2. Click on the chain icon between the layer thumbnail and the mask thumbnail to unlink the layer and mask. Disable the Layer Mask by right-clicking the mask thumbnail and choose Disable Layer Mask or choose Layer > Layer Mask > Disable (Figure 13.93).

FIGURE 13.93 Unlink the thumbnails (left) and disable the mask (middle). The red X on the mask thumbnail is a visual clue that the mask in disabled.

By unlinking the thumbnails and disabling the Layer Mask, the gradient can be modified independently from the mask. The mask and linking will be restored after the filters have been applied.

3. Click on the layer thumbnail to select the paint portion of the layer. With the thumbnail selected, you can apply filters to the gradient square.
4. Open the Add Noise filter by choosing Filter > Noise > Add Noise.
5. In the Add Noise dialog box, set the Amount to 30, the Distribution to Uniform, and uncheck the Monochromatic box (Figure 13.94, left). Click OK.

These settings pepper the gradient with pixels of uniformed color creating a speckled look that will be smoothed with a Motion Blur.

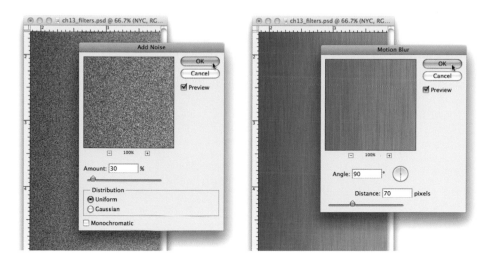

FIGURE 13.94   The Add Noise dialog box (left). The Motion Blur dialog box (right).

6. Choose Filter > Blur > Motion Blur. In the Motion Blur dialog box, set the Angle to 90° and the Distance to 70 pixels (Figure 13.94, right). Click OK.

This filter, when combined with the Noise filter, creates a brushed metal look that will work nicely in the NYC mask. Combining filters is a great way to get unique effects.

7. Enable the Layer Mask by choosing Layer > Layer Mask > Enable and link the layer thumbnail by clicking the space between the layer and mask thumbnails (Figure 13.95).

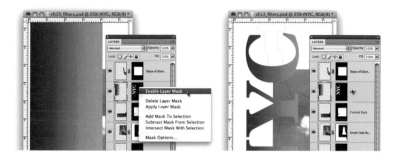

FIGURE 13.95   Enable the mask (left) and relink the two thumbnails (right) to make the NYC graphic appear whole again.

Dust & Scratches Filter

The cloud image is quite grainy, but you can use the Dust & Scratches filter to remove that graininess.

1. Select the Clouds layer in the ch13_filters.psd file.
2. Unlink the thumbnails and disable the Layer Mask.

Remember that this is done to ensure the integrity of the Layer Mask. Follow the directions from the previous example if you need to.

3. Choose Filter > Noise > Dust & Scratches.
4. Set the Radius to 5 and the Threshold to 5 (Figure 13.96). Click OK.

FIGURE 13.96   The Dust & Scratches dialog box.

You can uncheck the Preview box so that you can see the original image and compare it to the preview shown in the dialog box. Notice how the clouds seem fluffier and the pixelated look of the sky is gone. The clouds seem almost impressionistic.

5. Enable the Layer Mask and link the thumbnails.

With the cloud layer intact again, zoom out and take a look at the full image after the filters have been applied. It is starting to come together (Figure 13.97).

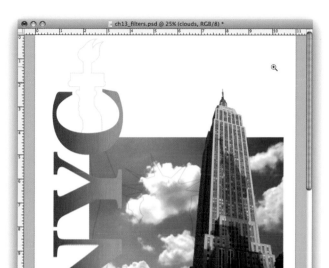

FIGURE 13.97   The montage after having several filters applied to it.

Sharpen and Unsharp Mask Filters

Sharpening enhances the edge of an image. Almost all digital photographs, whether from a camera or from your scanner, could benefit from sharpening. Sharpening varies depending on the quality of your scanner and digital camera. With today's technology, the digital process is becoming better and the quality of the image is quickly getting on par with film cameras. The greater the number of pixels in the image, the better the quality will be. Still, nothing is perfect. At least we have the Sharpen filters.

Sharpening increases the contrast of the image and often clips some highlights and shadows. If there is noise in the image, remove the noise (with the filters discussed in the previous section) so that it doesn't get worse.

It is easy to oversharpen an image. Be careful and alert as you sharpen images. Not every Sharpen filter needs to be used on every image. Use this as a basic guide for knowing when to use the various Sharpening filters.

The Sharpen, Sharpen Edges, and Sharpen More filters do not have any options and are automatic. Figure 13.98 shows examples of an image with each filter applied to it. Notice that the only one that really improved was the image that was merely sharpened using the Sharpen filter (top right). You can see that the fence in the lower left of the image is sharper and more defined, but in the other images, the edges are oversharp, and it distracts from the image.

FIGURE 13.98   Clockwise from top left: Original image, Sharpen filter, Sharpen More filter, and the Sharpen Edges filter.

The Unsharp Mask filter gives you the most control of any of the Sharpening filters:

1. Using the ch13_filters.psd from the previous exercises, use the scroll bars of the Hand tool (H) to focus on the image of the taxis in the lower-left corner.
2. Select the Taxis layer in the Layers panel.
3. Choose Filter > Sharpen > Unsharp Mask.
4. Make sure the Preview box is checked.

Use the Preview box to look around the image. Use the + and – buttons to zoom in and out.

5. Set the Amount to 175, the Radius to 1.5, and the Threshold to 45 (Figure 13.99). Click OK.

The *Radius* determines the number of pixels around the edge pixels that affect sharpening. A value of between 1 and 2 is recommended for the best results. A lower value sharpens the edge pixels, whereas a higher number sharpens a greater number. You won't really see it on-screen, but you will in the printed piece.

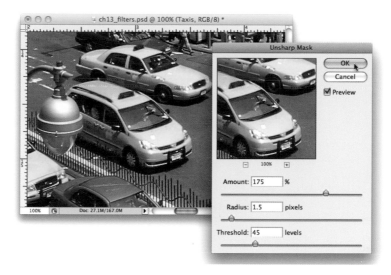

FIGURE 13.99 The Unsharp Mask dialog box.

The *Amount* controls the contrast of the pixel affected. If you have a high-resolution image, use a number between 100% and 200%.

The *Threshold* controls how different the sharpened pixels are from each other before they can be considered edge pixels. If the Threshold is set to 0, it will sharpen all the pixels in the image.

Using Text in Photoshop

The last thing that needs to be done to complete this design is to insert a paragraph of text that describes the topic (much like what was done in the Type Poster project in Chapter 12).

The Type tool (T) works exactly the same way in Photoshop as it does in Illustrator. Follow these simple directions to add a text box to the design:

ON THE CD

1. Open the file named ch13_text.psd in the Chapter 13 folder on the CD-ROM.
2. Open the Character panel by choosing Window > Characters.
3. Choose the Horizontal Type tool (T) from the Tools panel.
4. Create a text box using the guides shown in Figure 13.100.
5. Type some text in the text area. Use Figure 13.101 as a guide.
6. Highlight all the text within the box using the Horizontal Type tool.
7. In the Character panel, change the Font Family, Font Style, Font Size, and Leading to fit the text box.

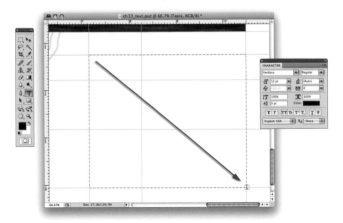

FIGURE 13.100   Create a text box in the lower-right corner of the design by clicking at the upper left and dragging down and to right with the mouse.

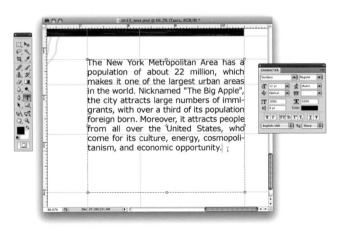

FIGURE 13.101   After the text box is made, type some text into it.

In this example, the Font Family is Univers, and the Font Style is 47 Light Condensed. The font size is 13 points, and the leading is 27 points. With those values and choices, the text fits in the box perfectly (Figure 13.102). You probably do not have the same fonts, so use your best judgment when choosing the font and size.

8. With the Move tool (V) selected, click on the text field and move it to the left .5 inch so that it is centered under the Empire State Building (Figure 13.103).

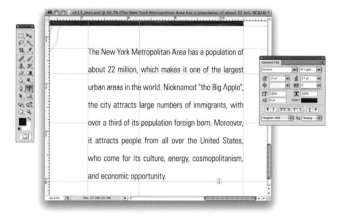

FIGURE 13.102   The new values help to make the text fit the box.

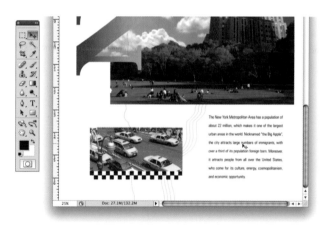

FIGURE 13.103   Move the text over as shown here.

Finishing Up the Design

As has been said in other projects, experiment with the things that you have learned and apply them to your designs.

Work with the picture frame and see if there are interesting crops that you can make to the design to make it harmonize and create balance. For example, the design seems to be too centered due to the white margins around the entire design. To remedy that, you can use the Crop tool to crop the image so that the right side of the clouds and building will become the right edge of the design.

1. With the Crop tool (C) selected, crop the image as shown in Figure 13.104. Click the Confirm button or double-click the selection to set the crop.
2. Save the file to your computer or drive.

FIGURE 13.104   Use the Cropping tool to remove the right margin of the image as shown.

Printing It Out

Printing in Photoshop CS4 is similar to printing in Illustrator CS4. You can set up the printer and the paper size and even preview the design to see if it will fit on your paper or allow you to tile it as you can in Illustrator.

1. Choose File > Print.

This allows you to view certain attributes of your design before you print it. Consult your software manual or the manual that came with your printer for specifics of paper size, ink, and paper types (Figure 13.105).

2. From the Printer menu, choose your printer.

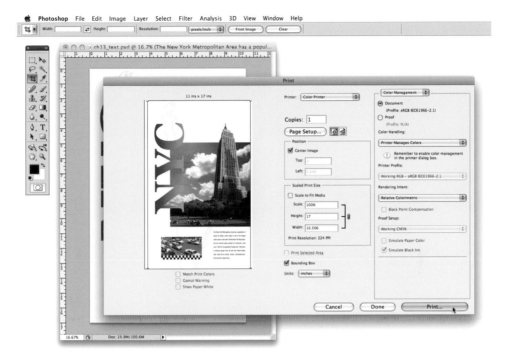

FIGURE 13.105   The Print dialog box.

3. Choose Page Setup to select your paper size, orientation and other options according to your software.
4. Set the position of your image relative to the paper using the Position section of the Print dialog box.
5. You can scale the area of the print to the media or a specific percentage in the Scaled Print Size section.
6. Click Print to print it. Follow any other prompts that you might be given.
7. After it dries, trim the design using a metal straight edge and an X-Acto knife.

Craftsmanship is a sign of professionalism. Do the best job that you can and be careful.

8. Mount the design to mat board or foam core for your class.

If you do not have a printer that can handle that size paper (you will have to print it out on 13" × 19" paper and trim it), you should plan ahead and take it to your local printer, print shop, or service bureau. ✂

SUMMARY

Now that you know everything about design, there is an easy test for you to take. Go back to an art museum or gallery you visited before you read this book. Take another look at one of the works of art you remember. Does it look the same? Can you analyze it visually and determine why you either liked or hated it? Do you feel differently about it now? Take some time when you go shopping or driving and pay special attention to a label, store sign, or billboard. Can you analyze it visually and determine why you either liked or hated it? You should be able to see design more clearly and appreciate great design that you may have previously passed by. You may also wonder why there are so many poor designs in the world.

In the "Summary" section of Chapter 10, the following statements and questions were asked:

As you make your design decisions, a personal style will begin to emerge. A preference for certain subject matter is only a superficial beginning. What types of compositions do you prefer: asymmetrical or symmetrical, closed form or open form? Did you use mostly curvilinear or rectilinear shapes for this project? What is the dominant line direction? Do you have a preference for designs that emphasize unity or variety? Will you be experimenting with low-key values or high-key values for future designs? Will you be using mainly realistic, stylized, abstract, or nonobjective shapes in your compositions?

Are you any closer to answering these questions? Can you look back and see if there are any similarities to your project solutions?

If you put in the time and energy to complete the projects in this book and thoroughly studied the theories and concepts, you have a fundamental background in the field of design. The information and projects were designed for the person who looks at the computer as a creative tool and has the desire to see more than function in everyday design. The reading and projects were not easy. They are reflective of the work you will face as a designer. Design isn't always fun, but if you try to follow the ideals discussed in this book you will always find it challenging.

A

ABOUT THE CD

The CD-Rom included in this book contains the files used with the tutorials in the latter chapters of the text. Follow the directions within the tutorials for opening the files.

To access these files, you will need the correct software. For files with the extension .psd or .tif you will need Adobe® Photoshop® CS4, and for files with the extension .ai, Adobe Illustrator® CS4 is required.

The files are contained within chapter folders for those chapters with tutorials only (for example, Chapter 10, "Design Project 4: Value," will have the files associated with the Value tutorial).

TUTORIALS FOLDER

- Chapter 4
- Chapter 5
- Chapter 6
- Chapter 7
- Chapter 9
- Chapter 10
- Chapter 11
- Chapter 12
- Chapter 13

Feel free to use the files to help you learn the concepts within the tutorials.

The files for the tutorials were created using the commercial versions of Adobe Illustrator CS4 and Photoshop CS4. These files will work in both the trial and commercial versions of the software.

TRIAL SOFTWARE FOLDER

Windows and Macintosh trial versions of the software can be downloaded for free from Adobe's Web site. You will need an Adobe ID. Registration is free and only takes a few minutes.

Adobe Illustrator CS4

- For Windows (1.1GB download): www.adobe.com/go/tryillustrator_win
- For Macintosh (1.44GB download): www.adobe.com/go/tryillustrator_mac

Adobe Photoshop CS4

- For Windows (815.5MB download): www.adobe.com/go/tryphotoshop_win
- For Macintosh (1.1GB download): www.adobe.com/go/tryphotoshop_mac

SYSTEM REQUIREMENTS

The following are the minimum system requirements for the effective use of Illustrator CS4 and Photoshop CS4.

Windows

- 1.8GHz or faster processor
- Microsoft® Windows® XP with Service Pack 2 (Service Pack 3 recommended) or Windows Vista® Home Premium, Business, Ultimate, or Enterprise with Service Pack 1 (certified for 32-bit Windows XP and 32-bit and 64-bit Windows Vista)
- 512MB of RAM (1GB recommended)
- 1GB of available hard-disk space for installation; additional free space required during installation (cannot install on flash-based storage devices)
- 1,024 × 768 display (1,280 × 800 recommended) with 16-bit video card
- Some GPU-accelerated features require graphics support for Shader Model 3.0 and OpenGL 2.0
- DVD-ROM drive

Macintosh

- PowerPC® G5 or multicore Intel® processor
- Mac OS X v10.4.11–10.5.4
- 512MB of RAM (1GB recommended)
- 2GB of available hard-disk space for installation; additional free space required during installation (cannot install on a volume that uses a case-sensitive file system or on flash-based storage devices)
- 1,024 × 768 display (1,280 × 800 recommended) with 16-bit video card
- Some GPU-accelerated features require graphics support for Shader Model 3.0 and OpenGL 2.0
- DVD-ROM drive

INDEX